PRINCIPLES OF BANKRUPTCY LAW

By

David G. Epstein

Professor of Law
Southern Methodist University
Dedman School of Law
Of Counsel Haynes and Boone

Steve H. Nickles

C.C. Hope Chair in Law and Management
Wake Forest University

CONCISE HORNBOOK SERIES®

Mat #40375512

610 Opperman Drive
P.O. Box 64526
St. Paul, MN 55164–0526
1–800–328–9352

Printed in the United States of America

ISBN–13: 978–0–314–16192–5
ISBN–10: 0–314–16192–9

We dedicate this book to –

Thomas K. and Laura Hearn

and

John P. and Cissie Anderson

to whom we are very deeply grateful for giving
us friendship and, especially, hope.

David G. Epstein
Steve H. Nickles

*

First Comments to Students

The phrase "teaching to the test" is generally a heresy both to law professors and real educators. Not to us in writing this book. While it might be heresy to say it, we are saying (as only someone who used to live in Arkansas can say) "look here, see how to make your bankruptcy/creditors rights grade your best grade in law school."

We think that this book can be helpful to the lawyer who wants to excel in her law firm bankruptcy work or the law student who still wants to be a "gunner" in his third year of law school. That is not why we wrote the book though. Again, we have written the book with the primary objective of making your grade on your bankruptcy/creditors rights test, your best grade in law school.

We understand that different teachers teach and test bankruptcy law differently. We have taught at 20 different law schools, and we teach and test the basic bankruptcy/creditors course differently each time that we teach. We have taught courses that separate business bankruptcy from consumer bankruptcy and courses that combine business bankruptcy and consumer bankruptcy; we have taught courses primarily from problems and courses primarily from cases; we have used take-home exams and in-class exams and essay questions, multiple choice questions and true-false questions.

Regardless of how your professor teaches or how she tests, all that you need to understand is

(1) a handful[1] of basic bankruptcy concepts

(2) the relationship among these basic bankruptcy concepts

(3) what legal issues can arise in a business bankruptcy case and what legal issues can arise In a consumer bankruptcy case and

(4) how the basic bankruptcy concepts affect these legal issues.

---

1. Large hands perhaps. Not O.J. Simpson size hands *http://www.cnn.com/US/OJ/evidence/glove/* but rather Oral Roberts University size hands *www.landmarktour.com/landmarktour2004/88-prayinghands.*

This short book, unlike "our"[2] three-volume bankruptcy treatise, does not cover all of bankruptcy law. We just cover all of the bankruptcy law that your exam is going to cover.

One final comment [that we hope that you wait to read until after you have bought this book.] If your teacher cared enough about her students to adopt our casebook, BANKRUPTCY (INCLUDING BAPCPA): 21ST CENTURY DEBTOR-CREDITOR LAW, you don't need this book or any other student guide. Our casebook is that clear and straightforward. If, on the other hand, your teacher adopted either the bankruptcy casebook co-authored by Professor Elizabeth Warren and Professor Jay Westbrook or the bankruptcy casebook co-authored by Professor Barry Adler and Professor Douglas Baird, then you probably need to buy more than one copy of this book.

DAVID G. EPSTEIN
Dallas, TX

STEVE H. NICKLES
Winston-Salem, NC

---

2. David G. Epstein, Steve H, Nickles & James J. White, Bankruptcy (3 vols. 1992). We understand that Jim White's name is on the book but Jim "gave" the book to us so that he would never have to do another book with us again.

Summary of Contents

*

Table of Contents

*

PRINCIPLES OF BANKRUPTCY LAW

*

Part One

INTRODUCTION TO BANKRUPTCY

Unit 1

QUESTION ONE: WHAT IS BANKRUPTCY LAW?

Table of Sections

The question "what is bankruptcy law" will not be a question on your exam. It is, however, a question that you have to be able to answer in order to answer the questions that will be on your exam.

§ 1.1 Federal Law and State Law

Bankruptcy law is federal law. Article I of the Constitution empowers Congress to "establish uniform laws on the subject of Bankruptcies throughout the United States." For most of the 20th century, bankruptcy law was the Bankruptcy Act of 1898, commonly referred to as the "Bankruptcy Act." It was replaced in 1978 by a law commonly referred to as the "Bankruptcy Reform Act of 1978" or "Bankruptcy Code." The Bankruptcy Code has been regularly amended; the most comprehensive bankruptcy amendments were enacted in 2005.

Bankruptcy law is also in large part state law. We are not here suggesting that there are state bankruptcy laws. Since Article I of the Constitution empowers Congress to enact uniform laws of bankruptcy and Congress has enacted such laws, principles of federal supremacy preclude state legislatures from enacting bankruptcy laws. Rather, bankruptcy law is in large part state law because (1) in places, the Bankruptcy Code expressly incorporates state law [every time you see the phrase "applicable law" in the Bankruptcy Code, think state law and, to a lesser extent, federal law other than the Bankruptcy Code] and (2) in other places, courts applying the Bankruptcy Code look to state law to determine questions such as what are the property rights of the debtor and what are the claims of the creditors to that property.

While the Bankruptcy Code looks to state law to determine important questions such as (1) what are the property rights of the debtor and (2) what are the claims of the creditors to that property. bankruptcy law is very different from state debt collection law. More specifically, you should know three critical differences:

First, state law focuses on individual action by a particular creditor and puts a premium on prompt action by a creditor. The first creditor to attach the debtor's property, the first creditor to execute on the property, etc. is the one most likely to be paid. Bankruptcy, on the other hand, compels collective creditor collection action and emphasizes equality of treatment, rather than a race of diligence. While bankruptcy law does not require equal treatment for all creditors, all creditors within a single class are treated the same. After the commencement of a bankruptcy case, a creditor cannot improve its position vis-a-vis other creditors by seizing the assets of the debtor. Similarly, the debtor's ability to make preferential transfers to creditors before bankruptcy is considerably limited.

Second, the prospects for debtor relief are much greater in bankruptcy. For individual debtors, this bankruptcy relief may take the form of relief from further personal liability for debts because of a discharge. While no debtor is guaranteed a discharge, most individual debtors do receive a discharge. "One of the primary purposes of the bankruptcy act is to 'relieve the honest debtor from the weight of oppressive indebtedness and permit him to start afresh....' " *Local Loan Co. v. Hunt* (1934). For business debtors, this bankruptcy relief may take the form of a restructuring of debts by reason of a confirmed Chapter 11 plan.

Third, the vocabulary of bankruptcy law is different from the vocabulary of state collection law. The Bankruptcy Code uses technical terms such as "property of the estate" and "automatic stay" that are not a part of state law. And the Bankruptcy Code uses other terms that are a part of state law such as "claim" and "secured claim" differently than state law. Accordingly, it is very important that you consistently and persistently check for the Bankruptcy Code's definition of terms used in the Bankruptcy Code.

§ 1.2 Statutory Law and Case Law

Look first to the language of the federal statute, the Bankruptcy Code, for answers to bankruptcy questions. It will also be necessary to look to case law for answers to questions that are (1) not addressed by any language in the Bankruptcy Code, (2) addressed by less than clear language in the Bankruptcy Code.

Most of the cases used in most of the bankruptcy casebooks used in law school classes are "illustrative," rather than leading. This book will cover (1) the leading cases and (2) the illustrative cases that are most likely to be important on your exam.

§ 1.3 Working With the Bankruptcy Code

The Bankruptcy Code is in Title 11 of the United States Code. For most of the 20th century, Title 11 was the Bankruptcy Act of 1898. That was replaced in 1978 by the Bankruptcy Reform Act of 1978 ("Bankruptcy Code"), The Bankruptcy Code has been amended periodically, most recently and most significantly in 2005 by the misnamed Bankruptcy Abuse Prevention Consumer Protection Act ["BAPCPA"].

The Bankruptcy Code is divided into 9 numbered chapters. Eight of the nine numbers are odd numbers: 1, 3, 5, 7, 9, 11, 12, 13 and 15. That is because Congress thought that bankruptcy (and anybody who studies bankruptcy) is odd and because Congress wanted to leave room to add new stuff such as Chapter 12 for "family farmers" which was added after 1978.

(a) Always Bankruptcy Code Chapters 1, 3, and 5

Chapters 1, 3, and 5 of the Bankruptcy Code apply in all bankruptcy cases, in all bankruptcy exam questions. Indeed, most bankruptcy exam questions are mostly about some provision in Chapter 5. And most bankruptcy exam questions require your use of two sections in Chapter 1: section 101 and section 105.

(b) Sections 101 and 105

Section 101 has most but not all of the definitions in the Bankruptcy Code. As we have said before (and will say again), "it is very important that you consistently and persistently check for the Bankruptcy Code's definition of terms used in the Bankruptcy Code." Even for words that you have been using all of your life.

Consider the section 101 definition of "debtor" ["a person ... concerning which a case under this title has been commenced"] and the following example: *C* makes a loan to two brothers, *A* and *B*. Both *A* and *B* sign the loan documents; the loan documents provide that *A* and *B* are jointly and severally liable to *C*. If brother *A*, and only brother *A*, files for bankruptcy, then *A* is a "debtor" and only *A* is a "debtor" for purposes of the Bankruptcy Code.

Section 105 is the Bankruptcy Code section judges, lawyers (and law students) rely on when they cannot find any other Bankruptcy Code support for a requested court order. More specifically, the first sentence of section 105: "The court may issue any order ... that is necessary or appropriate to carry out the provisions of this title."

Proponents of the requested order focus on the phrase "necessary or appropriate" and argue that the bankruptcy court can issue the order because it is "necessary," it is appropriate. Opponents of the requested order focus on the phrase "provisions of this title" and argue that the bankruptcy court can issue an order only if there is some basis for the order in some provision of title 11 (i.e., some section of the Bankruptcy Code) other than section 105.

Each judge (each professor) seems to have her own view of the role of section 105. Know your judge (AND PROFESSOR).

(c) Either 7 or 11 or 13 (or 9 or 12 or 15)

Every bankruptcy case (and to some extent every bankruptcy exam question) will also involve EITHER chapter 7. OR 9 OR 11 OR 12 OR 13 OR 15. Usually Chapter 7, 11, or 13.

Chapter 7 is the most common form of bankruptcy, and, as we will see, serves as a sort of "base line" for Chapters 11 and 13, Chapter 7 provides for the independent liquidation (i.e., sale) of the debtor's assets owned at the time of the bankruptcy filing and distribution of the net proceeds of the sale to creditors, pro rata, in accordance with statutory rules.

Chapter 11 does permit but does not require a sale of assets. Rather, Chapter 11 contemplates that a debtor will keep its (or his or her) assets and with these assets generate earnings that will fund a plan of creditor payment–a plan that has been negotiated with and voted on by creditors and also approved by the court.

While business entities or individuals can use either Chapter 7 or Chapter 11, only individuals can use Chapter 13. Like Chapter 11, Chapter 13 contemplates that the debtor will keep his or her assets. Like Chapter 11, Chapter 13 contemplates payments to creditors pursuant to a plan. Unlike Chapter 11, Chapter 13 does not require that the plan be either negotiated with or voted on by creditors.

[Chapter 9 is limited to bankruptcy cases filed by a "municipality," i.e., local political subdivision or instrumentality. Chapter 12 is limited to a case filed by a "family farmer." Chapter 15 is limited to a case filed by a debtor who has a bankruptcy case pending in some other country. If you are relying on this book, your time is so limited and so we will not ask you to read anything more about Chapter 9, 12 or 15].

§ 1.4 Building Blocks

The easiest way to understand bankruptcy is to understand three basic policies and five important concepts.

(a) Three Basic Policies

(1) Equality of Distribution

Bankruptcy judges in their opinions and law professors in their articles and classes consistently describe "equality of distribution" as an important, or even the most important, purpose of bankruptcy. The Bankruptcy Code nowhere uses the phrase "equality of distribution." Section 726(b) which mandates a pro rata distribution to non-priority unsecured claims in Chapter 7 cases is probably the most direct expression of the policy of equality of distribution. Section 547 "preference" law discussed infra in Unit 10 (and often) in law school bankruptcy classes is probably the most common exam opportunity for you to mention equality of distribution.

In bankruptcy (as elsewhere), equality does not always mean everybody gets treated the same. We will see that Bankruptcy treats some debtors different from others—e.g., individual debtors whose debts are primarily consumer debts. The Bankruptcy Code also treats some creditors different from other creditors—e.g., creditors who have a lien on the debtor's property.

(2) "Adequate Protection" of an Interest in Property

Creditors with a lien on the debtor's property have more than a contract right to be repaid. These lien creditors also have a property interest. In your first year property course, your teacher mentioned (if not covered) mortgages: the reason that she did is that a mortgage is an "interest" in property.

You can have rights in stuff even though someone else is in possession. Your landlord has property rights in your apartment even though you are now in possession of the apartment. Similarly, a creditor with a lien such as a mortgage or a judgment lien has a right in property subject to its lien (i.e., its collateral) even though the debtor is in possession.

The Constitution's Fifth Amendment protects interests in property—federal law cannot deprive a person (such as a creditor) of its interest in property (such as a lien) without just compensation. If the debtor owes creditor *C* $100 and *C* has a first lien on property of the debtor that has a value of $60 then *C* cannot be deprived of its lien without being paid $60.

We will see that a bankruptcy case can and does delay lien creditor *C*'s right to recover its $60 property interest. We will also see several Bankruptcy Code provisions requiring that throughout the bankruptcy case *C*'s right to be paid at least the $60 value of its property interest be adequately protected.

Again, adequate protection is limited to a creditor's property rights—not a creditor's right to payment under contract law or other law. *C* who has a lien on property valued at $60 to secure its debt of $100 has no right under the Bankruptcy Code to adequate protection of its right to be paid $100; adequate protection will be limited to *C*'s property right of $60.

(3) Fresh Start for Debtor

The basic bankruptcy policy of "fresh start" is, in a sense, the "debtor counterpart" to "the basic bankruptcy policy of equality of distribution." Bankruptcy judges in their opinions and law professors in their articles and classes consistently describe "fresh start" as an important, or even the most important, purpose of bankruptcy. The Bankruptcy Code nowhere uses the phrase "fresh start."

Courts and law professors consistently connect the bankruptcy "fresh start" policy with the bankruptcy concept of discharge. The term "discharge" does appear in the Bankruptcy Code. A lot.

(b) Five Basic Bankruptcy Concepts

(1) Discharge

The Supreme Court has stated, "The federal system of bankruptcy is designed not only to distribute the property of the debtor, not by law exempted, fairly and equally among his creditors, but as a main purpose of the act, intends to aid the unfortunate debtor by giving him a fresh start in life, free from debts, except of a certain character, after the property which he owned at the time of bankruptcy has been administered for the benefit of creditors. Our decisions lay great stress upon this feature of the law—as one not only of private but of great public interest in that it secures to the unfortunate debtor, who surrenders his property for distribution, a new opportunity in life." *Stellwagen v. Clum* (1918).

Again, the phrase "fresh start" nowhere appears in the Code. Again, courts and commentators however consistently connect the bankruptcy "fresh start" policy with the bankruptcy discharge. Again, the term "discharge" does appear in the Code and on law school exams. A lot.

A debtor who receives a bankruptcy discharge is relieved from any further personal, legal liability on her dischargeable debts. Reread this sentence and notice the limitations on the concept of discharge.

First, not every person who is a debtor in a bankruptcy case receives a discharge. The tests for whether a debtor receives a discharge vary from chapter to chapter.

In Chapter 7 cases, corporations and business entities other than humans cannot receive a discharge, section 727(a)(1). With respect to humans, Section 727(a)(2)–(12) lists eleven other bases for withholding a discharge from an individual debtor in a Chapter 7 case. Most of these "objections" to discharge are based on a debtor's misdeeds before or during the bankruptcy case.

In Chapter 11 cases involving debtors who are business entities such as corporations or limited liability companies or partnerships, the biggest hurdle for obtaining a discharge is court approval of the plan of reorganization. Under section 1141(d), a business entity in Chapter 11 generally receives a discharge on the "confirmation of a plan." The business debtor's completion of payments under the plan is not a condition precedent to a Chapter 11 discharge.

By contrast, in Chapter 13 cases, individual debtors receive discharges only if there has been both (1) confirmation of the plan and (2) payments under the plan have been made or judicially excused and (3) a course on personal financial management has been completed. Similarly, in Chapter 11 cases involving individual debtors, there will generally be no discharge until payments under the plan have been made.

Second, a discharge does not make a debt disappear; it does not vaporize or obliterate it. The discharge only relieves the debtor from *personal* liability on the debt. Accordingly, if *D*'s debt is guaranteed by *X*, *D*'s discharge does not affect *X*'s guarantee. The creditor can sue *X* on the guaranty and not worry about *D*'s discharge. And, if *D*'s debt to *M* is secured by a mortgage on Blackacre, then *D*'s discharge does not affect *M*'s rights as a mortgage holder with respect to Blackacre. This means that, if done correctly, *M* may foreclose and evict *D* regardless of *D*'s discharge.

Third, a discharge does not relieve the debtor from personal liability on *all* debts. A discharge only affects "dischargeable" debts. Whether a debt is dischargeable depends on:

- whether the case is a 7, 11, or 13 case;
- when the debt arose; and
- whether the debt is excepted from discharge.

[We consider nondischargeability of debts because of exceptions to discharge later.]

Saying the same thing another way, there are three discharge issues that you might see on your exam:

(1) What is a discharge?

(2) Who gets a discharge?

(3) Which debts are affected by a discharge?

If you can't answer these three questions, then reread the above materials on discharge.

(2) Property of the Estate

You need to be able to answer two questions about property of the estate: first, what is the bankruptcy law importance of property of the estate and second, what is included in property of the estate. Taking first things first, the bankruptcy importance of property of the estate.

a. What is the Bankruptcy Law Importance of Property of the Estate?

"Property of the estate" is one of the most important, most basic bankruptcy concepts. The filing of any bankruptcy petition automatically creates an "estate," and that estate includes the assets of the debtor. After the bankruptcy filing, these assets "belong" to the estate not the debtor.

In a Chapter 7 case, "property of the estate" is collected by the bankruptcy trustee and sold; the proceeds from the sale of the property of the estate are then distributed to creditors. In other words, the loss of property of the estate is the primary cost of Chapter 7 bankruptcy to the debtor; the receipt of the net proceeds from the sale of property of the estate is the primary benefit creditors derive from a Chapter 7 bankruptcy.

In other kinds of bankruptcy cases, the importance of property of the estate is less obvious. Nonetheless, property of the estate is an important concept in cases filed under Chapter 11, 12, or 13.

In most Chapter 11 and 12 cases and in 13 cases, the debtor will remain in possession of "property of the estate." However, the Chapter 11 or Chapter 12 or Chapter 13 debtor's use of the property of the estate will be subject to bankruptcy court supervision.

In both Chapter 12 and Chapter 13 cases, the value of the property of the estate determines the minimum amount that must be offered to holders of unsecured claims in the debtor's plan of repayment, sections 1225(a)(4), 1325(a)(4). Chapter 11 imposes a similar requirement as to nonassenting holders of unsecured claims, section 1129(a)(7)(A)(ii).

Finally, a number of general provisions in Chapters 3 and 5 that are applicable in all bankruptcy cases use the phrase "property of the estate." For example, the automatic stay bars a creditor from collecting a claim from property of the estate, section 362(a)(3), (4).

In short, in all bankruptcy cases and in all bankruptcy classes, it is necessary to be able to answer the question "what does property of the estate include?"

b. What is Included in Property of the Estate Under Section 541(a)(1)?

Section 541 is the primary section to turn to in answering the question "what is included in property of the estate." Section 541 applies in all bankruptcy cases. [In Chapter 13 cases, section 541 needs to be read together with section 1306. In Chapter 11 cases in which the debtor is an individual and not some business entity, section 541 needs to be read together with section 1115].

1. What is Included in the Phrase "Interests of the Debtor in Property as of the Commencement of the Case"?

The seven numbered subparagraphs of section 541(a) specify what property becomes property of the estate. Paragraph one is by far the most comprehensive and significant. Section 541(a)(1) provides that property of the estate includes "all legal or equitable *interests of the debtor* in property *as of the commencement of the case*" (emphasis added).

This is a very broad statement. Property of the estate thus includes both real property (such as a company's manufacturing facility or an individual's house) and personal property (such as a store's inventory or an individual's car), both tangible (the manufacturing facility, the car, etc.) and intangible property (such as an account receivable or a license), both property in the debtor's possession and property in which the debtor has an interest that is held by others.

This language in section 541(a)(1) raises two important litigable issues. Please reread the statutory excerpt again. Focus on the italicized phrases.

First, note the phrase "interests of the debtor in property." If the debtor has a limited interest in some asset, it is that limited interest that is property of the estate. Consider the following two examples:

(1) Back when they lived in Arkansas, Epstein and Nickles owned a double-wide mobile home as tenants in common. If Nickles filed a bankruptcy petition, only Nickles' limited interest in the mobile home would be property of the estate.

(2) Epstein and Nickles borrowed the money to buy the mobile home from the Bank of Elkins (BOE) which retained a mortgage. That mortgage or lien is a property interest in the double-wide. Outside of bankruptcy then, Epstein, Nickles and BOE all have

property interests in the double-wide. Accordingly, if Nickles files a bankruptcy petition, under section 541 of the Bankruptcy Code, only Nickles' property interest in the double-wide is property of the estate.

Second, consider the phrase "as of the commencement of the case" in section 541(a)(1). "Commencement of the case" is synonymous with the filing of a bankruptcy petition, sections 301, 303. Thus, generally assets that the debtor acquired prior to the petition become property of the estate; property acquired after the petition generally is not property of the estate. For example, if *D* files for bankruptcy on April 5, the money she earns from the work that she does after April 5 is not property of the estate, section 541(a)(1), (6) ("earnings from services performed by an individual after the commencement of a case" excepted from property of the estate).

2. *What Else is Included in Property of the Estate?*

While property of the estate is determined primarily by section 541(a)(1)—"the interests of the debtor in property as of the commencement of the case," property of the estate also includes

#1 "Any interest in property that the trustee recovers," section 541(a)(3)

As we will see later, the bankruptcy trustee (and the debtor in possession in a Chapter 11 case) is empowered by the Bankruptcy Code to recover certain payments and other transfers of the debtor's interest in property. The trustee's use of these avoidance powers increases the property of the estate. Assume, for example, *D* pays $1 million to one of his creditors, *C*, on January 10th and *D* then files for bankruptcy on January 15th. If the bankruptcy trustee is able use her avoidance powers under sections 547 and 550 to avoid that January 10th payment, then *C* would have to return the $1 million, and that $1 million would become property of the estate.

#2 "Proceeds, product, offspring, rents or profits of or from property of the estate," section 541(a)(6)

Assume that Homer and Marge Simpson file a bankruptcy petition and the next day their house is destroyed by an explosion of the Springfield nuclear power plant. Any insurance proceeds would be property of the estate.

Similarly, if Trump Realty Co. files for bankruptcy, both the buildings it owns as of the bankruptcy petition and the postpetition rents from the buildings would be property of the estate. And, if Trump Hotel and Casino Resorts, Inc., files for bankruptcy, property of the estate would include the corporation's postpetition earnings.

Reconsider the last sentence. The postpetition earnings of a corporation or any other "person" other than an "individual" are property of the estate under section 541(a)(6). It is only postpetition earnings of an individual from the services that she performs after the bankruptcy are excluded from property of the estate—unless the debtor has filed a petition for relief under Chapter 13 or 11.

#3 "Earnings from services" that an individual debtor acquires after filing a petition for relief under Chapter 13 or Chapter 11

If an individual debtor files a petition for relief under Chapter 11 or Chapter 13, property of the estate will be determined not only by section 541 but also by section 1115 or 1306. Under these provisions, postpetition earnings are property of the estate.

#4 Property that the debtor acquires or becomes entitled to within 180 days after the filing of the petition by (a) bequest, devise, or inheritance; (b) property settlement or a divorce decree; or (c) as beneficiary of a life insurance policy, section 541(a)(5).

c. *What is Excluded From Property of the Estate?*

There are some very specific exclusions from property of the estate in section 541(b) and 541(c). For example, section 541(b)(5), added in 2005, provides that funds placed in an educational retirement account at least 365 days prior to a bankruptcy filing, within limits established by the Internal Revenue Code and for the benefit of the debtor's children or grandchildren, are excluded from the debtor's estate with a $5,000 limit on funds contributed between one and two years before filing.

If your professor is going to test you on insignificant stuff like that, even this book is not going to help.

The most significant section 541(b) or section 541(c) exclusion from property of the estate is section 541(c)(2). Even though neither the words "spendthrift trust" nor "ERISA" appear in section 541(c)(2), it has been read to exclude traditional spendthrift trusts and ERISA accounts from property of the estate, *Patterson v. Shumate* (1992). Since most bankruptcy law professors do not understand ERISA, you probably do not need to understand more about section 541(b) and (c).

In both law school classes and bankruptcy cases, the most significant exclusions from property of the estate are not based on section 541(b) or (c). Rather, the most significant exclusions are (I) property acquired by the debtor after the bankruptcy filing which was considered earlier in this unit and (II) exemptions which will be considered later in another unit.

(3) Claims

Bankruptcy is all about "claims." Claims are what are discharged by bankruptcy: the discharge ends the debtor's personal liability on claims. Claims are what are paid in bankruptcy: in a Chapter 7 case, property of the estate is liquidated and the proceeds are distributed to holders of claims under section 726 and in a Chapter 11 case or a Chapter 13 case, the plan provides for distributions to holders of claims.

The term "claim" is defined in section 101(5). The most important part of the definition is "right to payment, whether or not such right to is reduced to judgment, liquidated, unliquidated, fixed, contingent, matured, unmatured, disputed, undisputed, legal, equitable, secured or unsecured." First, focus on the phrase "right to payment."

Assume *D* owes his neighbor, *N*, or a government agency, EPA, the costs of remediating *D*'s pollution. *N* or the EPA has a "claim"—a right to payment.

Now, assume *N* or the EPA has merely obtained a "sin no more" order, an injunction that bars *D* from engaging in future activities. That injunction does not create a claim—not a right to payment. And, if *N* or the EPA has a court order that requires *D* to clean up its pollution, that requires a discussion of *Ohio v. Kovacs* (1985).

Kovacs was the debtor; he had filed for personal bankruptcy. A major part of the reason for Kovas' bankruptcy was pollution caused by Chem–Dyne Corp. (C–D–C)–Kovacs was CEO and shareholder of C–D–C. Prior to Kovacs' personal bankruptcy, the State of Ohio had obtained a judgment against both C–D–C and Kovacs that required, inter alia, cleanup of the pollution. After Kovacs' bankruptcy filing, the State of Ohio filed a complaint in bankruptcy court seeking a determination that Kovacs' obligation to clean up the pollution was not dischargeable because it was not a "claim." Section 727(b) only discharges "debts," and "debt" is defined in section 101 as liability on a "claim." The essence of the State of Ohio's argument was that the cleanup order was not a "claim" because it was not a "right to payment."

The Supreme Court concluded that the cleanup order was a "claim." In so ruling, the Court emphasized that a receiver had been appointed prior to bankruptcy and that after the appointment of a receiver "the only performance sought from Kovacs was the payment of money."

Remember that a right to the payment of money is a "claim" even if that right to payment is "unmatured," "contingent".... If *D* borrows $100 from *C* and *G* guarantees *D*'s repayment and *D* files for bankruptcy before either *D* or *G* had paid *C*, then both *C* and *G* have a "claim" in *D*'s bankruptcy.

(4) Secured Claims

Recall that the section 101 definition of "claim" includes "secured or unsecured" claims. Under the section 506 definition of "secured claim," a creditor will have a secured claim if (1) it has a right of payment from the debtor and (2) this right of payment is "secured" by a right of setoff or a lien against property of the estate. Let's focus on "liens" for now.

Under nonbankruptcy law, certain creditors have greater rights than other creditors because they have liens. These liens are property interests in the debtor's property. Perhaps the most familiar example of a lien is a real estate mortgage. If you are taking a secured credit course, you are familiar with consensual liens on personal property called security interests. When you took civil procedure you were familiar with execution liens, garnishment liens, judgment liens, i.e., liens created by judicial proceedings. And, some creditors are granted liens by statute: federal tax liens and mechanics' liens are examples of statutory liens.

When the debtor defaults, these creditors with liens (also known as secured creditors) have all of the rights of other creditors (also known as unsecured creditors). Lien creditors also have additional rights because of their property interests.

Under nonbankruptcy law, a secured creditor has greater rights than unsecured creditors have in both the property subject to its lien and the proceeds from any disposition thereof. More specifically, under nonbankruptcy law, a secured creditor can seize and sell the property subject to its lien and use the proceeds to satisfy its claim.

Somewhat similar rights exist under the Code. First, bankruptcy law does not eliminate the right of a holder of a secured claim to seize and to sell the property subject to its lien. However, bankruptcy law makes such seizure and sale subject to the automatic stay (considered next): the creditor with a lien must obtain relief from the automatic stay before seizing its collateral, before selling its collateral.

Second, bankruptcy law, in its own way, recognizes that the holder of a lien enjoys special rights in the property subject to its lien and in the proceeds from any disposition thereof. Remember the definition of "property of the estate" in section 541: the phrase "interest of the debtor."

Because (1) property of the estate in limited to the "debtor's interest in property" and (2) a lien is the creditor's interest in property, if, at the time of *D*'s bankruptcy filing, *D* owns Blackacre which is worth $100,000 and *M* has a mortgage on Blackacre securing its $40,000 right to payment from *D*, then not all of the $100,000 value of Blackacre is property of the estate. Only *D*'s interest is property of the estate; *M*'s $40,000 property interest is not property of the estate. *M* has a $40,000 secured claim.

The concept of "secured claim" is such an important bankruptcy concept let's do it one more time. Do you see how a single credit transaction with a single debt instrument can create both a secured claim and a unsecured claim? If (1) *X* makes a loan to *D* secured by equipment and (2) *D* later files for bankruptcy still owing 100 and (3) the court determines that the value of *X*'s collateral (the equipment) is only 70, then *X* has a secured claim of 70 and an unsecured claim of 30.

Now, an exam "trick" to watch for. *D* borrows $10,000 from *C*. *G* guarantees repayment and grants *C* a mortgage on Blackacre to secure his guarantee. *D* later files for bankruptcy. In *D*'s bankruptcy case, *C* would have a claim, but not a secured claim. *C*'s mortgage is a "lien" but Blackacre which belongs to *G* is not "property of the estate" in *D*'s bankruptcy. Under section 506's definition of "secured claim," only a creditor with a lien on property that is "property of the estate" has a "secured claim" in a bankruptcy case.

(5) Automatic Stay

The automatic stay is one of the most important parts of any real world bankruptcy case and one of the more important parts of any law school bankruptcy exam. Going into your exam, you need to know that you know 5 things (a. through e. below) about the automatic stay.

a. What an Automatic Stay is

An automatic stay is a like an injunction or restraining order that becomes effective automatically, the instant a bankruptcy case is filed by either a debtor (i.e., a "voluntary" case) or by creditors (i.e., an "involuntary" case).

After the filing of a bankruptcy petition, a debtor needs immediate protection from the collection efforts of creditors. If the petition is a voluntary Chapter 7, the bankruptcy trustee needs time to collect the "property of the estate" and make pro rata distributions to creditors. If the petition is a voluntary Chapter 11 or Chapter 13, the debtor needs time to prepare a plan. And, if the petition is an involuntary Chapter 7 or Chapter 11, the debtor needs time to controvert the petition. Moreover, since creditors will receive payment through the bankruptcy process or the plan of rehabilitation and some claims will be discharged, continued creditor actions would interfere with orderly bankruptcy administration.

Accordingly, the filing of a voluntary petition under Chapter 7, Chapter 11 or Chapter 13, or the filing of an involuntary petition under Chapter 7 or Chapter 11 automatically "stays," i.e., restrains, creditors from taking further action against the debtor, the property of the debtor, or the property of the estate to collect their claims or enforce their liens, section 362.

b. *When Stay Starts*

The automatic stay is triggered by the filing of a bankruptcy petition. It dates from the time of the filing, not from the time that a creditor receives notice of or learns of the bankruptcy. If *D* files a bankruptcy petition on April 5, the stay becomes effective April 5. The stay dates from April 5 even if creditors do not learn of the bankruptcy until much later. If *C*, not knowing of *D*'s bankruptcy, obtains a default judgment against *D* on April 29, the default judgment violates the automatic stay and is invalid.

c. *What Stay Covers*

1. *Section 362*

Paragraph (a) of section 362 defines the scope of the automatic stay by listing all of the acts and actions that are stayed by the commencement of a bankruptcy case. It is comprehensive and includes virtually all creditor collection activity.

Subparagraphs (1) and (2) of section 362(a) cover most litigation efforts of creditors directed at collecting prebankruptcy debts. Section 362(a)(1) stays creditors from filing collection suits after the bankruptcy petition is filed or from continuing collection suits that were commenced prior to bankruptcy. Section 362(a)(2) bars creditors from enforcing judgments obtained prior to bankruptcy.

Section 362(a)(6) stays "any act to collect...." This has been read as barring informal collection actions such as telephone calls demanding payments and dunning letters.

Subparagraphs (3), (4), and (5) stay virtually all types of secured creditor action against property of the estate or property of the debtor. Creditors are barred from obtaining liens, perfecting liens, or enforcing liens after the bankruptcy petition is filed.

While paragraph (a) of section 362 indicates what is stayed, paragraph (b) lists actions that are not stayed, i.e., exceptions to the automatic stay. The most important exception is section 362(b)(2) which provides a somewhat limited exception for "domestic support obligations" (as defined in section 101). Such claims can be collected from property that is not "property of the estate."

Most of the other exceptions are very narrowly drawn. Most of the other exceptions apply in relatively few bankruptcy cases. For example, section 362(b)(21) only applies to a creditor with a mortgage or deed of trust on real property of a debtor who was not eligible to file the bankruptcy petition by reason of section 109(g) or a court order from a prior bankruptcy case.

There is an important limitation on the scope of section 362 that is not dealt with in paragraph (b) of section 362. The automatic stay of section 362(a) only covers the debtor, property of the debtor, and property of the estate. It does not protect third parties. Assume, for example, that *D* borrows $3,000 from *C* and *G* guarantees repayment. If *D* files for bankruptcy, section 362(a) will stay *C* from attempting to collect from *D*. Section 362(a) will not, however, protect *G*.

2. *Section 1301*

While section 362(a) will not protect *G*, section 1301 might if the case is a Chapter 13 case. By reason of section 1301, the filing of a Chapter 13 petition automatically stays collection action against guarantors and other co-debtors if

(1) the debt is a consumer debt and

(2) the co-debtor is not in the credit business.

Section 1301's automatic stay of actions against co-debtors applies only in Chapter 13 cases.

3. *Section 105*

Section 105 grants to bankruptcy courts the power to issue orders "necessary or appropriate to carry out the provisions of this title." Courts have used this section 105 power to enjoin or restrain creditor action against third parties.

There is an important procedural difference between section 105 and sections 362 or 1301. Sections 362 and 1301 are "automatic"—no court action is required. An injunction under section 105 will not be automatic. Rather, it will be granted according to the usual procedures for injunctive relief.

There is also an important substantive difference between section 105 and sections 362 or 1301. In acting under section 105, the bankruptcy court is not expressly limited by the restrictions in section 362 or section 1301.

If *D*, Inc. files for bankruptcy, a court cannot use section 362 to prevent creditors of *D*, Inc. from proceeding against *G*, who personally guaranteed *D*, Inc.'s debts. There are, however, numerous reported cases in which courts have invoked section 105 to protect *G* from *D*, Inc.'s creditors during the course of the bankruptcy.

Courts that have so ruled under section 105 have generally emphasized the importance of *G* to the success of *D*, Inc.'s bankruptcy—perhaps *G* is the chief executive officer who needs to devote all of her time and attention to *D*, Inc.'s bankruptcy, perhaps *G* is a possible source of the new funds that *D*, Inc. needs to reorganize. Accordingly, if you are using section 105 in an exam question on whether a court can enjoin actions against someone other than the debtor, emphasize how such an injunction might benefit the debtor.

d. When Stay Ends

Section 362(c)(1) and (2) describe two fairly common situations in which the automatic stay terminates automatically. Section 362(c)(1) provides that the automatic stay ends as to particular property when the property ceases to be property of the estate. Assume for example that *C* has a mortgage on *D* Corp.'s building. *D* Corp. files a bankruptcy petition. *C* is stayed from foreclosing its mortgage. The bankruptcy trustee sells *D* Corp.'s building to *X*, subject to the mortgage. *C* is no longer stayed from foreclosing its lien.

Section 362(c)(2) provides that the automatic stay ends when the bankruptcy case is closed or dismissed or the debtor receives a discharge. The typical Chapter 7 bankruptcy can be completed in a matter of months. In Chapter 11 cases and Chapter 13 cases, however, there can be a gap of several years between the filing of the petition and discharge. Accordingly, unless some action is taken, the stay can last several years.

The 2005 legislation added two new grounds for automatic termination of the automatic stay based on the debtor's recent bankruptcy filings. Section 362(c)(3) provides that if the debtor had been the debtor in an earlier bankruptcy case that was dismissed within one year of this bankruptcy case filing, then the automatic stay automatically terminates 30 days after the filing unless the debtor or some other party in interest can show that the second case was filed in good faith. Section 362(c)(4) deals with the even less common situation of a debtor who has had two or more bankruptcy cases dismissed within the past year.

e. What Can Creditors Do to Get Relief From the Stay?

A bankruptcy court may grant relief from the automatic stay on request of a "party in interest," section 362(d). The relief will not always take the form of termination of the stay. Section 362(d) provides for "relief" "such as by terminating, annulling, modifying, or conditioning such stay." The Rules provide that the "request" in section 362 takes the form of a motion, Rules 4001(a), 9014. The facts of the reported cases make clear that the "party in interest" in section 362 is usually a creditor, usually a secured creditor.

What does a creditor have to allege in its motion and establish in its proof in order to obtain relief from the stay? The grounds for relief from stay are set out in section 362(d).

1. Section 362(d)(1)

The most general statutory ground for relief from the stay is "for cause," section 362(d)(1). It is important—exam important—that you understand that the test for relief from stay under section 362(d)(1) is "cause." The "adequate protection" language that follows "cause" is simply ONE example of cause.

There is very little reported case law on what other than a lack of "adequate protection" constitutes "cause" for purposes of section 362(d)(1). Bankruptcy courts routinely find "cause" to lift the stay to allow tort suits against the debtor to go forward in state court to determine liability where the plaintiff agrees that any judgment will be collected only from the liability insurance carrier or some other third party.

Most of the reported section 362(d)(1) cases involve the specific example of cause set out in the statute—"lack of adequate protection of an interest in property of such party in interest." The quoted language raises four questions: (1) who is "the party in interest" (2) what is "the interest in property" (3) from what is it being protected and (4) how much protection is "adequate protection."

The party in interest is the person seeking relief from the stay. Again, typically, the party in interest under section 362(d)(1) will be a secured creditor.

Note that what is to be protected is the secured creditor's interest in property, not the secured party's claim. If, for example, *D* owes *C* $1 million and *C* has a security interest on equipment worth $600,000, section 362(d)(1) contemplates adequate protection of *C*'s $600,000 lien position, rather than *C*'s right to the payment of $1 million. You have to think of section 362(d)(1) as being about "adequate protection of an interest in property," not just "adequate protection."

The questions of what interest in property is protected and how much protection is adequate protection are closely related. These questions (and the answers to the questions) are relatively easy in a situation where the collateral is losing value through use, obsolescence or depreciation. Consider again the above example in which *D* owes *C* $1 million, and the debt is secured by equipment with a value of $600,000. Assume that the value of the equipment is declining by $5,000 a month. Section 362(d) contemplates that *C* will in some way be protected from a $5,000 a month loss due to decline in value of the collateral.

A more difficult question was whether section 362(d) also contemplates that a partially secured creditor such as *C* would be protected from a loss due solely to delay in realization of the value of the collateral. The Supreme Court finally resolved that issue in *United Savings Association of Texas v. Timbers of Inwood Forest Associates, Ltd.* (1988). There a Chapter 11 debtor, an apartment complex limited partnership, owed more than $4.3 million to *C*, a creditor that had a deed of trust on the apartment complex. The collateral was worth at most $4.25 million and was not depreciating in value. *C* moved for relief from the stay contending that "adequate protection" under section 362(d) included payment to it of "lost opportunity costs." More specifically, *C* argued

(i) part of its "interest in property" is the right to seize and sell its collateral when the debtor defaults;

(ii) if the debtor had not filed for bankruptcy, *C* could have sold the apartment complex for $4.25 million;

(iii) *C* could have then lent this $4.25 million to another debtor and received interest on this new $4.25 million loan;

(iv) accordingly, in order to provide "adequate protection" of *C*'s "interest in the property" as contemplated by section 362(d), the automatic stay should be conditioned on the debtor's making monthly payments to *C* equal to the amount that *C* would be receiving in interest payments on a new loan of $4.25 million. In sum, *C*'s argument was that "adequate protection" means that a debtor is compelled to pay a secured creditor for its "lost opportunity costs."

Looking to both legislative history and statutory language such as section 506, the Supreme Court in *Timbers* rejected this argument.

Section 361 does not define "adequate protection"; rather, section 361 specifies three nonexclusive methods of providing adequate protection. The first method of adequate protection specified is periodic cash payments to the lien creditor equal to the decrease in value of the creditor's interest in the collateral. If *C* has a security interest in *D*'s car and *D* files a bankruptcy petition, *D* can meet the adequate protection burden of section 362 by making cash payments to *C* equal to the depreciation on the car, section 361(1).

Section 361(2) indicates that adequate protection may take the form of an additional lien or substitute lien on other property. Assume, for example, that *D* files a Chapter 11 petition. *C* has a perfected security in *D*'s equipment. *D* needs to use the encumbered equipment to continue operation of its business, to accomplish a successful Chapter 11 reorganization. Such use will, however, decrease the value of the equipment and *C*'s lien in the equipment. Under section 361(2) adequate protection may take the form of a lien for *C* on other property owned by *D*; the new collateral does not necessarily have to be equipment.

Section 361(3) grants the debtor in possession or trustee considerable flexibility in providing adequate protection to a secured creditor. Section 361(3) recognizes such other protection, other than providing an administrative expense claim, that will result in the secured party's realizing the "indubitable equivalent" of the value of its interest in the collateral. The term "indubitable equivalent" is not statutorily defined. Even though sections 361 and 362(d) have remained unchanged since 1978, uncertainty remains as to (1) the importance of the "indubitable equivalent" language in section 361, and (2) the requirements of the "adequate protection" language in section 362(d). This uncertainty is attributable in part to the practice of negotiating rather than litigating section 362(d)(1) issues and in part to what is decided in section 362(d)(1) litigation. Section 362(d)(1) does not contemplate that the bankruptcy judge will decide what is adequate protection for a secured creditor and mandate that it be provided. Rather, in section 362(d)(1) litigation, the bankruptcy judge merely decides whether what the bankruptcy trustee or debtor in protection has offered to a secured creditor is adequate protection.

What if (i) there is section 362(d)(1) litigation, (ii) the bankruptcy judge decides that the debtor is providing adequate protection and (iii) the "adequate protection" proves to be inadequate? To illustrate, *X* has a perfected security interest in the inventory of *D*. *D* files a Chapter 11 petition. At the time of the petition, *D* owes *X* $100,000, and the encumbered inventory has a value of $60,000. *X* requests relief from the stay. The court concludes that *D*'s offer of a personal guarantee by *G* was "adequate protection," was an "indubitable equivalent." This conclusion turns out to be wrong. When *D*'s Chapter 11 reorganization fails, *G* is insolvent. The value of the inventory now securing *D*'s $100,000 claim is worth only $20,000. Obviously, *X* cannot sue the bankruptcy judge. What can *X* do?

Section 507(b) applies when "adequate protection" proves to be inadequate. It grants an administrative expense priority[1] for the losses. In the above hypo, *X* would have a $40,000 administrative expense priority claim. More about administrative expense priorities later.

1. The significance of an administrative expense priority is considered infra.

2. *Section 362(d)(2)*

Under section 362(d)(2) a lien creditor can obtain relief from the stay if

(A) the debtor does not have any equity in the encumbered property, AND

(B) the encumbered property is not necessary to an effective reorganization.

The application of section 362(d)(2)(A) would not seem to present any difficult legal issues: generally a debtor's equity in encumbered property is measured by the difference between the value of the property and the encumbrances against it. If, for example, property has a value of $100,000 and is subject to a $120,000 lien, "the debtor does not have any equity in such property."

A lien creditor cannot obtain relief from the stay under section 362(d)(2) merely by establishing no equity for purposes of section 362(d)(2)(A). Note the conjunction "and" connecting the no equity test of section 362(d)(2)(A) and section 362(d)(2)(B). A creditor relying on section 362(d)(2) then must satisfy both (A) and (B).

The language of paragraph (B) of section 362(d)(2) sets out two separate standards, provides two different opportunities for a creditor. The first possible creditor section 362(d)(2)(B) argument is that the encumbered property is not "necessary." Does the individual debtor need the car in order to get to her job so she can make the payments under her Chapter 13 plan? Does the business debtor need the equipment so that it can manufacture goods to make its Chapter 11 payments? The courts have been much more aggressive in deciding that an individual Chapter 13 debtor does not need a car or house than in deciding that a business debtor does not need equipment or a building.

Even if the collateral is necessary for the Chapter 11 or 13 debtor's reorganization efforts, the phrase "effective reorganization" in section 362(d)(2)(B) enables a creditor who invokes section 362(d)(2)(B) to question whether the debtor can reorganize. Some financial problems can be solved only by an Act of God, not by a mere Congressional bankruptcy act. Does this debtor have a realistic possibility of an "effective reorganization"? Dicta in the Supreme Court decision in *United Savings Association of Texas v. Timbers of Inwood Forest Associates, Ltd.* (1988), suggests that this should be a meaningful test. "What this requires is not merely a showing that if there is conceivably to be an effective reorganization, the property will be needed for it, but that the property is essential for an effective reorganization *that is in prospect.*"

3. *Section 362(d)(3)*

Section 362(d)(3) is available only to a creditor with a lien on "single asset real estate," a phrase defined in section 101. That definition looks not only to the nature of the real estate but also to the nature of the debtor and the amount of "secured debts."

The debt limit phrasing in the section 101 definition of "single asset real estate"—"noncontingent, liquidated secured debts in an amount no more than $4,000,000"—is very similar to the language in section 109(e) imposing debt limits for Chapter 13. Just as reported decisions under section 109(e) treat a $10,000 debt secured by collateral worth $2,000 as a $2,000 secured debt, courts are likely to find that a creditor owed $5,000,000 secured by real property worth only $4,000,000 has a secured debt of only $4,000,000 and so can invoke section 362(d)(3).

Under section 362(d)(3), a creditor with a lien on single asset real estate has a right to relief from stay unless the debtor, within 90 days after the order for relief, has either (A) filed a reorganization plan or (B) started monthly payments. If the debtor selects alternative A, the plan must be one that has "reasonable possibility of being confirmed within a reasonable time." If the debtor selects alternative B, the amount of the payment must equal interest at "a nondefault contract rate" on the value of the creditor's interest in the real estate.

Alternative B is in essence a partial legislative reversal of the *Timbers* case, discussed earlier. Under section 362(d)(3)(B), an undersecured creditor has a right to interest—or at least a right to monthly payments equal in amount to interest.

4. *Section 362(d)(4)*

New section 362(d)(4), like section 362(d)(2), is only helpful to creditors with secured claims. Section 362(d)(4) is more limited than section 362(d)(2) in that (1) section 362(d)(4) only applies to creditors with claims secured by real property and (2) section 362(d)(4) only applies to debtors who have made an unauthorized transfer of the encumbered real property or made multiple bankruptcy filings.

It is helpful to compare section 362(d)(4) not only with section 362(d)(2) but also with section 362(c)(3). Section 362(c)(3) provides for termination of the automatic stay in this bankruptcy case as to all creditors. Section 362(d)(4) provides for relief from the automatic stay in this case and any other case filed in the next two years but only for creditors secured by real estate.

5. *Relationship of Section 362(d)(1) or Section 362(d)(2) or Section 362(d)(3) or Section 362(d)(4)*

Note that section 362(d)(1), section 362(d)(2), section 362(d)(3), and section 362(d)(4) are connected by the conjunction "or." A creditor is entitled to relief from the stay if it is able to establish grounds for relief under either section 362(d)(1), section 362(d)(2), or section 362(d)(3), or section 362(d)(4). If, for example, a creditor is able to establish the lack of adequate protection, it is entitled to relief from the stay even though the property is necessary to an effective reorganization.

6. *Burden of Proof in Section 362(d) Litigation*

Section 362(g) allocates the burden of proof in stay litigation. The creditor or other party requesting the relief has the burden on the issue of whether the debtor has an equity in the property. The debtor or bankruptcy trustee has the burden on all other issues.

§ 1.5 People in the Bankruptcy Process

Bankruptcy takes place in lawyers' offices where lawyers representing debtors and creditors negotiate, Bankruptcy also takes place in a courtroom where lawyers representing debtors and creditors litigate. Here is a short list of the major people in the bankruptcy process:

- *Debtor*. The person, individual or business entity that is the subject of the bankruptcy case. Put another way, it is the person who owes money and is seeking some form of relief. *See* 11 U.S.C. § 101(13).
- *Debtor in Possession*. The debtor in Chapter 11 cases in which there is not a trustee. A debtor in possession (or "DIP") is the debtor, but with expanded duties as a representative of the bankruptcy estate. A DIP has fiduciary duties to the estate that the debtor does not. *See* 11 U.S.C. § 1101(1).
- *Creditor*. The holder of a "claim," i.e., a person to whom the debtor owes a monetary obligation. *See* 11 U.S.C. § 101(10).
- *Creditors' Committee*. Generally, this refers to a committee of unsecured creditors in a Chapter 11 case. Such committees are recognized by statute, 11 U.S.C. § 1102, and are given statutory duties, 11 U.S.C. § 1103(c). They may hire their own professionals, who will be paid from the estate and not by the individual members of the committee.
- *Trustee*. In every Chapter 7 case, every Chapter 12 case, every Chapter 13 case and some Chapter 11 cases, there will

be not only a bankruptcy judge but also a bankruptcy trustee. Generally, the bankruptcy trustee will be a private citizen, not an employee of the federal government.

A bankruptcy trustee is an active trustee. According to section 323 of the Bankruptcy Code, the bankruptcy trustee is "the representative of the estate." The filing of a bankruptcy petition is said to create an estate consisting generally of the property of the debtor as of the time of the bankruptcy filing. This estate is treated as a separate legal entity, distinct from the debtor. The bankruptcy trustee is the person who sues on behalf of or may be sued on behalf of the estate.

The powers and duties of a bankruptcy trustee vary from chapter to chapter. Recall that Chapter 7 bankruptcy is liquidation in nature. The duties of a bankruptcy trustee in a Chapter 7 case include:

1. collecting the "property of the estate," i.e., debtor's property as of the time of the filing of the bankruptcy petition
2. challenging certain prebankruptcy and postbankruptcy transfers of the property of the estate
3. selling the property of the estate
4. objecting to creditors' claims that are improper
5. in appropriate cases, objecting to the debtor's discharge, section 704.

Remember that there will be a bankruptcy trustee in every Chapter 7 case. And, in most Chapter 7 cases, most of the work is done by the Chapter 7 trustee.

There will also be a trustee in every Chapter 13 case, and in most Chapter 13 cases the trustee does most of the work. But, the person who works as a Chapter 13 trustee is different from the person who works as a Chapter 7 trustee, and the work that she does is different.

A Chapter 7 trustee is selected to serve as trustee in a particular Chapter 7 case. While a person often serves as trustee in more than one Chapter 7 case at a time, her work as a trustee is dependent on her being appointed or elected to serve as trustee in that case, sections 701 and 702. By contrast, one or more individuals is selected by the United States Trustee to serve as trustee for all of the Chapter 13 cases in his or her district—to be the "standing Chapter 13 trustee."

The duties of a Chapter 13 trustee also differ significantly from the duties of a Chapter 7 trustee. Section 1302 sets out the duties of a Chapter 13, and there seems to a considerable overlap between section 1302 and section 702 which sets out the duties of a Chapter 7 trustee.

The major differences between the work of a Chapter 13 trustee and the work of a Chapter 7 trustee mirror the major difference between Chapter 13 and Chapter 7: payments pursuant to a court approved plan as compared with payments pursuant to liquidation. Accordingly, a Chapter 13 trustee does not collect and liquidate the debtor's property. Instead, the Chapter 13 trustee reviews and, where appropriate, contests the debtor's plan of repayment, and, after court approval of the Chapter 13 plan of repayment, serves as disbursing agent for the payments to creditors under the plan.

While there is a bankruptcy trustee in every Chapter 7 case and every Chapter 13 case, there is rarely a bankruptcy trustee in a Chapter 11 case. In Chapter 11, a bankruptcy trustee will be appointed only if the bankruptcy judge decides, after notice and hearing, that there is "cause" or the "appointment is in the interest of creditors, any equity security holders, and other interests of the estate."

Remember also that Chapter 11, like Chapter 13, contemplates rehabilitation, not liquidation, and that Chapter 11, unlike Chapter 13, is available to corporations and partnerships as well as individuals. The typical Chapter 11 case involves a business that continues to operate after the bankruptcy petition is filed. If a bankruptcy trustee is named in such a case, he or she will take over the operation of the business. As noted above, generally there will not be a trustee in a Chapter 11 case. The debtor will usually remain in control of the business after the filing of a Chapter 11 petition; remember, such a debtor is referred to as a "debtor in possession."

The United States trustee is a government official, appointed by the Attorney General. More specifically, the Attorney General appoints a U.S. trustee for each of the various "regions" across the country; there are now 21 of these regions.

Essentially, the United States trustee performs appointing and other administrative tasks that the bankruptcy judge would otherwise have to perform. To illustrate, the United States trustee, not the bankruptcy judge, selects and supervises the bankruptcy trustees in Chapter 7, 11, 12, and 13 cases. Although the United States trustee can act as trustee in a Chapter 7 case or a Chapter 13 case (but not a Chapter 11 case), he or she is not intended as a substitute for private bankruptcy trustees. The United States trustee is more of a substitute for the bankruptcy judge with respect to supervisory and administrative matters.

- *Examiner.* In Chapter 11 cases only, an examiner may be appointed to investigate the prepetition activities of the debtor. In both the Enron bankruptcy case and in the WorldCom bankruptcy case, examiners were appointed and authored lengthy reports.

- *Bankruptcy Judge.* The judicial officer who presides over a bankruptcy case. Although a federal judge, bankruptcy judges are judges appointed under Article I of the Constitution. They thus do not have life tenure; they serve 14–year terms. Circuit judges select the bankruptcy judges for the circuits in which they sit. 28 U.S.C. § 152. Appeals from decisions of bankruptcy judges are to Article III district judges, or in some circuits, to Bankruptcy Appellate Panels (also known as "BAPs") which consist of three bankruptcy judges. *See* 28 U.S.C. § 158(b). Appeals from district court decision or BAPs are to the Circuit Courts of Appeal. 28 U.S.C. § 158(d).
- *Clerk of the Court.* In most districts, the bankruptcy court is a separate court, with separate records maintained by a separate person known as the clerk of the court. 28 U.S.C. § 156.

Unit 2

QUESTION TWO: WHY DO PEOPLE DO BANKRUPTCY (REQUIRING YOU TO BE ABLE TO DO BANKRUPTCY LAW)?

Table of Sections

---

§ 2.1 Problems

The problem that leads to bankruptcy is that an individual or a business is unable or unwilling to pay its debts. Debts plural. More than one debt. Usually the repayment problem affects all debts.

That problem is usually caused by other problems—problems that neither bankruptcy law nor any other law can fix. Maybe the business debtor continues to manufacture "Polaroid cameras" and consumers are buying cell phone cameras or maybe the individual debtor lost her job and her health insurance when General Motors "down-sized"....

If your bankruptcy professor's view is more narrowly that the problem is those greedy, overreaching credit card issuers and other creditors who force debtors to borrow money or those lazy shiftless deadbeats who refuse to accept responsibility, then....

§ 2.2 Possible "Legal" Solutions to the Debt Default Problem Outside of Bankruptcy

(a) For Creditors

The legal solutions for creditors outside of bankruptcy are expensive and largely ineffective.

When debtors default in paying obligations, creditors try to collect without hiring a lawyer and going to court. The creditor will first attempt "persuasion" to get the debtor to pay "voluntarily."

The creditor may even hire a collection agency to help persuade the debtor. When the debtor is a consumer debtor, these nonjudicial collection efforts are controlled by the Fair Debt Collection Practices Act and various state consumer protection statutes.

In the real world, creditors who are unable to collect their debts through these informal collection efforts often simply "write off" their bad debts. In some law professors' worlds, state collection law is still important. If you have been living in such a world this semester, here is what you need to know about state collection law.

At the broadest level, the law of creditors' remedies involves only two issues: (1) when and how a creditor gets a lien on property of the debtor (or the property itself), and (2) the lien's priority in relation to third parties' rights to the property, including other creditors' liens and the claims of transferees. These two issues are common to every kind of creditors' remedy.

A creditor cannot seize and sell its debtor's property unless it has some property interest in the debtor's property. The way a creditor acquires such an interest through the judicial process is to obtain a "lien" on that property.

Generally a creditor does not acquire or retain a lien or other property interest in the debtor's property until the creditor reduces her claim to judgment and enforces this judgment through appropriate postjudgment process. There are three important forms of postjudgment liens: (1) judgment liens, (2) execution liens, and (3) garnishment liens.

A judgment is no more than another form of debt; it is a new form of the obligation that the debtor owes the creditor. A judgment does, however, differ from the original obligation in that a judgment is the State's recognition of the legitimacy of the creditor's claim against the debtor. Along with this recognition comes (1) a judgment lien, which attaches by force of law to the debtor's real property once the judgment is appropriately recorded, and also (2) a willingness by the state to use its coercive power to enforce this lien and otherwise collect the amount of the judgment forcibly from the debtor's property (both real and personal) if the judgment debtor does not pay "voluntarily."

A creditor with a judgment initiates this state coercive process by applying to the court for a *writ of execution*. The writ of execution is ordinarily issued from the court that rendered the judgment and is directed to a sheriff. The writ orders the sheriff to seize property of the debtor, sell it, and apply the proceeds in satisfaction of the judgment. This seizure is commonly referred to as "levy" and creates an execution lien.

Garnishment is in essence a special form of execution—designed for reaching property of the debtor held by a third party. For example, when a creditor wishes to levy or execute upon a bank account, it seeks to obtain property of the debtor's held by a third person. In this context, the proper nomenclature regarding what occurs when, for example, the IRS tries to go against a delinquent taxpayer's (*T*) bank account at *B* Bank (*B*), the IRS is the garnishor, *B* is the garnishee, and *T* is the principal debtor.

Obviously, obtaining a judgment and getting a sheriff to seize and sell property of a debtor is both time-consuming and expensive ... and often unsuccessful for the following three reasons.

First, the debtor may not have property that can be seized or sold or the sheriff may not be able to find any property.

Second, even if the debtor has property, that property may be encumbered by other creditors' liens that have priority. These other liens may have been created by a earlier judicial collection effort by some other creditor. More likely, these prior liens were created by agreement (e.g., mortgage, security interest) or statute (e.g., tax liens, mechanics liens).

Third, the debtor might file for bankruptcy before its property is seized and sold. Bankruptcy law is the third reason for the decline in lawyers' use of (and professors' instruction in) state collection law. As we have seen, bankruptcy law only stops (i.e., "stays") not yet completed collection efforts. As we will see, bankruptcy law also often undoes (i.e., avoids) completed state collection actions.

(b) For Debtors

There is not much a debtor can do outside of bankruptcy to fix its debt problems. At least not much that a debtor can do without the help and support of its creditors.

A debtor can try to work out some sort of debt repayment agreement with its creditors. Professors who teach first year contracts courses call these agreements "compositions" and "extensions." Real lawyers and bankruptcy law teachers who want to sound like real lawyers call these agreements "workout agreements."

Whatever you call them, they are "agreements" and only bind the creditors who agree. If even one creditor refuses to participate in the workout agreement, that dissenting creditor, can in essence, "blow up" any deal by suing on its debt and using the execution process to levy on and sell assets of the debtor that are essential to the debtor's performing its workout obligations to the assenting creditors.

Assume, for example, that the Nickles Nabob Company has reached an agreement with nine out of ten of its largest creditors to pay 90% of their debts over three years at a new, higher interest rate. That tenth, nonassenting creditor is not bound. And, that creditor can sue on its debt, obtain a judgment, and levy on and cause the sale of equipment and inventory essential to Nickles Nabob's continued business operations.

If the debtor is an individual, state and federal laws exempt certain property of the debtor from the collection efforts of certain creditors. At most, these exemption statutes enable a debtor to keep some of his or her property from some of his or her creditors; exemption statutes do not enable a person with debt problems to "fix" the problems.

State exemption laws vary significantly from state to state. In most states, the amount of property that a debtor can designate as exempt is very limited. And, in all states, creditors with a mortgage or security interest in property that is designated as exempt can still seize and sell that property. If, for example, First Bank has a mortgage on Epstein's house and Epstein defaults, First Bank can seize and sell Epstein's house even if Epstein has designated the house as his exempt homestead.

§ 2.3 Possible Advantages of Bankruptcy

(a) For Debtors

We have already considered two of the three principal advantages of bankruptcy to debtors: (1) the automatic stay which protects the debtor from creditor collection efforts during the bankruptcy case, (2) the discharge which, if obtained, protects the debtor from creditor efforts to collect from him personally after the bankruptcy case. The third principal reason that debtors file for bankruptcy is to reduce the amount that they have to pay to their creditors.

In Chapter 7 cases, seizure and sale of property of the estate and distribution of the net proceeds from the sale to creditors very rarely results in full payment to all creditors. Similarly, in Chapter 11 cases and Chapter 13 cases, the payments pursuant to the court-confirmed plan very rarely result in full payment to all creditors.

(b) For Creditors

Less obvious are the possible advantages of bankruptcy to creditors. It should be obvious from the fact that less than 1% of the bankruptcy cases are filed by creditors that most creditors in most situations believe that they do not want to deal with the restrictions and costs of bankruptcy. Possible advantages to creditors of bankruptcy are (1) judicial supervision of the debtor's use of property of the estate protects creditors from fraud or waste and (2) the aggregate costs to all creditors of a bankruptcy are less than the total costs to individual creditors of individual collection efforts.

Unit 3

QUESTION THREE: WHERE DO LAWYERS DO BANKRUPTCY?

Table of Sections

---

§ 3.1 Allocation of Judicial Power Between Federal District Court and Bankruptcy Court

In the main, the substantive law of bankruptcy is in title 11 of the United States Code. Questions of judicial power over bankruptcy-related matters are, in the main, answered in title 28 of the United States Code.

The question of which court has the power to adjudicate the litigation that arises in bankruptcy can be an important one. Many attorneys that represent parties with claims against the bankrupt or parties against whom the bankrupt has claims prefer to litigate in some forum other than the bankruptcy court. Some believe that the bankruptcy judge has a pro-debtor bias; others are simply more comfortable or more familiar with state court procedures; others prefer state court for reasons of delay—a state court generally has a larger backlog of cases than a bankruptcy court so that filing in state court delays any litigation.

In considering the question of which court has the power to adjudicate the litigation that arises in bankruptcy, it is helpful to consider the kinds of matters that can arise in bankruptcy. Some matters will involve only bankruptcy law. For example, *D* files a Chapter 7 petition. The Chapter 7 trustee alleges that *B*'s payment of $40,000 to *C* a month before bankruptcy is recoverable by the estate under section 550 as a section 547 voidable preference. *C* contends that the $40,000 payment is protected from avoidance as a section 547(c)(2) ordinary course of business payment.

Other matters will involve both bankruptcy law and nonbankruptcy law. For example, *D* files a Chapter 7 petition. *C* files a secured claim that describes its Article 9 security interest. The bankruptcy trustee takes the position that *C*'s security interest is invalid because it was not properly perfected. If this is litigated, it will probably involve both the Bankruptcy Code's avoidance provisions and the Uniform Commercial Code's perfection provisions.

And, still other matters will not involve substantive bankruptcy law. For example, *D*, Inc., a Chapter 11 debtor, files a breach of contract claim against *X*.

(a) History

The allocation of judicial power over bankruptcy matters has been, and still is, one of the most controversial bankruptcy issues. A general familiarity with prior statutory schemes and prior controversies is helpful to understanding the present situation.

(1) 1898 Act and "Summary" Jurisdiction

Under the Bankruptcy Act of 1898, bankruptcy courts had limited jurisdiction. This jurisdiction was commonly referred to as "summary" jurisdiction. (The phrase summary jurisdiction is somewhat misleading. First, it incorrectly implies that under the Bankruptcy Act of 1898, bankruptcy courts had a second, nonsummary form of jurisdiction. Bankruptcy courts had only summary jurisdiction; other courts had plenary jurisdiction. Second, it incorrectly implies that in resolving controversies, the bankruptcy judge always conducted summary proceedings.)

Summary jurisdiction extended to (1) *all* matters concerned with the administration of the bankruptcy estate and (2) *some* disputes between the bankruptcy trustee and third parties involving rights to money and other property in which the bankrupt estate claimed an interest. The tests for which disputes with third parties were within the bankruptcy judge's summary jurisdiction turned on issues such as whether (1) the property in question was in the actual possession of the bankrupt at the time of the commencement of the case, (2) the property in question was in the constructive possession of the bankrupt at the time of the commencement of the case, and (3) the third party actually or impliedly consented to bankruptcy court jurisdiction.

There was considerable uncertainty over which disputes were within the summary jurisdiction of the bankruptcy court. This uncertainty gave rise to considerable litigation.

(2) 1978 Code Before Marathon Pipeline

To eliminate this uncertainty, Congress in 1978 decided to create a bankruptcy court with pervasive jurisdiction. For apparently political reasons, Congress also decided that this bankruptcy court should *not* be an Article III court.

As you recall from your Constitutional Law course in law school or civics course in high school, Article III of the Constitution vests the judicial power of the United States in the United States Supreme Court and such inferior tribunals as Congress might create. To insure the independence of the judges appointed under Article III (the so-called constitutional courts), Article III provides them with certain protections. These include tenure for life, removal from office only by congressional impeachment, and assurance that their compensation will not be diminished. The constitutional courts created under Article III include the United States Supreme Court, the United States Courts of Appeal, and the United States District Courts.

Congress, in the exercise of its legislative powers enumerated in Article I of the Constitution, may create other inferior federal tribunals—the so-called legislative courts. Judges of these legislative courts need not be granted tenure for life. In addition, they can be removed by mechanisms other than congressional impeachment, and their salaries are subject to congressional reduction. Historically, these Article I legislative courts and their judges have been granted jurisdiction over limited and narrowly defined subject matters, like the Tax Court. In other instances, jurisdiction has been limited to narrowly defined geographical territories, such as the territorial courts, the District of Columbia courts, etc.

In amending title 28 in 1978, Congress gave bankruptcy judges none of the protections found in Article III of the Constitution. Nevertheless, the 1978 amendments to title 28 gave bankruptcy judges much of the power and responsibilities of an Article III judge. Since bankruptcy debtors can be just about any kind of individual or business entity, this meant that litigation in the bankruptcy courts could deal with almost every facet of business and personal activity.

(3) Marathon Pipeline Decision

The 1978 grant of pervasive jurisdiction to a non-Article III bankruptcy court was successfully challenged in the *Marathon* case. *Northern Pipeline Constr. Co. v. Marathon Pipeline Co.* (1982).

In that case, Northern Pipeline, a Chapter 11 debtor, filed a breach of contract lawsuit against Marathon Pipeline in bankruptcy court. There was no question as to whether the bankruptcy court had jurisdiction over this lawsuit under the jurisdictional statute enacted in 1978, 28 U.S.C. § 1471(c). Marathon Pipeline did, however, question whether section 1471(c) conferred Article III judicial power on non-Article III courts in violation of the separation of powers doctrine and filed a motion to dismiss. A divided Supreme Court sustained Marathon's challenge.

The Court in *Marathon* was so divided that there was no majority opinion. Justice Brennan's opinion was joined by three other justices. Additionally, two justices concurred in the result. The holding of these six is perhaps best summarized in footnote 40 of Justice Brennan's plurality opinion which indicates that (1) the 1978 legislation does grant the bankruptcy court the power to hear Northern Pipeline's breach of contract claim, (2) the bankruptcy court, a non-Article III court, cannot constitutionally be vested with jurisdiction to decide such state law claims, and (3) this grant of authority to the bankruptcy court is not severable from the remaining grant of authority to the bankruptcy court.

After *Marathon*, Congress was urged to solve the constitutional dilemma by establishing bankruptcy courts as Article III courts. Congress rejected this solution. Instead, Congress in 1984 made the bankruptcy court a part of the federal district court, conferred jurisdiction in bankruptcy on the district court, and allocated judicial power in bankruptcy matters between the federal district judge and the bankruptcy judge.

It is easy for a law professor to criticize the provisions allocating judicial power over bankruptcy matters. It is more difficult (but probably more important) for a lawyer or law student to understand how these provisions operate.

(b) Provisions in Title 28 Allocating Judicial Power Over Bankruptcy

In understanding the present law allocating judicial powers over bankruptcy matters, it is necessary to understand three separate sections in title 28: (1) § 151, (2) § 1334, and (3) § 157. By understanding these three provisions you will understand that (1) bankruptcy courts are a part of the United States District Court but bankruptcy judges are different from district court judges, (2) bankruptcy cases are different from bankruptcy proceedings, (3) bankruptcy cases can be handled by either bankruptcy judges or federal district judges (depending on withdrawal of the reference), but not by state court judges and (4) bankruptcy proceedings can be tried by bankruptcy judges or federal judges (depending on withdrawal of the reference) or even state court judges (depending on where the lawsuit was filed and removal and abstention). To understand even more, please read the following descriptions of the three key sections in title 28:

(1) Bankruptcy Court as Part of the District Court

Section 151 refers to a bankruptcy judge and a bankruptcy court as a "unit" of the district court. It is important to keep this reference in mind when reading other sections in title 28 dealing with the allocation of judicial power in bankruptcy matters. When the term "district court" appears in section 1334 or section 157, it could be referring to the United States district judge and/or the bankruptcy judge. After all, the bankruptcy judge is a part of the district court–a "unit" of the district court.

(2) Grants of Jurisdiction to the District Court

Section 1334(a) vests original and exclusive jurisdiction in the district court over all cases arising under the Bankruptcy Code. "Case" is a term of art used in both the Bankruptcy Code and the Bankruptcy Rules. "Case" refers to the entire Chapter 7, 9, 11, 12, or 13–not just some controversy that arises in connection with it.

The term "case" is to be distinguished from the term "proceeding." A specific dispute that arises during the pendency of a case is referred to as a "proceeding." Section 1334(b) provides that the district courts have original but not exclusive jurisdiction over all civil proceedings, "arising under title 11, or arising in or related to cases under title 11."

"Proceedings" include "contested matters," [motions brought in the main bankruptcy case] and "adversary proceedings" [real lawsuits with complaints and answers and . . .]. Section 1334(b) grants the district court original but not exclusive jurisdiction over three types of "civil proceedings":

a. "Arising Under" Title 11

This involves adjudication of rights or obligations created by the Bankruptcy Code. For example, stay relief. A further example: preference litigation.

b. "Arising In" a Title 11 Case

This covers matters peculiar to bankruptcy but based on rights or obligations created by the Bankruptcy Code. For example, allowance or disallowance of claims. A further example: assumption or rejection of executory contracts.

c. "Related To" a Title 11 Case

This covers matters that impact on the bankruptcy case. While it is not a "catch-all," it certainly catches a lot. In *Celotex Corp. v. Edwards* (1995), the Supreme Court held that entry of an injunction prohibiting a judgment creditor from executing on a supersedeas bond of a third party surety of the debtor was "related to."

(3) Role and Power of the Bankruptcy Court

The title of section 157 is "Procedures." As this title suggests, section 157 is not a jurisdictional provision. It does not confer jurisdiction on the bankruptcy judge. Rather, it deals with procedure—the role that the bankruptcy judge, a unit of the district court under section 151, is to play in exercising the jurisdiction conferred by section 1334 on the district court.

Clearly, section 1334 confers jurisdiction over bankruptcy matters to the district court. It is equally clear that most federal district judges have neither the time nor the inclination to exercise this bankruptcy jurisdiction. Accordingly, section 157 empowers the district judge to refer bankruptcy matters to a bankruptcy judge. And, in every district, the federal district judges have issued a "blanket referencing," referring all bankruptcy cases and proceedings to the bankruptcy judge.

Section 157 differentiates between "core" and "noncore" proceedings. A nonexclusive list of core proceedings is set out in section 157(b)(2).

Obviously, if a matter is not a core proceeding, it is a "noncore proceeding." "Noncore proceeding" is neither defined nor illustrated in the statute. In noncore proceedings, the bankruptcy judge still can hold the trial or hearing, but generally[4] cannot issue a final judgment. She instead submits proposed findings of fact and law to the district court for review, section 157(c)(1).

Remember that a determination that a proceeding is noncore does not mean that the matter is withdrawn from the bankruptcy judge. Remember that a bankruptcy judge can hear noncore proceedings and prepare proposed findings of facts and law.

(4) The "Constitutional Escape Hatch"—Withdrawal of the "Reference"

Remember also that every district has entered an order authorized by Section 157(a) that "refers" all bankruptcy matters within the scope of Section 1334 to the bankruptcy court for that district. To preserve at least the pretense that district courts still are the residual keepers of Article III jurisdiction over bankruptcy, there has to be some way to get the case or parts of it "back" to the district court. In that way, the district judge can retain ultimate control over the role of the bankruptcy judge, and ensure that matters that should be decided by an Article III judge will be.

Remember that withdrawal under section 157(d) merely moves a matter from the bankruptcy judge to the federal district judge.

4. The bankruptcy judge can enter a final order or judgment in a noncore matter only if the parties consent, 28 U.S.C. § 157(c)(2). To help assist the parties in knowing when the bankruptcy judge may enter a final order, the Bankruptcy Rules require the parties' pleading to state that a matter is core or noncore, and to state affirmatively that they do not consent to entry of a final judgment by the bankruptcy court. BANKR. R. 7008(a).

Withdrawal under section 157(d) does not move a matter to a state court. That requires abstention.

(5) Abstention

Abstention moves litigation from the bankruptcy court to state court. Abstention is governed by section 1334(c).

The key to understanding abstention in bankruptcy is to remember that Congress provided for broad, pervasive jurisdiction in section 1334(b). Accordingly, some matters that are covered by this jurisdictional grant in section 1334(b) are not in any way bankruptcy matters but are matters that would be better left to other courts. Section 1334(c) empowers bankruptcy judges to leave such matters to other courts by abstaining.

§ 3.2 Multinational Bankruptcies

Obviously, businesses and their economic problems have become more global. BAPCPA establishes a new set of protocols for multinational bankruptcies in new Chapter 15. Chapter 15 is designed to encourage coordination among courts and bankruptcy representatives in different countries in the interest of avoiding inconsistent decisions that may hinder restructuring efforts.

A case under Chapter 15 is commenced by a petition filed in a United States bankruptcy court by an authorized representative from a foreign bankruptcy case seeking "recognition" of that "foreign proceeding." Recognition turns on the foreign representative's filing documents issued by a foreign court that establish that she is the authorized representative of a foreign insolvency proceeding. When the foreign representative is recognized, she then benefits from many of the substantive provisions of the Bankruptcy Code with respect to property in the United States. For example, the foreign representative many operate or sell the debtor's United States assets.

§ 3.3 Bankruptcy in the Conference Room and Other Places Deals Are Made

Use of bankruptcy law is not limited to the court room, to litigation. Bankruptcy law can also be important in the conference room or wherever deals are negotiated. Because an unanticipated bankruptcy can affect both the executory and executed parts of a contracts, good lawyers and "A" law students think about possible bankruptcy consequences when they are looking at a deal.

Part Two

THE BEGINNING OF A BANKRUPTCY CASE

Unit 4

QUESTION FOUR: HOW DOES AN INDIVIDUAL BANKRUPTCY CASE BEGIN?

Table of Sections

Any bankruptcy case, individual debtor or business entity debtor, begins with the filing of a bankruptcy petition. More than 99% of the bankruptcy petitions are filed by the person seeking bankruptcy relief, by the "debtor." Remember that these bankruptcy cases are called "voluntary cases" by both section 301 and law professors.

Less than 1% of the bankruptcy petitions are filed by creditors against a debtor. And, these bankruptcy cases are called "involuntary cases" by both section 303 and law professors. Both sections 301 and 303 provide that the case is "commenced" when a petition is filed by or against an eligible debtor.

Eligibility issues can involve challenges to (1) the person who is the debtor, (2) the petition and other papers that commence the case, and (3) the particulars that triggered the filing.

First, the person. Section 109 focuses on the person who is the debtor and provides the statutory basis for answering the questions:

(i) is this person eligible to be a debtor in a case under the Code?

(ii) is this person eligible to be a debtor in a bankruptcy case under this particular chapter of the Code?

Before the 2005 BAPCPA amendments, any individual was eligible to be a debtor in a case under Chapter 7 or Chapter 11 and was eligible to be a debtor in a case under Chapter 13 if she (1) had regular stable income to meet plan payment obligations and (2) came within the statutorily prescribed debt limits. As we will see later, one of the effects of BAPCPA is to make individual debtor Chapter 11 cases more similar to Chapter 13 cases than to Chapter 11 cases involving corporations, partnerships or other business entities.

A much more important "practical" effect of the BAPCPA amendments is to make it more difficult for individuals to file for bankruptcy. These 2005 changes affect the practice of lawyers who represent individuals and the lives of those individuals. Important changes in the real world. Kind of stuff that should be taught in continuing legal education programs and challenged in newspaper op-ed columns. Not the kind of stuff that should be covered in a law school class on basic bankruptcy.

For some law professors, however, railing against the credit card issuers and the rest of the consumer finance industry, their lobbyists, and their "bought Congress" is a cause. If your professor is in that group, then you need to read carefully the next two parts on what an individual has to do (and not do) before filing for before bankruptcy and what an individual must file with her bankruptcy petition because it might be on you exam.

§ 4.1 What an Individual Has to Do Before Filing a Bankruptcy Petition

Credit counseling is what an individual debtor has to do before bankruptcy. BAPCPA adds a requirement of prebankruptcy credit counseling. Section 109(h) makes an individual ineligible to file for bankruptcy under any of the chapters unless within 180 days before her bankruptcy filing she received credit counseling from an agency approved by the United States Trustee. This "counseling" can be a group briefing and can be by telephone or on the internet.

Again, subject to a very limited statutory exception, this credit counseling must be done before the bankruptcy filing. Courts routinely dismiss bankruptcy petitions filed by individual debtors who are unable to file with their bankruptcy petitions a certificate of briefing by an approved credit counseling agency. And, such a dismissal has continuing practical consequences. If after dismissal the debtor obtains the counseling and files another bankruptcy petition, she will have only a 30 day automatic stay which can be extended only on stringent terms, section 362(b)(3).

§ 4.2 What an Individual Debtor Has to File With Her Bankruptcy Petition

All debtors must file prescribed schedules of what they own (property) and what they owe (claims). And, almost all debtors must pay a filing fee (28 U.S.C. § 1930(f)[1] empowers the bankruptcy court to waive the filing fee for certain low income debtors).

As a result of BAPCPA, individual debtors must also file

—certificate of credit counseling;

—certificate that the debtor has received an informational notice required by section 342(b);

—tax return for the most recent tax year;

—statement of monthly net income and any anticipated increases in income or spending after filing.

This last item is especially important to the new "means test."

§ 4.3 What the "Means Test" Means in the Real World and on Your Exam in a Question in Which an Individual Debtor Files a Chapter 7 Petition

The term "means test" nowhere appears in the Bankruptcy Code. The term appears in real world cases in which the question is whether an individual debtor can use Chapter 7 or whether she is limited to Chapter 11 or Chapter 13 because she has the "means" to make meaningful payments to creditors.

The "means test" will appear on your exam if the fact pattern tells you that (1) the debtor is an individual and (2) her debts are primarily consumer debts and (3) she files a Chapter 7 petition, and (4) the fact pattern also gives you detailed information about how much the debtor earns and how much she spends. Such a fact pattern raises the question of whether the section 707(b)(2) means test will result in that Chapter 7 bankruptcy case being dismissed or converted to some other chapter.

As amended in 2005, section 707(b)(1) provides for dismissal of a Chapter 7 petition filed by an individual debtor with primarily consumer debts for "abuse." There are three different ways of establishing section 707(b)(1) "abuse":

First and second ways of establishing section 707 "abuse": reading section 707(b)(1) together with section 707(b)(3), "abuse" turns on (1) bad faith filing or (2) "totality of the circumstances of the debtor's financial situation."

Third way of establishing section 707 "abuse": reading section 707(b)(1) together with section 707(b)(2), "abuse" turns on what is generally referred to as a "means test."

The policy reason for the section 707(b)(2) means test is easy to state in class or on an exam. The section 707(b)(2) means test is based on the premise that if debtors can afford to pay their creditors at least between $6,000 and $10,000 over five years, they should pay instead of using Chapter 7 to avoid paying.

However, the particulars of the section 707(b)(2) means test are hard to explain in class or an exam. Before getting into the particulars of the section 707(b)(2) means test, you need to understand that in real bankruptcy cases, the particulars of the section 707(b)(2) means test will usually not be applicable.

More specifically, the applicability of the section 707(b)(2) means test turns primarily on a comparison of the debtor's "current monthly income" as defined in section 101 and "median family income" as defined in section 101. If the debtor's "current monthly income" times 12 is less than "median family income," for the state in which the debtor lives no one can file a motion to dismiss the Chapter 7 case based on the section 707(b)(2) means test, section 707(b)(7). And, in almost all real Chapter 7 bankruptcy cases in which the debtor is an individual whose debts are primarily consumer debts, the debtor's "current monthly income" multiplied by 12 will be less than "median family income" so it will not be necessary to consider the other particulars of the section 707(b)(2) means test.

For those debtors you encounter in the real world or in law school classes with "current monthly income" above "median family income," section 707(b)(2) creates a means test that compares 60 months of "current monthly income" as defined in section 101 with the total of the following:

(1) 60 months of expenses measured by Internal Revenue Service expense standards; and

(2) 60 months of other, actual expenses specified in section 707(b)(2); and

(3) payments due on secured and priority debts for the 60 months after the bankruptcy petition date.

More specifically, subtract the total of (1) and (2) and (3) above from the product of multiplying "current monthly income" by 60. If the difference is greater than either

(1) $10,000 or

(2) the greater of $6,000 or 25% of the debtor's nonpriority unsecured debts,

then section 707(b) "abuse" is presumed, section 707(b)(7).

Remember that the section 707(b)(2) computations in the previous paragraph do not establish "abuse." Rather, these computations establish a presumption of abuse that the debtor can rebut by swearing to and documenting "special circumstances" that increase expenses or decrease "current monthly income" so as to bring the debtor's income after expenses below the $10,000/$6,000 trigger points. More important, remember that these complicated section 707(b)(2) computations will be necessary only if a debtor's "current monthly income" exceeds "median family income."

As we will learn in the Unit on what happens in a Chapter 13 case, debtor's "current monthly income" as compared with "median family income" is also important in determining the Chapter 13 debtor's payment period and plan payment commitment. If the debtor's "current monthly income" exceeds "median family income," then

(1) the Chapter 13 plan payment period is "not less than 5 years" instead of 3 years, section 1325(b)(4) AND

(2) the minimum amount required to be paid under the plan is measured by the "means test" as discussed above instead of the "disposable income" test as applied by courts, section 1325(a)(3).

Unit 5

QUESTION FIVE: HOW DOES A BUSINESS BANKRUPTCY CASE BEGIN?

Table of Sections

Any bankruptcy case begins with the filing of a bankruptcy petition. Recall from Unit 4 that most bankruptcy petitions involving individuals are filed by the debtor under section 301. Similarly, most bankruptcy petitions involving businesses are filed by the debtor.

§ 5.1 Which Businesses Can File for Bankruptcy

Generally, any business entity can file for bankruptcy under Chapter 7 or Chapter 11. More specifically, here are the three things that you need know for your exam about which businesses can file for bankruptcy.

First, bankruptcy is limited to a "person" as that term is defined in section 101. The definition includes corporations, partnerships, limited partnerships, limited liability companies, . . .; it does not include sole proprietorships. If Epstein is owns and operates (1) the Law School Legend Laundry as a sole proprietorship and (2) the Law School Legend Lounge as a separate sole proprietorship, then Epstein can file bankruptcy petition but he cannot file a bankruptcy petition that is limited to one of his sole proprietorships.

Second, eligibility for bankruptcy never depends on insolvency. Even if a business entity is solvent, it can file for bankruptcy.

Third, business entities are not eligible to file for bankruptcy under Chapter 13. Only individuals can file for bankruptcy relief under Chapter 13.

§ 5.2 What Businesses Do Before Filing for Bankruptcy

The short answer to the question of what a business does before filing for bankruptcy is "a lot of stuff." The more immediate answer to that question is "it will not be on your exam." With the exception of (1) prebankruptcy payments to creditors which will be covered in the Unit on preferences and (2) prebankruptcy sales of assets which will be covered in the Unit on fraudulent transfers, and (3) prepackaged Chapter 11 plans which will be covered in the Unit on Chapter 11, the business decisions a business makes before filing for bankruptcy (such as who to hire and fire and who to tell) are not covered in a basic bankruptcy course.

§ 5.3 Where Businesses Can File for Bankruptcy

Most business bankruptcy cases involve small businesses and are filed in the bankruptcy court in the district in which the business operates. A very small number of Chapter 11 cases involve large corporations. These cases are usually filed in Delaware or the Southern District of New York.

The venue of bankruptcy case is governed by 28 U.S.C. § 1408. You need to know two things about section 1408.

First, a debtor may file for bankruptcy in its state of domicile. A corporation is "domiciled" in its state of incorporation. Most large corporations are incorporated in Delaware, and so filing in Delaware is a venue choice for these corporations.

Second, under the affiliate rule of section 1408(2), a corporation may file for bankruptcy in a state in which an "affiliate"(i.e., any related corporation) has filed. If, for example, *P* Corp. has a subsidiary, *S*, Inc., with its principal place of business in New York and *S*, Inc. files a bankruptcy petition in New York, then *P* Corp. can also file a bankruptcy petition in New York even though *P* Corp. is incorporated in North Carolina and all of its business operations are in North Carolina.

Unit 6

QUESTION SIX: WHAT ARE THE IMMEDIATE LEGAL CONSEQUENCES OF A BANKRUPTCY FILING?

Table of Sections

There are three "exam-important" immediate legal consequences of a bankruptcy filing. First, what has been property of the debtor now becomes property of the estate. Second, that property of the estate and the debtor are protected from creditors' collection efforts by the automatic stay. Third, the date the petition was filed is treated as the date of the commencement of the case, an important point of reference for a number of important bankruptcy concepts.

§ 6.1 Property of the Estate (Again)

Property of the estate is one of the important bankruptcy concepts that uses "commencement of the case," i.e., the date that the bankruptcy petition, was filed as a point of reference. Under section 541 an estate is created the instant the bankruptcy petition is filed regardless of whether the petition is for Chapter 7 relief, Chapter 11 relief, or Chapter 13 relief.

The importance of property of the estate is most obvious in Chapter 7 cases. In Chapter 7 cases, a trustee will take possession of the property of the estate. Even though it will take time for a Chapter 7 trustee to be appointed and for the Chapter 7 trustee to take possession of property of the estate, all of the debtor's interests in property becomes property of the estate the instant that the bankruptcy petition is filed.

If in the gap period between *D*'s filing for Chapter 7 bankruptcy, and the trustee's taking possession of property of the estate, *D* gives his bass boat to his fishing buddy *F*, the trustee can bring a conversion action against *D*. *D* did not own the bass boat. It was not his to give away. Although the trustee had not yet taken possession of the bass boat, the bass boat belonged to the bankruptcy estate—it was property of the estate.

§ 6.2 Automatic Stay (Again)

Similarly, the automatic stay protecting the property of the estate from creditors becomes legally effective from the moment that a bankruptcy petition is filed. Not the time that a creditor learns of the bankruptcy filing but the time of the bankruptcy filing.

If *D* files for bankruptcy on the morning of January 15th and *S*, an unpaid creditor with a security interest in *D*'s bass boat repossesses the boat that afternoon, *S* has violated the automatic stay. Regardless of whether *S* knew about the bankruptcy filing when it repossessed the boat, *S* was stayed from repossessing and must return the boat.

§ 6.3 Date of Petition as a Point of Reference

The commencement of the case (i.e., the date of the filing of a petition) is an important point of reference in doing bankruptcy law, an important dividing line. In the "racier language" used by many courts, the date of the filing of the petition is "the date of cleavage."

Property of the estate is generally limited to interests of the debtor in property "as of the commencement of the case" and proceeds thereof. Section 541(a)(1), (6).

A payment obligation that arose before the bankruptcy filing is often treated different from a payment obligation in applying basic bankruptcy concepts For example,

—Automatic stay: Many of the automatic stay provisions contain the limiting phrase "that arose before the commencement of the case," section 362(a)(1), (2), (5), (6), and (7). If, for example, *D* files for bankruptcy on April 5, a lawsuit to collect a debt owed by *D* before April 5 will be stayed, regardless of whether that suit was brought before or after the April 5 bankruptcy filing. On the other hand, a lawsuit to collect a debt *D* incurred after April 5 would not be stayed. [If that law suit on the post-April 5th debt resulted in a judgment against *D*, any effort to collect that judgment from property of the estate would be stayed]

—Allowance of claims: The amount of an allowable claim is generally fixed "as of the date of the filing of the petition," section 502(b). To illustrate, *D* borrows $10,000 from *C* and promises to repay the loan with interest. At the time of *D*'s bankruptcy petition, she owes *C* $10,900, including interest. Subject to two very limited exceptions,[3] *C*'s allowable claim will be limited to $10,900. Interest will stop accruing as of the date of the bankruptcy filing.

—Administrative expense priority: Determination of whether an obligation is an administrative expense often turns on the phrase "after the commencement of the case," cf. section 503(b).

For example, Nickles moonlights as a security guard for *D* Trailer Park. At the time of *D* Trailer Park's bankruptcy, it owes Nickles $100. Nickles continues to work as a security guard after *D* Trailer Park files for bankruptcy and *D* Trailer Park continues not to pay Nickles.

The amount owed Nickles for his postbankruptcy work would be an administrative expense priority. The $100 owed for exactly the same work done before *D* Trailer Park's bankruptcy filing would not be an administrative expense.

And the date of the filling of the petition becomes an important part of applying a number of important Bankruptcy Code time periods. For example, section 547, the preference provision which is discussed in Unit 10, refers to transfers "90 days before the date of the filing of the bankruptcy petition." Similarly, section 507(a)(4), the wage priority provision, refers to wages earned "180 days before the date of the filing of the petition."

There are other Bankruptcy Code provisions that focus on the date of the "order for relief." For example, a Chapter 7 discharge only affects "debts that arose before the date of the order for relief," section 727(b).

What is important for you to remember is that for voluntary bankruptcy cases, i.e., the more than 99% of all bankruptcy cases in which the debtor filed the bankruptcy petition, the date of the filing the bankruptcy petition is BOTH the date of the commencement of the case and the date of the order for relief. If *D* files a voluntary Chapter 7 bankruptcy on July 13th, then July 13 is the date of the commencement of the case and the date of the order for relief.

No formal adjudication is necessary in a voluntary case. In the language of section 301: (a) the filing commences the case and (b) "commencement of a voluntary case ... constitutes an order for relief."

It is only in involuntary cases, the less than 1% of the cases in which creditors file the bankruptcy petition, that a formal adjudica-

3. If *C*'s claim is secured and the value of the security is greater than the $10,900 amount of the debt, then *C*'s claim will continue to accrue interest under section 506(b). Or, if *D* is that once in a lifetime Chapter 7 debtor whose property of the estate yields more than enough to pay all creditors, then *C*'s will be paid postpetition interest under section 726(a)(5).

tion is necessary. While the filing of an involuntary petition effects a commencement of the case, it does not operate as an adjudication, as an "order for relief." The debtor has the right to file an answer. If the debtor does not timely answer or if one of the two section 303(h) grounds is established by the petitioning creditors, then the court will order relief. In involuntary cases then (and only in involuntary cases), there will usually be a gap of several weeks between the date of the filing of the petition (the commencement of the case) and the order for relief.

To review, *D*'s creditors file an involuntary Chapter 7 petition against her on July 13th. The court orders relief pursuant to section 303(h) on September 9th. In determining whether any of *D*'s pre-bankruptcy transfers is a section 547 preference, July 13th is the relevant date for the 90–day requirement. In determining which of *D*'s debts are affected by a discharge, September 9th is the relevant date.

Part Three

DURING THE BANKRUPTCY CASE

Unit 7

QUESTION SEVEN: WHAT HAPPENS DURING A CHAPTER 7 CASE?

Table of Sections

A lot happens in a Chapter 7 case after the bankruptcy petition is filed, starting the case

—a trustee is appointed

—the trustee collects the property of the estate

—the trustee sells the property of the estate (if there is any property of the estate to be sold)[6]

—the trustee distributes any net proceeds from the sale of the debtor's assets to creditors

—the debtor usually receives a discharge protecting her from any further liability on debts that arose before the filing of the bankruptcy petition.

Not much of what happens in a Chapter 7 case turns on the resolution of interesting bankruptcy law questions. And so not much of what happens in a Chapter 7 case is important to know for your bankruptcy exam. More specifically, we believe that you need to watch for two (at most three) legal problem areas that can be part of a Chapter 7 law school exam fact pattern:

6. Most Chapter 7 cases are "no asset cases." The phrase "no asset case" is commonly used to describe in which the debtor has assets but so because of exemptions and encumbrances the proceeds from the trustee's liquidation of the assets is not enough to pay administrative expenses, i.e., there are no assets (or proceeds from assets) available to pay unsecured claims.

(1) exemptions

(2) [and least important] distributions to creditors in a Chapter 7 case and

(3) discharge and dischargeability.

§ 7.1 Possible Exemption Issues

Only individual debtors have "exempt property" and possible exemptions issues. While exemptions issues are limited to individual debtors, exemptions issues are not limited to individual debtors in Chapter 7 bankruptcy cases or even to individual debtors in bankruptcy cases.

All states constitutionally or statutorily restrict creditor recourse to certain property belonging to individuals. Property designated in these exemption provisions *cannot* be reached by creditors through judicial collection efforts. A three-pronged purpose is commonly attributed to exemption statutes: protection of the debtor, protection of the family of the debtor, and protection of society. By allowing the debtor to retain certain property free from appropriation by creditors, exemption statutes extend to a debtor an opportunity for self-support so that he will not become a burden upon the public.

All states exempt certain personal property from creditor process. In some jurisdictions, the exempt property is identified by type (e.g., the family bible, a rifle); in others, by value (e.g., personal property of a value of $5,000); in still others, by both type and value (e.g., an automobile with a value of not more than $1,500). In most states, some specific provision is made for the exemption of life insurance, wages and retirement benefits.

Almost all states also have homestead laws designed to protect the family home from the reach of certain classes of creditors. Homestead laws only protect real property interests of the debtor and so are of no aid to the urban apartment dweller.

The protection afforded by an exemption statute is not absolute. The federal tax lien reaches and may be satisfied from "exempt property." A number of states make similar exceptions for state taxes, claims for alimony and child support, materialmen and mechanics' liens. By statute in most states, case law in others, mortgages and security interests are generally not affected by an exemption statute. Thus, the bank that finances the purchase of a home or car will be able to seize and sell the encumbered property notwithstanding the fact that the property is covered by an exemption statute.

In this book and in your Bankruptcy Code, you will see that these state laws are generally applicable in bankruptcy cases and are applicable in a bankruptcy case involving an individual debtor regardless of whether the case in a Chapter 7, 11, or 13 case. On law school exams, however, exemption issues arises primarily in fact patterns in which an individual has filed for Chapter 7 protection. Watch for a fact pattern that has (1) an individual debtor who (2) is eligible for Chapter 7 because of his relatively insignificant "current monthly income" and (3) still has significant property that he wants to claim as exempt.

(a) Which Law Determines What Property is Exempt in Bankruptcy

(1) Role of State Law

Section 522 provides that an individual debtor in a bankruptcy case—7, 11, or 13—can assert the exemptions to which she is entitled under the laws of the state of her domicile [as determined by section 522(b)(3)] and under federal laws other than Title 11.

In less than 1/4 of the states, individual debtors have the choice of asserting either these nonbankruptcy exemptions or the exemptions in section 522(d). The exemptions in section 522(d) are available only to individual debtors in states that have not enacted "opt out" legislation under section 522(b). Under section 522(b), a state legislature can preclude its residents from electing to utilize section 522(d). And, more than 3/4 of the states have enacted this "opt-out" legislation. Accordingly, we have "opted out" of coverage of section 522(d).

(2) Role of Bankruptcy Code in Determining Which State's Law Determines Exemptions

Recall that (1) exemption laws vary significantly from state to state and (2) the exemption law of the state of the debtor's domicile generally determines what property is exempt. Congress was concerned that individuals would change their domiciles before filing for bankruptcy—move from states with limited exemptions to states with more generous exemptions and then file for bankruptcy.

In 2005, Congress addressed that concern in three different provisions that you need to know. The most significant limitation on a debtor's choice of exemption statutes is section 522(b)'s new two-year residency inquiry for state exemption laws. As a result of the 2005 legislation, the debtor can choose the exemption law of the state in which she was living at the time of the bankruptcy filing only if that was the only state in which she was domiciled for the entire two years preceding bankruptcy. If the debtor has not maintained her domicile in the same state for the 730 days (two years) before her bankruptcy filing, the governing exemption law is the exemption law of the state in which the debtor lived in the 180 days before that 730 days. In other words, what is then determinative is where that debtor lived between 2 years and 2.5 years before the filing.

To illustrate, *D* files a bankruptcy petition in January 2006. In the two years before bankruptcy, she lived in Texas, California and Iowa. Now that we know that *D* did not maintain her domicile in a single state for the two years before her bankruptcy filing, we don't care where she lived in that two-year period. Instead, we want to know where she lived for most of the six-month period before that two-year period. If from September through December of 2003, *D* lived in Minnesota, then *D*'s exemptions in bankruptcy would be determined largely by Minnesota state law.

(3) Role of Bankruptcy Law in Limiting Conversion of Nonexempt Property Into Other Forms of Exempt Property

The 2005 amendments also added two limitations on a homestead exemption: First, a state homestead exemption will be reduced by the amount that the homestead is attributable to the debtor's disposition of nonexempt property in the ten years prior to bankruptcy with the intent to hinder, delay or defraud creditors, section 522(*o*). Second, value added to the homestead within 1,215 days before the bankruptcy filing is capped at $125,000, section 522(p).

The Bankruptcy Code does not expressly deal with the consequences of a debtor converting nonexempt property into exempt property on the eve of bankruptcy. What if, just before filing for bankruptcy, *D* takes funds from her bank account, nonexempt property under relevant law, and invests the money in a homestead? A number of different reported cases have answered this question—in a number of different ways. One common judicial approach is the "pig to hog analysis" in which the court compares the amount of property converted, the total amount of debt, and the total amount of other property still available to pay that debt and concludes that "when a pig becomes a hog, it is slaughtered."

To illustrate, *D*, an individual who lives in a state with an unlimited homestead exemption, owns a home that is encumbered by a $500,000 mortgage. *D* sells her Microsoft stock for $200,000 and uses the $200,000 to prepay her mortgage so that she only owes $300,000 to the mortgagee. Four weeks later, *D* files for bankruptcy. Section 522(p)'s $125.000 limit would apply, regardless of whether *D* intended to "hinder, delay or defraud a creditor" so that $75,000 of the value of the homestead would be property of the estate, available for distribution to creditors in a Chapter 7 case.

If instead of filing for bankruptcy four weeks after prepaying a part of her mortgage deed, *D* waited four years to file for bankruptcy, then section 522(p) would not apply. Section 522(*o*), however, might apply if, and only if, at the time *D* sold her Microsoft stock, she did so with the intent to hinder, delay or defraud creditors. And, if section 522(*o*) applies it would apply without any "exceeds . . . $125,000" limit so that $200,000 of the value of the homestead would be property of the estate, available for distribution to creditors in a Chapter 7 case.

New section 548(e) imposes the same sort of ten-year rule on self-settled trusts that section 522(*o*) imposes on homesteads. Because it takes so much class time to explain what a self-settled trust is, it is unlikely that you covered section 548(e) in class, unlikely that it will be on your exam.

The Bankruptcy Code does not expressly deal with the consequences of a debtor converting nonexempt property into other forms of nonexempt property. What if just before filing for bankruptcy, *D* takes funds from her bank account, nonexempt property under relevant state law, and uses that money to acquire some other form of exempt property? A number of different reported case have used this fact pattern to raise a number of different bankruptcy questions:

(1) Is the property acquired exempt under section 522?

(2) Is the transfer a fraudulent transfer under section 548?

(3) Is the transfer a basis for withholding discharge under section 727?

A common judicial approach in law school casebooks in answering these question is the "pig to hog" analysis of the United States Court of Appeals for the Eighth Circuit in *In re Tveten* (1988), in which the court compares the amount of property converted, the total amount of the debt, and the total amount of other property still available to pay that debt—"when a pig becomes a hog, it is slaughtered."

Dr. Tveten, a very successful doctor and very unsuccessful real estate investor, owed $19 million on a real estate partnership. His attorney recommended that he (1) maximize his exemptions and then (2) file for bankruptcy. Dr. Tveten followed this advice: he (1) invested $700,000 from selling nonexempt property and closing nonexempt accounts in an exempt annuity account with the Lutheran Brotherhood and (2) filed a bankruptcy petition. The bank that had financed Tveten's real estate investments and had obtained a personal guarantee from Tveten objected to his discharge. A divided Eighth Circuit denied the discharge.

(b) What the Bankruptcy Significance of Exempt Property is

Generally, an individual debtor is able to retain his or her exempt property. Exempt property is not distributed to creditors in the bankruptcy case and is protected from the claims of *most* pre-petition creditors after the bankruptcy case.

Note the italicized qualifier "most." Section 522(c) identifies the prepetition claims that are, in essence, exempt from the exemptions. After bankruptcy, there are basically four groups of prepetition creditors who have recourse to property set aside as exempt in a bankruptcy case:

#1 creditors with tax claims excepted from discharge by section 523(a)(1);

#2 spouses, former spouses and children of the debtor with domestic support obligations excepted from discharge by section 523(a)(5);

#3 creditors whose claims arise from the debtor's fraud in obtaining funding for higher education;

#4 creditors with liens on exempt property that are neither avoided nor extinguished through redemption.

(1) Section 522(f)

As #4 suggests, some liens on exempt property that are valid outside of bankruptcy can be invalidated because of bankruptcy. The general invalidation provisions, discussed infra in Unit 10, are applicable to liens on exempt property. And section 522(f) empowers the debtor to avoid judicial liens that impair exemptions and to avoid security interests that are both nonpurchase money and nonpossessory on certain household goods, tools of the trade, and health aids.

The most important thing for you to understand about section 522(f) is that it is not very important in the "real world." Again, it only affects (a) judicial liens and (b) certain kinds of consensual liens on certain kinds of exempt property.

Because of increases in the costs of obtaining a judicial lien and the increases in bankruptcy filing, creditors' use of judicial liens has decreased significantly. If a creditor does obtain a judicial lien on exempt property, the debtor can invoke section 522(f)(1)(A) to avoid that judicial lien "to the extent that such lien impairs an exemption."

Section 522(f)(2) explains the quoted phrase "to the extent that...." The following examples "explain" section 522(f)(2).

#1 Assume *D*'s house is worth $100,000 and *F* has a $40,000 first mortgage on the house and *J* has a $50,000 judicial lien on the house and the relevant exemption lien permits *D* a $15,000 homestead. Add (a) the amount of the exemption—$15,000, plus (b) the amount of the judicial lien—$50,000 and (c) the amount of all other liens on the homestead—$40,000. The total in this hypothetical is $105,000. Subtract from that the value of the house—$100,000. Under these facts, the amount of impairment is $5,000 and so the debtor could use 522(f) to avoid $5,000 of *J*'s judicial lien—to reduce that lien from $50,000 to $45,000.

#2 Now increase the amount of *F*'s first mortgage by $50,000 to $90,000. This increases the amount of the impairment to $55,000 and so the debtor could use 522(f) to avoid all of *J*'s $50,000 judicial lien.

We have used the example of a "judicial lien" to illustrate the application of section 522(f) because that is when you will use section 522(f)—if you ever use section 522(f). Recall that section 522(f) also applies to certain kinds of consensual liens on certain kinds of exempt property. In particular, recall our limiting phrase "certain kinds of."

Section 522(f)(1) does not apply to purchase money liens. It does not affect Circuit City's lien on the home entertainment center that it sold the debtor on credit; it does not apply to First Bank's lien on the dental equipment it financed. More limiting, section 522(f)(1) does not apply to any consensual lien on houses and cars—the two most valuable exempt assets of most individuals. Section 522(f)(1)(B) only applies to nonpurchase money security interests in the kinds of exempt property described in section 522(f)(1)(B)(i), (ii), or (iii).

The use of section 522(f) to avoid consensual liens on exemptions is further limited by section 522(f)(3). Even if the consensual lien is nonpurchase money and even if the exempt assets subject to the lien come within one of the categories described in section 522(f)(1)(B), the debtor may be precluded from avoiding the lien by section 522(f)(3).

It is not clear when section 522(f)(3) applies or how section 522(f)(3) applies. In general, you will look at section 522(f)(3) only if the debtor has job-related or farm-related exempt property that is worth more than $5,000 and that exempt property is subject to nonpurchase money consensual liens.

(2) Section 722

Possessory security interests in exempt personal property, purchase money security interests in exempt personal property, and any security interests on exempt personal property not covered by section 522(f) may be extinguished through "redemption." Section 722 authorizes an individual debtor to redeem or extinguish a lien on exempt personal property by paying the lienor in cash the replacement value of the encumbered property. To illustrate, assume that *D* owes *C* $3,000. *C* has a security interest in *D*'s Subaru.

If *D* files a bankruptcy petition and the value of the Subaru is only $1,200, *D* can eliminate *C*'s lien by paying *C* $1,200 in cash.

Section 722 applies to all liens on "tangible personal property intended for personal, family or household use" that secures a "dischargeable consumer debt." So, in theory, there is considerable overlap between section 522(f) and section 722. Is there any real overlap? If you understand what happens under section 522(f) and what happens under section 722, you understand that there is no practical overlap. A debtor will not invoke 722 to redeem property from liens by paying cash if she can invoke 522(f) to avoid such liens without paying.

§ 7.2 Trustee's Distribution of Proceeds Pursuant to Statutory Guidelines

Think again about how Chapter 7 cases end. Costs and benefits. In every Chapter 7 case, the costs to the debtor include (i) attorneys's fees, and (ii) loss of "property of the estate." In every Chapter 7 case, the benefit to creditors is the trustee's distribution of the money received from the sale of property of the estate in the manner set out in section 726. Section 726 distribution is a part of the end game in every Chapter 7 case: Chapter 7 cases involving debtors who are individuals, Chapter 7 cases involving debtors who are corporations or other business entities.

(a) What Property is Distributed to Creditors in Chapter 7 Cases

The bankruptcy trustee has a statutory duty to sell the "property of the estate," section 704(1). The net proceeds received from the liquidation of the "property of the estate" are to be distributed to the holders of unsecured or general claims. Such claimants do not, however, receive the net proceeds from the sale of all of the "property of the estate":

- Some "property of the estate" will be turned over to the debtor as exempt property, section 522.
- Some "property of the estate" will be validly transferred after the filing of the bankruptcy petition to third parties, section 549.
- Some "property of the estate" will be subject to liens that are valid in bankruptcy. Encumbered property or the proceeds thereof must be first used to satisfy the holders of secured claims, cf. section 725.
- Some "property of the estate" must be used to satisfy the administrative expenses of the bankruptcy proceeding.

Subject to these four exceptions, holders of unsecured or general claims in Chapter 7 cases receive the net proceeds from the bankruptcy trustee's sale of the "property of the estate." As noted earlier, the great majority of Chapter 7 cases are "no asset" cases, at least in the sense that there are no assets available to pay unsecured claims.

(b) What the Order of Distribution is

In a bankruptcy case, certain allowed unsecured claims are entitled to priority in distribution over other unsecured claims. Section 507(a) sets out the levels of priorities. In its proof of claim form, a creditor can assert a priority and state the amount and basis therefore. Most of the litigation over whether a claim is entitled to a priority involve assertions of section 507(a)(2) administrative expense status.

Chapter 7 requires that the various priority classes are paid in the order in which they are listed in section 507, section 726(a)(1). In other words, each section 507(a)(1) first priority claim is to be paid in full before any section 507(a)(2) second priority claim is paid at all. If there are not sufficient funds to pay all claims within a particular class, then generally all claims entitled to that priority are paid pro rata.

Section 726 establishes the rules for distribution in a Chapter 7 case to the holders of unsecured claims. Basically, the distribution is to be as follows:

1. priorities under section 507 (section 507 is considered below)

2. allowed unsecured claims which were either timely filed or tardily filed by a creditor who did not know of the bankruptcy

3. allowed unsecured claims which were tardily filed by creditors with notice or actual knowledge of the bankruptcy

4. fines and punitive damages

5. postpetition interest on prepetition claims.

Each claim of each of the five categories must be paid in full before any claim in the next category receives any distribution. Each claim within a particular category shares pro rata if the proceeds from the liquidation of the property of the estate is insufficient to satisfy all claims in that category.

Assume, for example, that there is $20,000 available to pay to holders of unsecured claims and the following unsecured claims:

$11,000 claims entitled to priority under section 507

$4,800 claim by *X* that was timely filed

$7,200 claim by *Y* that was timely filed

$3,000 claim by *Z* that was not timely filed even though *Z* knew of the bankruptcy case.

The distribution would be:

$11,000 to holders of priority claims

$3,600 to *X*[7]

$5,400 to *Y*.

§ 7.3 Resolution of Possible Discharge Issues in Individual's Bankruptcy Case

Again, think about how a Chapter 7 bankruptcy case ends. Benefits and costs. For most individual debtors, the most significant benefit of Chapter 7 bankruptcy is discharge. And for most creditors of these individual debtors, the most significant cost of the Chapter 7 case is the discharge.

For your exam, you will need to be able to answer the following three questions [(a), (b), and (c) below] about a bankruptcy discharge: (1) what does a discharge do, (2) which Chapter 7 debtors do not receive a discharge, and (3) which debts are not affected by a discharge.

(a) What Discharge Does

Sections 524 and 525 answer the question "what does a discharge do?" Primarily section 524.

Under section 524 a discharge protects a debtor from any further personal liability on discharged debts. After a bankruptcy discharge, creditors cannot sue the debtor to collect discharged debts; creditors cannot even call the debtor to ask her to pay a discharged debt.

The title of section 525 suggests that the debtor is also protected from discriminatory treatment. The Boy Scouts could refuse to let someone serve as a scoutmaster because he filed for bankruptcy—even straight bankruptcy. More importantly, a store could refuse to extend credit or a bank could refuse to make a loan because of a person's bankruptcy history.

Notice that two of the three lettered subsections, 525(a) and 525(c), only apply to "governmental units." And, notice that two of

7. The first $11,000 must be used to pay priority claims. The remaining $9,000 ($20,000 − $11,000) must be distributed pro rata to $12,000 ($4,800 + $7,200) of timely filed claims. Accordingly, each timely filed claim will be paid at the rate of 75¢ on the dollar ($9,000 ÷ $12,000). Accordingly, *X* will receive $3,600 for its $4,800 claim.

the three subsections, 525(a) and 525(b), require proof that the adverse action occurred "solely" because of the bankruptcy history.

For your exam, it is more important to understand what a discharge does not do than what a discharge does. It only protects the debtors from further personal liability on the debt and provides limited protection from discrimination. A discharge does not cancel or extinguish debts.

(1) No Protection of Co–Debtors

Section 524(e) limits the protection of the discharge to the debtor. A bankruptcy discharge does not automatically affect the liability of other parties such as co-debtors or guarantors. For example, the discharge of an insured tortfeasor does not affect the liability of the insurance company.

(2) No Effect on Liens

A bankruptcy discharge has no effect on a lien. Remember, a discharge only eliminates a creditor's right to collect a debt from the debtor personally. It does not eliminate the debt; discharge does not eliminate liens securing payment of the debt.

To illustrate, *D* owes *C* $10,000. The debt is secured in part by *D*'s car which is worth $6,000. *D* files for relief under Chapter 7. The trustee abandons the car to the debtor under section 554. *D* receives a discharge. The discharge does not extinguish *C*'s security interest. If *D* is in default, *C* can repossess the car. The discharge does, however, wipe out *C*'s rights against *D* personally. If *C* repossesses and resells the car, *C* cannot obtain a deficiency judgment against *D*.

(b) Which Chapter 7 Debtors Do Not Receive a Discharge

Some Chapter 7 debtors do not receive a discharge. Section 727 set out the twelve grounds for withholding a discharge from a Chapter 7 debtor. These twelve "objections" to discharge are the only statutory grounds for withholding a discharge in a Chapter 7 case.

Section 727(a)(1) denies a Chapter 7 discharge to business entities such as corporations or partnerships. Only an individual is eligible to receive a discharge in a Chapter 7 case.

The other eleven objections to discharge in section 727(a) apply to individual debtors. Most of these statutory grounds for withholding a discharge have their foundation in some form of dishonesty or improper conduct either before or after the bankruptcy filing.

The most frequently tested objection to discharge is aimed at "frequent filers." If a debtor has received a discharge in a Chapter

7 case in the past eight years, she will be denied discharge, section 727(a)(8).

The eight-year time period test is measured from filing date to filing date. So, if *D* obtains a discharge on April 5, 2000, in a Chapter 7 case filed on January 15, 2000, section 728(a)(8) would not bar *D*'s bankruptcy discharge in a Chapter 7 bankruptcy case filed in March of 2008.

Now that you understand what section 727(a)(8) does, be sure you understand what this provision does not do. Section 727(a)(8) only limits the availability of a discharge in a Chapter 7 case. It does not affect the debtor's right to file a voluntary petition or creditors' right to file involuntary petitions under Chapter 7 or any other chapter.

(c) Which Debts Are Not Affected by a Discharge

Even if a Chapter 7 debtor receives a discharge, that discharge does not always cover all of the Chapter 7 debtor's debts. Certain debts are not affected by a discharge. Issues as to whether a debt is covered by the discharge are commonly referred to as "dischargeability issues."

(1) Section 727(b) and the Time That a Debt Arises

Section 727(b) raises a dischargeability issue by limiting the Chapter 7 discharge to debts that "arose before" the date that the bankruptcy petition was filed. If D files her Chapter 7 bankruptcy petition on January 15, then borrows $20,000 from C on February 16 and then receives a discharge on March 4, the $20,000 debt owed to C would not be affected by the discharge.

(2) Section 523 and Exceptions to Discharge

Most dischargeability issues arise under section 523. Section 523, entitled "Exceptions to discharge" lists the kinds of debt that are not covered by a bankruptcy discharge.

The phrase "exceptions to discharge" is unfortunately similar to the phrase "objections to discharge." It is important to understand the difference between an "objection to discharge" under section 727 and an "exception to discharge" under section 523.

Proof of an objection to discharge benefits all of that debtor's creditors. Proof of an exception to discharge benefits only the very creditor that established that its debt was excepted from discharge.

Assume, for example, that Epstein files for bankruptcy and his creditors included Nickles, Higgins, and West. If Nickles or any other creditor or, more likely, the Chapter 7 trustee, is able to establish a section 727 objection to Epstein's bankruptcy discharge, then Epstein will not receive a discharge. Higgins and West as well as Nickles will be able to proceed against Epstein personally to collect the remainder of their claims.

If, on the other hand, Nickles establishes a section 523 exception to discharge, then Epstein will still receive a discharge. Neither Higgins nor West will be able to proceed against Epstein personally to collect the remainder of their claims. Only Nickles, whose debt was excepted from the discharge, will be able to proceed against Epstein personally after the bankruptcy discharge.

The previous topic—objections to discharge—like the topic before it—exemptions—affects the Chapter 7 debtor and all holders of unsecured claims. This topic—exceptions to discharge—like the topic after it—reaffirmation—affects only the debtor and a particular creditor.

Section 523(a) sets out 18 exceptions to discharge. Some of these statutory exceptions are based on the nature of the debt; other exceptions are based on the conduct of the debtor in incurring that debt.

Taxes [section 523(a)(1)], domestic support obligations [section 523(a)(5)] and and educational loans [section 523(a)(8)] are the three most important discharge exceptions based on the nature of the debt. If your teacher covered any of these three, she most likely covered educational loans. Pandering to students, teachers cover dischargeability of educational loans because they think students will be interested.

Section 523(a)(8) excepts from discharge student loans and other obligations to repay "educational benefits." The debtor has to prove "undue hardship" to have her student loans discharged.

Most of the cases under section 523(a)(8) simply address the question of what is "undue hardship." These cases look to the totality of the circumstances.

There are, however, a number of section 523(a)(8) reported cases that address the legal question of whether the bankruptcy court can grant a partial discharge—e.g., it would be a hardship for the debtor to pay the $100,000 in college loans that she owes but she can pay $40,000 and so $60,000 is discharged and the remaining $40,000 is excepted from discharge under section 523(a)(8).

There is no language in section 523(a)(8) or anywhere else in the Bankruptcy Code that empowers a court to except a part of a debt from discharge. The courts that have granted partial discharge of student loans look to the policy objectives of section 523(a)(8) and "the discretionary equitable powers reserved by the bankruptcy court by section 105."

Credit card debt is not specifically excepted from discharge. Indeed the phrase "credit card" nowhere appears in section 523(a) or any Bankruptcy Code provision.

If the phrase "credit card" appears on your bankruptcy exam, you need to turn to section 523(a)(2) which is based primarily on the conduct of the debtor incurring the debt. Accordingly, your answer must focus on the conduct of the debtor in incurring the credit card debt.

Section 523(a)(2) dealing with fraudulently incurred obligations is the most frequently involved exception to discharge in real world bankruptcy proceedings and in law school exam questions on credit cards. Section 523(a)(2)(A) and section 523(a)(2)(B) describe two different fact patterns.

Section 523(a)(2)(B) deals specifically with the fact pattern that includes the debtor's providing the creditor with a written false financial statement. Section 523(a)(2)(A) applies if the creditor alleges "false pretenses, a false representation, or actual fraud, other than a statement respecting the debtor's or an insider's financial condition."

Even though dischargeability of credit card debt involves 523(a)(2)(A), it is easier to understand section 523(a)(2) by starting with section 523(a)(2)(B). A creditor faces difficult problems of proof under section 523(a)(2)(B). A creditor seeking an exception to discharge based on the debtor's providing false or incomplete financial information must establish:

(1) materially false written statement respecting the financial condition of the debtor or an "insider";

(2) its reasonable reliance on the statement;

(3) the debtor's intent to deceive.

Merely establishing the falsity of a written statement involving the debtor's financial condition will not suffice. The creditor will also have to establish its reliance, the reasonableness of the reliance, and, most difficult of all, the debtor's intent to deceive.

A close comparison of the language of section 523(a)(2)(B) with the language of section 523(a)(2)(A) raises the more important question of whether the reasonable reliance and intent to deceive requirements that are expressed in section 523(a)(2)(B) should be implied under section 523(a)(2)(A). Courts, including the Supreme Court in *Field v. Mans* (1995), have held that section 523(a)(2)(A) does require proof of both the debtor's intent to deceive and the creditor's reasonable reliance.

Section 523(a)(2)(A) needs to be read together not only with section 523(a)(2)(B) but also together with section 523(a)(2)(C) which deals with luxury goods and services and cash advances. More specifically, consumer debts incurred for luxury goods and services owed to a single creditor in excess of $500 incurred within 90 days of the bankruptcy filing are "presumed nondischargeable." Similarly, obligations to pay cash advances of $750 obtained within 70 days of the bankruptcy filing are "presumed to be nondischargeable."

Note section 523(a)(2)(C)'s use of the phrase "presumed to be nondischargeable." How can this presumption be rebutted? Section 523(a)(2)(C) begins with the phrase "for purposes of subparagraph (A) of this subsection." Section 523(a)(2)(A) deals with false representations. When a person buys something on credit with a credit card, he impliedly represents (1) an ability to pay and (2) an intent to repay. Section 523(a)(2)(C) seems to presume that with respect to the described luxury purchases and cash advances the debtor lacks that ability and/or intent. Accordingly, it would seem that the debtor can avoid section 523(a)(2)(C)'s exception from discharge by showing that he had both the ability and the intent to repay at the time of the transaction.

And, it is necessary to read section 523(a)(2) together with section 523(d). Under section 523(d), a creditor who unsuccessfully asserts a section 523(a)(2) exception to the discharge of a consumer debt may be required to pay the debtor's costs including an attorney's fee. Section 523(d)'s test is whether the creditor was "not substantially justified." Even if the position of the creditor was "not substantially justified," it can avoid section 523(d) liability if "special circumstances would make the award unjust."

(3) Reaffirmation Agreements

A debtor can affect which debts are affected by a bankruptcy discharge by entering into a reaffirmation agreement with a creditor, after she has fled for bankruptcy and before she has received a discharge. A reaffirmation agreement is an agreement between a debtor and one of her creditors that the debtor will pay a debt she incurred before her bankruptcy filing that, but for the reaffirmation agreement, would have been dischargeable in the bankruptcy case. Under contract law, such an agreement is legally enforceable even though there is no bargained-for exchange, i.e., no consideration.

Why would a debtor make such an agreement? The most common reason for a debtor's reaffirming a debt is to keep encumbered property. Assume, for example, that *D* owes GMAC $16,000 on her car loan at the time of her bankruptcy filing. *D*'s bankruptcy discharge will affect GMAC's contract rights against *D*—GMAC's ability to collect the $16,000 from *D* personally. The bankruptcy discharge will not, however, affect GMAC's property interest in the car—GMAC's ability to foreclose on its lien and take the car. Accordingly, *D* might enter into a reaffirmation agreement with GMAC to keep her car.

Most of the bankruptcy law issues relating to reaffirmation relate to concern that a creditor might pressure a debtor into reaffirming its debt.

Section 524(c) and (d) limit the enforceability of reaffirmation agreements by

1. requiring that the agreement be executed before the discharge is granted, section 524(c)(1);

2. giving the debtor a right to rescind, section 524(c)(4);

3. requiring that, before any reaffirmation agreement is signed, the creditor provided the debtor with disclosures detailed in section 524(k);

4. requiring the reaffirmation agreement be filed with the court, section 524(c)(3);

5. requiring a hearing if the debtor is an individual and not represented by an attorney in the reaffirmation negotiations, section 524(d), section 524(c)(6);

6. requiring the attorney who represented the debtor in the reaffirmation to certify inter alia that the debtor was fully informed and that either the agreement does not impose an undue hardship or the debtor has the ability to make the reaffirmation payments, section 524(k)(5).

§ 7.4 Review: Comparison of Reaffirmation Agreements and Redemption

We covered "redemption" earlier in this Unit as a part of section 7.1 on exempt property. If you get an exam question on redemption of reaffirmation agreements, it will probably invoke both.

Either redemption or reaffirmation can be involved in a Chapter 7 debtor's paying secured claims from postpetition earnings and loans. Recall that (i) most of the debtor's interests in property as of the date of the filing of the bankruptcy petition becomes property of the estate, (ii) the debtor can retain property that is exempt under section 522, and (iii) if such property is encumbered by liens, the liens remain enforceable after a discharge. Accordingly, if Nickles' prized bass boat is exempt property and *F* has a lien on the boat, Nickles keeps the boat and *F* keeps its lien on the boat.

Because *F* retains its lien notwithstanding the discharge, Nickles may be willing to pay *F* from postpetition earnings or borrowings in order to keep the boat. If so, Nickles should look to section 524 reaffirmation agreement and section 722 redemption.

Recall that section 524 does not require the payment of any particular amount. Recall also that section 524 does require an agreement: the debtor and creditor must agree as to the amount that is to be paid and other terms.

Section 722, on the other hand, does not require any agreement, but does require the payment of a particular amount. Section 722 empowers Chapter 7 debtors to extinguish liens on certain property by paying the holder of the secured claim an amount equal to the "amount of the allowed secured claim," i.e., an amount measured by the value of the collateral not the amount of the debt.

The following chart compares the debtor's payment of a secured claim under section 524 with the debtor's payment of a secured claim under section 722.

	524	**722**
Amount of payment	Determined by agreement between debtor and creditor	Determined by the value of the collateral which is fixed at the replacement price
Form of payment	Determined by agreement between debtor and creditor	Cash

Remember, section 722 redemption only applies to secured claims. A section 524 reaffirmation agreement is not limited to secured claims.

Unit 8

QUESTION EIGHT: WHAT HAPPENS DURING A CHAPTER 13 BANKRUPTCY CASE?

Table of Sections

In Chapter 13, an individual debtor with a regular source of income (1) proposes a plan of repayment, (2) obtains court approval of the plan and (3) makes the plan payments over a number of years. Generally, the Chapter 13 plan is prepared by the debtor's attorney before the bankruptcy petition is filed so that the plan is filed with the petition.

There is a trustee is every Chapter 13 case. In most districts, the United States trustee for that district appoints one or more persons to serve as the Chapter 13 trustee for all cases in that district.

The Chapter 13 trustee has the responsibility of reviewing the Chapter 13 plan before the court approves the plan. More specifically, the Chapter 13 trustee makes a preliminary determination of (1) whether the plan is feasible, i.e., whether the debtor will be able to make the payments that she proposes to pay under the plan and (2) whether the plan can be "confirmed," i.e., whether the plan meets the legal requirements for court approval.

While the Chapter 13 trustee reviews the plan, the court will decide whether to confirm the plan at "a hearing." Generally, the Chapter 13 trustee will be heard (and heeded) on the general question of whether the plan should be confirmed.

After the court confirms (approves) the plan, the Chapter 13 trustee collects plan payments from the debtor and makes the plan payments to the creditors. When a Chapter 13 debtor fails to make plan payments as required by the court-approved plan, the Chapter 13 trustee initiates appropriate remedial action.

We think it is helpful to think of Chapter 13 (and Chapter 13 exam questions) in terms of the four different stages in the "life" of a Chapter 13 case:

#1 "Planning"

#2 Obtaining court approval of a plan

#3 Living with a Chapter 13 plan

#4 Ending a Chapter 13 plan

This Unit will cover the possible Chapter 13 exam issues that you might encounter in each of these four stages and then review Chapter 13 by comparing what happens in a Chapter 13 case with what happens in a Chapter 7 case.

§ 8.1 "Planning"

Again, every Chapter 13 debtor must file a plan, section 1321. At a hearing, the court will look at that plan to determine if it meets the requirements of section 1325. If the court "confirms" (approves) the plan, then you look to the plan for the answers to the two most important questions in any bankruptcy case: (1) how much does the debtor has to pay and (2) who gets paid.

(a) Planning: How Much a Chapter 13 Debtor Has to Pay

Section 1325, which sets out the confirmation requirements, has a two-part test for establishing the minimum amount that a Chapter 13 debtor must pay.

First, payments under a Chapter 13 plan must at least enable unsecured creditors to receive as much as t hey would have received if this had been a Chapter 7 case and nonexempt, unencumbered property of the estate had been sold, with net proceeds distributed to creditors, section 1325(a)(4). This is commonly referred to as the "best interest test."

[It is in your "best interest" not to spend much time (now or on your test) worrying about the "best interest test." Recall that most of what individuals have when they file for bankruptcy is exempt or encumbered or both.]

Second, section 1325 requires a Chapter 13 debtor to pay all of her projected "disposable income" to creditors under the plan for a three to five year commitment period, section 1325(b) This is commonly referred to as the "best efforts tests" or the "disposable income requirement." You do need to use your "best efforts" to understand the "disposable income requirement."

At the very least, you need to know that "disposable income" is based on the Chapter 13 debtor's current monthly income less certain living expenses. If you professor is requiring you to know more than that then you need to read again about two Chapter 7 concepts

—"current month income"

—"median family income."

Recall "current monthly income," as defined in section 101, is subjective. It looks to this particular debtor and is a six-month average of monthly income from all sources of this particular debtor.

"Median family income," as defined in section 101, is objective. It looks to U.S. Census Board tables for the debtor's state for the median income of a household in that state with the same number of persons as the debtor's.

A comparison of "current monthly income" and applicable "median family income" can affect the number of months that a Chapter 13 debtor must commit all of her disposable "disposable income" to the Chapter 13 plan. Thirty-six months is the required "commitment period" if the debtor's current monthly income is less than the applicable median family income. Sixty months is the required commitment period is *D*'s current monthly income is more than the applicable median family income.

This comparison of *D*'s "current monthly income" and applicable "median income" not only determines how many months *D* must pay all of her disposable income to unsecured creditors under the Chapter 13 plan but also affects how much of *D*'s income will be "disposable income."

Remember "disposable income" is determined by "current monthly income" less certain allowable expenses. What expenses the Chapter 13 debtor can deduct from her "current monthly income" in calculating "disposable income" depends on whether the "current monthly income" is above the relevant "median income."

If the debtor's "current monthly income" is less than the applicable "median income" then "reasonably necessary" expenses can be deducted. Lots of questions about what expenses are "reasonably necessary"—fact questions, not exam questions.

If the debtor's household monthly income exceeds the median income, reasonable expenses are determined by applying the means test formula. That formula permits the deduction of four distinct types of expenses:

1. Living expenses, as determined by the Internal Revenue Service guidelines;
2. Monthly secured debt payments;
3. Amount required to pay priority debts in full;
4. Other administrative and special purpose expenses, including up to 10% of the projected Chapter 13 plan payments for administrative expenses, and most charitable contributions.

The "best interest test" and the "disposable income test" simply set a floor on the amount that a Chapter 13 debtor must pay. Sometimes a debtor will be required to pay more than the floor amount in order to confirm a plan, because Chapter 13 imposes requirements that can be met only if the debtor pays more. For example, the debtor must pay priority claims in full, in order to confirm a plan. The most common types of priority claims that Chapter 13 debtors have are the costs of the Chapter 13 case (trustee charges and debtor's attorney fees paid through the plan), support obligations and certain tax obligations. If the amount of the priority claims exceeds the amount that the debtor must pay to meet the best interests test and the disposable income requirement, then the minimum amount that the debtor must pay is the amount necessary to pay the priority claims.

Sometimes a debtor will have to pay more than the floor amount to confirm a plan that accomplishes what the debtor wants to accomplish. If, for example, the debtor is behind on her house or car payments and she wants to keep the house or recently purchased car, she will either need to cure the default though the plan payments (bring the house or car loan current) or will have to pay the entire debt through the plan. Sections 1322(b)(2)–(5) and 1325(a)(5).

(b) Planning: Who Gets Paid

As the preceding paragraphs remind us, there are three types of claims in bankruptcy: priority claims, unsecured claims and secured claims.

(1) Priority Claims

Priority claims are those claims identified in section 507 for "special treatment." Recall that in Chapter 7 cases, the special treatment for priority claims is "paid first." While Chapter 7 does not require that priority claims be paid in full, it does require that priority claims be paid first—that unsecured claims get nothing from the Chapter 7 trustee's distribution of the net proceeds from the liquidation of property of the estate until priority claims are paid.

The "special treatment" of priority claims in Chapter 13 cases is completely different. There is no requirement that priority claims be paid first; instead, Chapter 13 requires that the plan must pay priority claims in full over the life of the plan, unless a particular priority creditor agrees to a different treatment.

(2) Unsecured Claims

Section 726 governs the payment of unsecured claims in a Chapter 7 case and requires a pro rata treatment: each holder of an unsecured claim is paid the same percentage of what it is owed. The Chapter 13 plan governs the payment of unsecured claims in a Chapter 13 case. A Chapter 13 plan may classify claims and pay some classes of claims more than others.

A Chapter 13 debtor often wants to make certain that some creditors are paid in full by her Chapter 13 plan. Especially debts guaranteed by a family member or friends and debts excepted from the Chapter 13 discharge.

To get credit, the debtor may have had to get some more credit-worthy—a relative or close friend—to guarantee payment of the obligation. To the extent that the Chapter 13 plan does not pay that obligation, the creditor can and will collect from the co-debtor. *Cf.* section 1301(c)(2).

And, some debts such as student loans are not covered by a Chapter 13 discharge. The debtor will, of course, want to pay all such nondischargeable debts in full in her Chapter 13 plan; otherwise the debtor will have to pay the balance after completing the Chapter 13 plan payments.

A Chapter 13 debt can use claim classification to pay one or more of her creditors in full even though she does not have sufficient disposable income to pay all of her creditors in full.[8] Under section 1322(b)(1), a Chapter 13 plan can divide unsecured claims into more than one class and treat the various classes differently.

The primary limitation on this discrimination in the plan treatment of unsecured claims is that the classification may not "discriminate unfairly." The key word is, of course, "unfairly": any

8. A Chapter 13 debtor can also use section 1322(b)(5) to make preferential plan payments on long-term debts. Section 1322(b)(5) only applies if the last payment on the debt is due after the last plan payment. With respect to such debts, a Chapter 13 debtor can simply make payments according to the contractual terms. The advantage to this approach is that more of the debt can be paid during the Chapter 13 case. The disadvantage to this approach is that, even if the debt was otherwise dischargeable, the debtor will have to complete the payments under the contract notwithstanding any Chapter 13 discharge. *Cf.* section 1328(a).

classification discriminates—what is required is that the discrimination not be unfair.

Most reported opinions under section 1322(b)(1) set out some sort of multi-factor test. The factor that seems most important is the difference in the amount of payment to the various classes. Obviously, it will be easier to get court approval of a plan that pays Class 2 100% and all other classes 90% than a plan that pays Class 2 100% and all other classes 10%.

Put Chapter 13 plan classification in context. All Chapter 13 plans must meet the "best interests" test of section 1325(a)(4). In other words, even the creditors in the classes receiving least favorable Chapter 13 plan treatment are still receiving at least as much as they would have received if the debtor had filed for Chapter 7 relief instead of Chapter 13.

(3) Secured Claims Other Than Home Mortgages

In most Chapter 13 plans and in all law school exam questions involving secured claims, each secured claims is the subject of a separate plan provision that modifies the contract rights of the secured creditor. Assume, for example, that *D* owes *S* $7,000 and the debt is secured by *D*'s bass boat. The installment sales contract between *D* and *S* provides for 10% interest and 30 equal monthly payments. *D*'s Chapter 13 plan can modify *S*'s contract rights by reducing the total amount to be paid to *S*, change the interest rate, change the number of payments, and change the amount of each payment.

A Chapter 13 plan can propose modifications of a secured claim to which the holder of the claim consents. For example, the creditor might agree to wait longer for payment if the payment is increased. If the modification is acceptable to the holder of the secured claim, it will be acceptable to the court, section 1325(a)(5)(A). No secured claim plan confirmation issue.

Alternatively, a Chapter 13 plan can propose to surrender the encumbered property to the holder of a secured claim. Assume, for example, that *D* owes *S* $200,000, secured by a first mortgage on Blackacre. If *D*'s Chapter 13 plan surrenders Blackacre to *S*, then *S* no longer has a secured claim. If Blackacre's value is less than $200,000, *S* might still have a claim. Just not a secured claim. Accordingly, a plan that "surrenders the property securing such claim" will be acceptable to the court, section 1325(a)(5)(C). Again, no secured claim plan confirmation issue.

Secured claim plan confirmation issues arise only if the plan proposes that (i) the debtor retain the encumbered property and (ii) the secured claim be modified and (iii) the holder of the secured claim does not accept the plan. These issues are called cram down issues (or cramdown issues).

It's not the Bankruptcy Code that uses the phrase "cram down." Neither cram down nor cramdown appears anywhere in the Bankruptcy Code. Rather it is the bankruptcy lawyers, judges, and law professors who have come to use the term cram down to describe court approval of a plan provision that effects changes in the payment of a claim that the claim holder objects to.

In order to cram down a Chapter 13 modification of a secured claim, the bankruptcy court must apply section 1325(a)(5)(B). And, in order to apply section 1325(a)(5)(B), it is necessary to determine the nature of the proposed modification.

Prior to the 2005 legislation, the most common form of secured debt modification was a "strip down," i.e., reducing the amount that was to be paid to the holder of the secured debt to the value of its collateral. And, prior to the 2005 legislation, in applying section 1325(a)(5)(B) to a "strip down," the bankruptcy court would make the following two determinations:

(1) what is the value of the collateral;[9]

(2) is the present value of the plan payments at least equal to the value of the collateral?[10]

To illustrate, *D*, an independent trucker, owes *S* $60,000. *S* has a security interest in *D*'s tractor and trailer rig. *D* files a Chapter 13 plan that proposes to pay *S* $1,000 a month for 36 months. *S* does not consent.

In applying section 1325(a)(5)(B) to this proposed strip down, the court would first have to determine the value of the collateral, the value of the tractor and trailer rig. Looking to *Associates Commercial Corp. v. Rash* (1997), discussed supra, the court would look to the replacement value of the tractor and trailer rig.

If the replacement value of the tractor and trailer rig was $36,000, then the proposed plan payments must have a present value of $36,000. Obviously, a Chapter 13 debtor's promise to pay $1,000 a month for 36 months has a present value significantly less than $36,000. The debtor would also have to pay cram down interest as measured by the "formula approach" of *In re Till* (2002).

9. The relevant language in section 1325(a)(5) is "allowed amount of SUCH CLAIM." The antecedent of "such claim" is "secured claim." Section 506 ties the amount of the secured claim to the value of the collateral.

10. The relevant language in section 1325(a)(5) is "value, as of the effective date of the plan, of property to be distributed under the plan. . . ."

In *Till*, Debtors purchased a used truck from Creditor for $6,725.75 (including fees and taxes). Debtors paid $300 down and financed the balance over 136 weeks at 21% interest, with payments due biweekly. Creditor retained a security interest in the truck.

One year after Debtors purchased the truck, they filed Chapter 13. Debtors owed $4,894.89 on the truck obligation at the time of bankruptcy, but the truck was worth only $4,000. Debtors' plan proposed to pay Creditor's $4,000 secured claim over a period not to exceed three years with interest at 9.5%, which was prime rate plus 1.5%. Creditor objected, claiming it should be paid interest at 21%.

The question was what methodology should be used in deciding how much compensation a creditor has to receive so that the present value of the payments it receives under a plan equals its allowed secured claim as required by § 1325(a)(5)(B). Compensation for delay in payment is required because of the risk of nonpayment (except in Justice Thomas' view), the risk that inflation may make the dollars paid at a future date worth less than dollars paid today, and the fact that if the creditor had the dollars today, it could invest the money and make a rate of return, commonly referred to as the time value of money.

Before this decision, courts had used four different methods to determine the compensation required: the formula rate, the coerced loan rate, the presumptive contract rate, and the cost of funds rate. In a 4–1–4 decision, the plurality accepted Debtors' argument that the formula rate should apply. That rate is calculated by starting with the prime rate, which is a rate that a commercial lender would charge a commercial borrower with good credit. The prime rate includes the amounts necessary "to compensate for the loan's opportunity costs, the inflation risk, and the relatively slight default risk." Add to the prime rate such additional percentage points as is necessary to compensate the creditor if the debtor poses a greater risk of nonpayment than a commercial borrower with good credit. The adjustment should not be so high "as to doom the plan." Generally, the adjustment is in the 1%–3% range.

The plurality identified three reasons for adopting the formula rate. First, bankruptcy judges should be uniform in their approach to determining interest rates. The formula approach requires less expensive evidentiary hearings than the other approaches, and is familiar to the financial community. Second, the fact that the Chapter 13 debtor has proposed a feasible plan, as determined by the bankruptcy court, and payments are being made through the bankruptcy estate, reduces the risk of default. Third, the formula rate uses objective criteria, thereby assuring uniform treatment for similarly situated creditors, which is what the Bankruptcy Code requires.

Under the formula approach, as adopted, the creditor bears the burden of proving how many points should be added to prime rate. The dissent would have adopted the presumptive contract rate which starts with a presumption that the original contract interest rate will apply. Either the debtor or the creditor can rebut the presumption by providing evidence that a lower or higher rate should apply.

As the plurality observed, it is really the burden of proof that divides the plurality and the dissent, because "if all relevant information about the debtor's circumstances, the creditor's circumstances, the nature of the collateral, and the market for comparable loans were equally available to both debtor and creditor, then in theory the formula and presumptive contract rate approaches would yield the same final interest rate."

The 2005 legislation significantly limits a Chapter 13 debtor's ability to strip down secured loans. No strip down is allowed on any debt incurred within one year prior to the bankruptcy filing. And, no strip down is allowed on a purchase money loan incurred within 910 days before the bankruptcy filing if it is secured by a motor vehicle acquired by the debtor for her personal use.

Think about what the 2005 legislation does and what it does not do. Think about what the typical Chapter 13 debtor can and cannot do with respect to the typical car loan.

A post–2005 Chapter 13 debtor who owes $13,000 on a car that she wants to keep will now have to make payments with a present value of $13,000.[11] While she cannot cram down a change in the principal to be paid, she can, consistent with *Till*, cram down a change in the interest rate, and she can, consistent with the requirements of new section 1325(a)(5)(B)(iii)[12] change the number of payments and the amount of the each payment.

Remember that strip down is simply one form of cram down. A cram down is any change in the payment obligation approved by the court over the creditor's objection. The change can be changes in the interest rate, changes in the number of payments, changes in the amount of payments, etc. Or the change can be a change in the amount to be paid, i.e., a strip down.

And, remember strip down is still possible in a case with the same facts as *Rash*. A strip down is still possible so long as (1) the

11. Prior the 2005 amendments, present value calculation would be pegged to the replacement value of the car, not the amount she owed on the car.

12. Section 1325(a)(5)(B)(iii) requires that the payments be monthly and be adequate to provide "adequate protection."

debt was not incurred within a year of bankruptcy and (2) the collateral is not a personal use automobile. And (3), the collateral is not the debtor's home.

(4) Secured Claims Secured Only by a Mortgage on the Debtor's Principal Residence

Most home mortgages are protected from the cram down, protected from nonconsensual modification by a Chapter 13 plan. Section 1322(b) excepts claims "secured only by a security interest in real property that is the debtor's principal residence" from plan modification.[13] This is known as the "anti-modification rule."

So, if *D* owes $100,000 on her home mortgage to *M* at the time that she files for Chapter 13 and her payments are $625 a month and the mortgage interest rate is 10%, *D* cannot use section 1322(b) to change her mortgage payment schedule or interest rate. Nor can *D* use section 1322 to reduce the amount of that secured claim, regardless of the value of the home. If, for example, the value of the home is only $70,000, *D* cannot use her Chapter 13 plan to "strip down" *M*'s secured claim to $70,000.

That is what the Bankruptcy Code says. That is what the United States Supreme Court said in *Nobleman v. American Savings Bank* (1993).

In *Nobelman*, *S*'s $71,335 claim was secured by a mortgage on *D*'s condo that was worth $23,500. *D* filed for Chapter 13 relief and proposed a plan that (1) bifurcated *S*'s claim into a $23,500 secured claim and a $47,385 unsecured claim and (2) provided for payment in full of the $23,500 secured claim but no payment on the $47,385 unsecured claim. The Supreme Court held that the plan impermissibly modified *S*'s rights in violation of section 1322(b)(2).

In so ruling, the Court focuses on the "rights of holders" phrase in section 1322(b)(2). It is not the secured claims in residences that cannot be modified but the rights of holders of claims secured by residences. Although *S* has a secured claim of $23,500 under section 506, that does not mean its "rights" protected by section 1322(b)(2) are limited to the value of its secured claim.

13. Reread the quoted language and identify the three "litigable" (i.e., "law school testable") issues. First, is the residence the only security for the loan, or did the creditor take a lien on some other collateral such as the debtor? What if the home loan is secured not only by a mortgage on the home but also a lien on the debtor's bank account? By a credit life insurance policy? By fixtures or furniture? Second, for North Carolina students and lawyers, is the double-wide mobile home (pronounced mo-beal home) that the debtor lives in "real property"? Third, is a mixed use property such as a combination home/business office protected?

In the real world, a judge expects a lawyer to know how she has ruled on each of these questions. In law school, a law professor expects a student to "spot" and raise each of these questions.

"Rights" under state law include the right to retain its line until the debt is paid in full and the right to recover any deficiency.

While the Supreme Court has ruled that home mortgages cannot be "stripped down" in Chapter 13 cases, courts are divided as to whether a home mortgage can be "stripped off." So you need to know (1) the factual difference between a "strip down" and a "strip off" and (2) possible legal differences between the two.

Assume again that *M* has a $100,000 first mortgage on *D*'s $70,000. Now also assume that *S* has a $25,000 second mortgage. As noted above, *D* cannot "strip down" *M*'s "secured claim" from $100,000 to $70,000. How is *S*'s "secured claim" different from *M*'s? Under section 506, the value of *S*'s zero, *i.e.*, the value of "SUCH" creditor's interest (*i.e.*, the second mortgage interest) in the house. Does *S* even have a "secured claim"?

The majority of the courts that have considered the question, including all six federal courts of appeal that have considered the issue, focus on the section 1322(b)(2) requirement that the creditor hold a secured claim. Under section 506(a), a creditor has a secured claim only if it has a security interest in the debtor's property and that security has actual value. If the security interest does not have actual value, the antimodification rule does not apply. The minority view interprets section 1322(b)(2) to prohibit modification of the claim of any creditor whose debt is secured solely by the debtor's residence, regardless of whether the security interest has actual value. To understand the point, consider again the following factual scenario:

D has a residence worth $70,000.

D owes *N* $100,000 secured by a first mortgage on her residence.

D owes *S* $25,000 secured by a second mortgage on her residence.

Under the majority view, *D*'s Chapter 13 plan can treat *S* as an unsecured creditor. Under the minority view, debtor must pay *S* in full because of the antimodification provision of § 1322(b)(2). Again, there is not yet a Supreme Court view.

Even though section 1322(b)(2) generally prohibits a Chapter 13 plan from cramming down changes in a home mortgage debt, a Chapter 13 plan can provide for curing defaults on home mortgages. Assume for example that D missed three home mortgage payments to M of $700 a month and under the terms of her home mortgage this default triggered an acceleration clause which made the entire loan balance due immediately. D can use her Chapter 13 plan to cure these defaults "within a reasonable time." In other words, D's Chapter 13 plan can provide that each month D will not only pay M $700 a month but will also pay M some additional amount that will cure the $2,100 default within a reasonable time.

§ 8.2 Obtaining Court Approval of the Plan

There is very little that creditors can do in a Chapter 13 case. Only the debtor can propose a plan of repayment. Creditors do not vote on the plan of repayment. Chapter 13 requires only court approval, i.e., confirmation, of the plan. The standards for judicial confirmation are set out in section 1325; the section 1325 standards likely to be involved in exam questions are covered in section 8.1 above.

§ 8.3 Living "Under" a Chapter 13 Plan

Confirmation of a plan binds the debtor and all of his preconfirmation creditors to the terms of the plan—regardless of whether the creditor objected to confirmation. The debtor must make the regular plan payments to the Chapter 13 trustee for distribution to creditors. For the duration of the plan which will generally be 3 or 5 years, the debtor must live on the budget that was the basis for determining "disposable income."

Most people are not able to stick to a budget. Most Chapter 13 debtors were not able to stick to a budget before filing for Chapter 13. Most Chapter 13 debtors are not able to stick to the budget after Chapter 13 plan confirmation.

§ 8.4 Ending a Chapter 13 Case

A Chapter 13 case can end with either (1) the debtor's receiving a discharge, (2) the case being dismissed, or (3) the case being converted to Chapter 7. Discharge requires the debtor to make the required plan payments.

Because most Chapter 13 debtors are not able to stick to their budget at Chapter 13 plan confirmation and make the required plan payments, most Chapter 13 cases are either dismissed or converted to Chapter 7. Approximately 2/3 of Chapter 13 debtors never receive a discharge. That means 2/3 of the Chapter 13 debtors get the short-term benefits of the automatic stay but not the lasting benefit of a bankruptcy discharge

(a) Discharge

Section 1328 is entitled "Discharge."

Section 1328 contemplates that a Chapter 13 debtor will complete all plan payment obligations, section 1328(a). A section 1328(a) discharge is subject to most but not all of the exceptions to discharge in section 523. For example, a section 1328(a) discharge, unlike a discharge in a Chapter 7 case, will cover debts for willful and malicious injury to property and debts for divorce or separation property settlements. Cf. section 1328(a)(2), (4).

The bankruptcy court may grant a discharge in a Chapter 13 case even though the debtor has not completed payments called for by the plan. Section 1328(b) empowers the bankruptcy court to grant a "hardship" discharge if:

1. the debtor's failure to complete the plan was due to circumstances for which she "should not justly be held accountable;" and

2. the value of the payments made under the plan to each creditor at least equals what that creditor would have received under Chapter 7; and

3. modification of the plan is not "practicable."

A section 1328(b) "hardship" discharge is not as comprehensive as a section 1328(a) discharge. A "hardship" discharge is limited by all of the section 523(a) exceptions to discharge, section 1328(c)(2).

Section 1328 imposes two additional requirements for obtaining any Chapter 13 discharge:

(1) First, the debtor must complete a personal finance management course and

(2) Second, any family support obligations—whether due prepetition or accrued postpetition—must have been paid in full.

(b) Dismissal or Conversion

Again, most Chapter 13 cases do not end in a discharge. Most Chapter 13 cases are either dismissed or converted to Chapter 7 cases.

§ 8.5 Comparing Chapter 13 Cases With Chapter 7 Cases

As should be obvious from reading Units 7 and 8 of this book, Chapter 7 and Chapter 13 are quite different. Just in case that is not yet obvious,

- **What the debtor gives up**. In Chapter 7, the debtor surrenders his nonexempt assets, which are liquidated for the benefit of the debtor's creditors. In Chapter 13, the debtor commits part of her future income which, along with any other assets the debtor has committed to the plan, is distributed to creditors.
- **What the debtor gets**. The ability of a Chapter 7 debtor to deal with a secured creditor whose debt is in default and who does not want to make a deal with the debtor is limited. In

Chapter 13, the debtor has the right to cure defaults over a period of time, even if the secured creditor does not agree. And, in the case of some undersecured debts, the debtor has the cramdown changes in secured debt payments.

- **How long it takes**. Obtaining a discharge in Chapter 7 is relatively quick; it usually takes four to six months. In Chapter 13, obtaining a discharge takes much longer, usually three to five years, and, more important, most Chapter 13 debtors do not receive a discharge . .
- **Who gets what**. In Chapter 7, the Code determines what is distributed and to whom. Central to Chapter 13 is a plan that establishes how much and when creditors will be paid.

And just in case your test is in part multiple choice or true false, here is a more complete comparison, in chart form, of the differences that "choice"[14] of chapters make that might make your exam:

	Chapter 7	Chapter 13
1. Automatic Stay	Automatic stay of section 362 protects the debtor from creditors' collection efforts.	Automatic stay of section 362 protects the debtor from creditors' collection efforts. Automatic stay of section 1301 protects certain co-debtors.
2. Loss of Property	"Property of the estate" as described in section 541 is distributed to creditors.	Except as provided in the plan or in the order of confirmation, debtor keeps "property of the estate."
3. Availability of Discharge	Section 727(a) lists grounds for objection to discharge.	Section 727 is inapplicable. Discharge depends on completing payments required by the plan, 1328(a). A "hardship" discharge to a debtor who makes some but not all payments required by the plan, 1328(b).
4. Debts Excepted from Discharge	Section 523(a) excepts 19 classes of claims from operation of the discharge.	A section 1328(a) discharge is subject to most of the important section 523(a) discharge exceptions. A section 1328(b) discharge is subject to all

14. Remember, as a result of section 707 as amended in 2005—the "means test"—some debtors who are in Chapter 13 are in Chapter 13 because if they filed for Chapter 7, their petitions would be dismissed.

	Chapter 7	Chapter 13
		of section 523(a)'s exceptions to discharge.
5. Effect on Future Chapter 7 Relief	A debtor who receives a discharge in a Chapter 7 case may not obtain a discharge in another Chapter 7 case for eight years.	A Chapter 13 discharge does not affect the availability of discharge in a future Chapter 7 case if the Chapter 13 plan was the debtor's "best effort" and paid 70% of all general claims, section 727(a)(9).
6. Whether Debtor's Postpetition Earnings are Property of the Estate	No, section 541(a)(6) ("earnings from services performed by an individual").	Yes, section 1306.
7. Debtor's Ability to Terminate the Case	"Only for cause," section 707.	"On request of the debtor at any time," section 1307(b).
8. Amount Required to be Distributed to Holders of Claims	Focus on property of the estate, section 541.	Plan controls, confirmation requires that holders of claims receive at least as much as they would in Chapter 7 and that plan commits all focus on disposable income, sections 1325(a)(4), 1325(b).

Unit 9

QUESTION NINE: WHAT HAPPENS DURING A BUSINESS CHAPTER 11 CASE?

Table of Sections

The last Unit on Chapter 13 focused on "real people." Only "real people"—men and women—can file for Chapter 13 bankruptcy. Business entities such as corporations or partnerships cannot file for Chapter 13 relief.

Both business entities and real people can file Chapter 11 cases. Chapter 11 is not limited to business debtors. Chapter 11 is not limited to insolvent debtors.

While Chapter 11 is not limited to operating businesses, the typical Chapter 11 debtor on law school exams is a business debtor that is attempting to continue its business operations by restructuring its financial obligations. And, while Chapter 11 is not limited to insolvent debtors, the typical Chapter 11 debtor on law school exams and in the real world is in Chapter 11 because its business operations do not generate enough cash to meet its financial obligations as presently structured.

It is easy to understand why the owners and employees *would* prefer for a financially troubled business to continue operating, instead of liquidating. You need also to understand why the creditors of a troubled business *might* also prefer that the business continue operating.

Some businesses have more economic value if kept together and operating than taken apart and liquidated. Chapter 11 was designed to (1) preserve this higher, going concern value by permitting continued business operations and (2) pay creditors more than they would receive from liquidation pursuant to a plan approved by the requisite majorities of creditors and the bankruptcy court.

As the previous paragraph suggests that are four primary stages in the life cycle of a Chapter 11 case

First, operating the business after the debtor's filing a bankruptcy petition and before the court's approval of a repayment plan;

Second, preparing a plan of repayment;

Third, obtaining the necessary creditors' approval of the plan of repayment; and

Fourth, obtaining court approval of the plan of repayment.

Let's start with the first days of a Chapter 11 case.

§ 9.1 First Day(s) of a Chapter 11 Case

The filing of a Chapter 11 petition, like the filing of a 7 petition or a Chapter 13 petition, (i) triggers the s automatic stay and section 541 property of the estate a "date of cleavage" for purposes of the avoiding powers treated in Unit 10 infra and the treatment of claims treated in Unit 15 infra. Most Chapter 11 petitions are unlike Chapter 7 petitions or Chapter 13 petitions in that (i) the filing triggers business and legal issues that need to be resolved immediately and (ii) creditors have a statutory role in the resolution of those issues.

(a) Organizing the Creditors

In many Chapter 11 cases, the debtor has hundreds, if not thousands, of creditors. It would not be practical for the Chapter 11 debtor to attempt to negotiate with each creditor individually.

Accordingly, section 1102 directs the United States trustee to appoint a committee of unsecured creditors as soon as practicable after the order for relief. Note that it is the United States trustee and not the bankruptcy judge who appoints committee members. And, note that section 1102 suggests, but does not require, that the committee have seven members, and that the seven have the largest claims.

Section 1102(b)(1) does require that the committee members be "representative of the different kinds of claims." If, for example, *D* owed significant amounts to lenders, vendors and tort claimants, the creditors' committee should have representatives from each "kind" of claim.

A creditors' committee performs a number of functions. It may:

(1) consult with the trustee or debtor in possession concerning the administration of the case

(2) investigate the debtor's acts and financial condition

(3) participate in the formulation of the plan

(4) request the appointment of a trustee

(5) "perform such other services as are in the interest of those represented," section 1103(c).

The creditors' committee may also appear at various hearings as a party in interest, section 1109(b). And, the committee may file a plan in those situations where the debtor ceases to have the exclusive right to do so, section 1121.

To state the obvious, a creditors' committee acts on behalf of all the unsecured creditors. Case law has consistently held that members of a committee have a fiduciary duty to other holders of unsecured claims.

The 2005 legislation requires committees to provide their non-member creditor constituents with "access to information," section 1102(b)(3).

The selection of a creditors' committee takes time. In many Chapter 11 cases, however, there are problems that need to be resolved immediately—on the first day of the case.

(b) First Day Orders

The phrase "First Day Orders" does not appear in either the Bankruptcy Code or the Bankruptcy Rules. Nonetheless, "First Day Orders" appear in virtually every Chapter 11 case.

"First Day Orders" are orders which the Chapter 11 debtor seeks to have entered by the bankruptcy court immediately, on the same day as the filing of the petition or soon thereafter. Many First Day Orders deal with administrative matters such as notices and appointment of professionals are usually noncontroversial.

More problematic are First Day Orders dealing with business emergencies such as obtaining financing and making payments to employees for work they have done prepetition and other essential prepetition creditors ("critical vendors") for goods or services they provided prepetition. In dealing with these business emergencies in the first day of the case or in an exam question, bankruptcy courts or law students have to balance the argument by the debtor that immediate action is required or the business will close against the argument by creditors that they have the right to be heard and need more time and the argument by the U.S. Trustee that this early payment of some prepetition claims is inconsistent with the provisions and policies of the Bankruptcy Code.

§ 9.2 Operating in 11: Authority to Continue Business Operations

A debtor's authority to continue operating its business in Chapter 11 comes from section 1108: "Unless the court orders otherwise, the trustee may operate the debtor's business. . . ." Note that section 1108 does not require prior court authorization.

§ 9.3 Operating in 11: Who—Debtor in Possession or Trustee; Examiner

(a) Debtor in Possession (a/k/a "the DIP")

Notwithstanding section 1108's use of the word "trustee," the debtor will remain in control of business operations in most Chap ter 11 cases. Prebankruptcy management will continue to oper the business as a "debtor in possession" unless a "request" motion) is made for the appointment of a trustee, and the ruptcy court, after notice and hearing, orders the appointr trustee.

[There is considerable language in case law and commentary that the debtor in possession is a new entity, separate and legally distinct from the debtor. We are not clear what such statements mean. And we are not even clear that the statement that a debtor in possession is a separate legal entity is even accurate.]

(b) Trustees and Examiners

(1) Statutory Grounds for Appointment

Section 1104 sets out the grounds for the appointment of a trustee. A trustee is to be appointed if there is "cause" (fraud, dishonesty, mismanagement, or incompetence) or if the appointment of a trustee is "in the interest of creditors, any equity security holders, and other interests of the estate." Section 1104 specifically instructs the court to disregard the number of shareholders or the amount of assets and liabilities of the debtor in deciding whether to appoint a trustee.

(2) Statutory Procedures for Appointment of Trustee

Under section 1104 the court decides whether to appoint a trustee in a Chapter 11 case. The United States trustee then decides which person to appoint, subject to the court's approval, unless the creditors act to select the trustee themselves.

(3) Statutory Duties

The duties of a trustee are enumerated in section 1106. Essentially, the trustee has responsibility for the operation of the business and formulation of the Chapter 11 plan.

(4) Business Considerations

Who serves as trustee in Chapter 11 cases? Remember, the trustee has responsibility for operating the business. Are lawyers prepared to run a troubled business? What about appointing an outstanding, experienced business person as Chapter 11 trustee?

Even an outstanding, experienced business person is going to need time to familiarize herself with this particular business. And, if she is such an outstanding, experienced business person, why is she available to serve as trustee—why isn't she already running some other business?

These business considerations caused Congress to decide to keep the debtor in possession unless a party in interest establishes cause, section 1104. And, in most cases, these business considerations cause the various parties in interest not to try to establish cause for the appointment of a Chapter 11 trustee.

(5) Examiner

If a trustee is not appointed, the court can order the appointment of an "examiner." Again, the court decides whether to appoint and the United States trustee decides which person to appoint, with the court's approval.

In theory, the role of an examiner is different from that of a trustee. An examiner does not run the debtor's business or run the debtor's Chapter 11 case. An examiner merely examines: she investigates the competency and honesty of the debtor and files a report of the investigation, sections 1104(b), 1106(b). In practice, the bright lines between the roles of an examiner and the roles of a trustee are sometimes blurred.

§ 9.4 Operating in 11: Using and Selling Encumbered Property Under Section 363

Remember that "encumbered property" is a shorthand way of describing property of the debtor that is covered by a creditor's lien such as a mortgage or security interest or.... In the typical Chapter 11 case, most of the debtor's property is encumbered by liens.

Remember also that section 362 stays a creditor with a lien on the property of a debtor in a bankruptcy case from repossessing the encumbered property. And in doing Chapter 11 questions on your exam, remember to read section 362 together with section 363.

(a) Overview of Section 363

Section 363 empowers the debtor in possession or trustee to continue using, selling, and leasing encumbered property. The interest of the lien creditor is safeguarded by section 363's requirement of "adequate protection," section 363(e).

Section 361 is entitled "adequate protection." Note that sections 363 and 361 provides for "adequate protection" of "an interest of an entity in property," not adequate protection of an entity in having its debt repaid. Note further that section 361 does not define "adequate protection." Rather, it provides examples of "adequate protection."

And, examples are the easiest way to understand "adequate protection." Assume, for example, that *D* files for bankruptcy owing *S* $1 million secured by equipment, which is worth $800,000. *S* has an interest in property that is worth $800,000. The purpose of adequate protection is to assure that at the end of the bankruptcy case *S* has (i) collateral worth $800,000; or (ii) payments $800,000 or (iii) a combination of collateral and payments that $800,000.

In the equipment example, assume further that the court concludes that the value of the equipment is declining by $10,000 a month. Under sections 361 and 363, the bankruptcy court could require the debtor to make monthly payments to *S* of $10,000. If the bankruptcy lasts 14 months and the court was correct about the decline in the value of the equipment, then at the close of the bankruptcy case, *S* who had a lien on property worth $800,000 at the start of the bankruptcy case would have a lien on property worth $660,000 and $140,000 in adequate protection payments at the end of the bankruptcy case.

Consider a second example. *D* files for bankruptcy owing *M* $500,000 secured by a first mortgage on Greenacre which is worth $300,000. If the bankruptcy court concludes that the value of Greenacre will not decline during the course of the bankruptcy case, the bankruptcy court could conclude that Greenacre itself is adequate protection.

Adequate protection works so long as the bankruptcy judge correctly foresees the future of the encumbered property. What if the value of the creditor's interest in property drops more significantly than the bankruptcy judge anticipated?

Under section 507(b), a creditor may seek an administrative expense claim for the amount by which the adequate protection ordered proves to be inadequate. Section 507(b) should always be read together with section 726(b). If the debtor's Chapter 11 efforts are not successful and the case is converted from Chapter 11 to Chapter 7, the administrative expenses from the 11 are not paid until the administrative expenses from the 7 are paid in full.

While a Chapter 11 debtor's use or sale of encumbered property is always subject to "adequate protection," the rules as to who has the burden of raising the adequate protection issue depend on the nature of the encumbered property and the nature of the debtor's use.

(b) Using Encumbered Property that is NOT "Cash Collateral"

Encumbered property that is not "cash collateral" as defined in section 363(a) may be used, sold, or leased in the ordinary course of business without a prior judicial determination of "adequate protection," section 363(c)(1). On "request" of the lien creditor, the court shall condition the use, sale, or lease of encumbered property so as to provide "adequate protection," section 363(e).

For example, if *D* Department Store, Inc., *D*, files a Chapter 11 petition and *C* Bank, *C*, has a perfected security interest in *D*'s inventory, *D* may continue to sell inventory in the ordinary course of business. *D* will not have to obtain court permission in order to make such sales; rather, *C* will have the burden of requesting the court to prohibit or condition such sales so as to provide "adequate protection" of *C*'s security interest.

Notice and a hearing on the issue of "adequate protection" is required before a Chapter 11 debtor uses, sells, or leases encumbered property in a manner that is *not* in the ordinary course of business, section 363(b). If for example, *D*, after filing its Chapter 11 petition, decides to discontinue its furniture department and wants to make a bulk sale of its furniture inventory, *C* must be first given notice and the opportunity for a hearing on the issue of "*adequate protection*."

(c) Using "Cash Collateral"

Use of "cash collateral" is treated different from the use of other collateral. Accordingly, it is necessary to understand (i) which collateral is "cash collateral" and (ii) when a debtor can use cash collateral.

(1) What Cash Collateral is

"Cash collateral" is defined in section 363(a). There are three components to the definition. First, cash collateral must be collateral, i.e., property that a creditor has an interest in because its lien extends to the property. Second, cash collateral must be cash or cash equivalent. Third, cash collateral can be derived from other collateral, i.e., proceeds, rents, etc. from other collateral.

In the above hypothetical of *D* Department Store, cash received by *D* from the postpetition sale of prepetition inventory would be *C*'s cash collateral. Cash received from the sale of land or other property not subject to *C*'s lien would not be cash collateral. And, accounts receivable generated by the postpetition sale of prepetition inventory would be *C*'s cash collateral only when collected.

(2) Use of Cash Collateral Only Upon Consent or Adequate Protection

Cash collateral may be used only if the lienholder *C* consents, or if the court, after notice and hearing, finds that *C*'s collateral position is adequately protected and authorizes such use under section 363(c)(2). Until the use of cash collateral is authorized under section 363(c)(2), the debtor in possession must segregate and account for all cash collateral, section 363(c)(4).

To understand how section 363(c) typically works, it is necessary to understand (i) how the Uniform Commercial Code works, (ii) how the Bankruptcy Code works and (iii) how the real world works.

First, how the Uniform Commercial Code works. Under Article 9 of the UCC, a creditor who extends credit secured by inventory o accounts receivable can (and usually does) obtain a security interest in not only the accounts and inventory a debtor has at the time it extends credit but also the accounts and inventory that the debtor later acquires. Thus, in the *D* Department Store example, *C*'s collateral could be all of *D* Department Store's inventory, whenever acquired. The UCC authorizes "floating liens."

Now, how the Bankruptcy Code works. If *D* Department Store files for Chapter 11, section 552(a) limits the extent to which *C*'s lien can "float" to after-acquired property. More specifically, under section 552(a), *C*'s prepetition security interest does not cover inventory that *D* Department Store acquires after the date of the Chapter 11 filing. Accordingly, a Chapter 11 debtor such as *D* Department Store can offer its prepetition secured creditors a replacement lien in postpetition inventory and accounts receivable as "adequate protection" for *D* Department Store's use of cash collateral.

And, if you understand how the "real world" works you will understand that such an offer is generally the proverbial "offer he cannot refuse."

Recall that a Chapter 11 debtor cannot use cash collateral unless the creditor with a lien on the cash collateral consents or the court approves the use, section 363(c). *D* Department Store is like most Chapter 11 debtors in that most of the cash it generates from business operations is cash collateral. Unless the business can use the cash collateral, the business will close.

Understandably, bankruptcy judges are sympathetic to the debtor's argument that unless it is permitted to use cash collateral, it will close and all of its employees will lose their jobs, their health insurance, their retirement benefits, etc. Understanding this, creditors generally agree to the debtor's use of cash collateral in exchange for some sort of replacement lien on postpetition inventory and receivables and some sort of administrative expense priority. Most court orders approving the use of cash collateral are consent orders.

While use of cash collateral is typically the debtor's initial source of credit, cash collateral alone is generally not a sufficient source of credit. Accordingly, one of the first problems confronting a debtor in possession or a Chapter 11 trustee is financing the operation of the business pending the formulation and approval of a plan of rehabilitation.

§ 9.5 Operating in 11: Funding the 11 (Finding the Money to Operate the Business)

If a business files for Chapter 11 because it does not have enough money to operate, why will it have enough money to operate in Chapter 11? In the prior section on "cash collateral," and section 363(c), we have seen the legal basis for a business' continuing to use earnings from business operations to pay the costs of continued operations.

(a) Savings From Not Paying Prebankruptcy Claims Until Confirmation of a Plan

There is no provision of the Bankruptcy Code that expressly states that a Chapter 11 debtor cannot pay prebankruptcy claims until confirmation of a plan. Nonetheless, lawyers, their clients and bankruptcy judges know that this is how Chapter 11 works. Now you do too.

(b) Sale of Assets

Recall that the Chapter 11 debtor continues to operate its business and is statutorily (section 363(c)(1)) authorized to continue selling inventory in the ordinary course of business, without court authorization. With court authorization under section 363(b), the debtor can even do asset sales that are not in the ordinary course of business. The proceeds from these sales are often important to funding business operations in a Chapter 11 case.

(c) New Credit and Section 364

Generally a Chapter 11 debtor needs additional credit and funding. To counter the understandable reluctance of vendors and creditors to extend credit to Chapter 11 debtors, section 364 provides incentives.

The incentive in subsections (a) and (b) of section 364 is an administrative expense priority. The differences between (a) and (b) are

(1) (a) is limited to "ordinary course"

(2) because (b) is not limited to "ordinary course," (b), but not (a), requires court approval after notice and hearing.

Subsections (c) and (d) of section 364 are available only if an administrative expense priority is not a sufficient incentive to induce the need credit or funding. The phrase "debtor in possession financing" (a/k/a "dip lending") is used to describe section 364(c) or (d) loans.

The major difference between subsection (c) of section 364 and subsection (d) is that 364(d) empowers the court to authorize a "priming lien." If your exam question covers dip lending, it will probably cover either a priming lien or cross collateralization.

(d) Obtaining Priming Secured Credit

Under section 364(d), the court, after notice and hearing, may authorize the obtaining of postpetition credit secured by a priming lien on property that will come ahead of existing liens on that property. Section 364(d) is the "last resort" provision. Section 364(d) has two requirements: (1) the trustee is unable to obtain such credit otherwise and (2) the interests of prepetition lienholders on the property whose liens are primed by the borrowing are adequately protected.

Court approval of a postpetition lien that primes prepetition liens is very uncommon. Most of the few reported cases granting a section 364(d) lien look to an equity cushion (i.e. value of collateral exceeds the amount of the prepetition secured debts) as the basis for adequate protection. If *D* owes *C* $2 million and *C* has a first lien on Greenacre, the strongest argument for *P*, a postpetition lender, seeking a section 364(d) priming lien for its proposed postpetition $1 million loan will be that Greenacre is worth more than $3 million. (*C*'s obvious response is that if it is so clear that Greenacre is worth more than $3 million then there is no need for *P*, the postpetition lender, to seek a priming lien. In other words, if being second in line is so damn "adequate," why does the new lender insist on being first in line?)

(e) Cross–Collateralization

Recall that frequently, postpetition credit is provided by prepetition lenders. A prepetition lender who is unsecured or undersecured may attempt to improve its position on its prepetition claim by agreeing to lend postpetition funds to the debtor with "cross-collateralization."

The term "cross-collateralization" does not appear in the Bankruptcy Code. It is a creation and creature of the case law and commentary.

In theory, cross-collateralization can take two different forms. First, cross-collateralization results when a postpetition extension of credit is secured by both prepetition collateral and postpetition collateral. A second form of cross-collateralization involves securing prepetition claims with postpetition collateral as a condition for new credit. It is this second form of cross-collateralization that is controversial.

Effectively, this second form of cross-collateralization by which a creditor gets new postpetition collateral to secure an old prepetition debt is inconsistent with the priority scheme of the Bankruptcy Code. The debtor is dealing with the prepetition debt owed to its postpetition lender more favorably than the debtor's other prepetition debts.

The Bankruptcy Code nowhere deals with cross-collateralization. Relatively few reported cases deal with cross-collateralization.

The two "leading" reported cases on this second form of cross-collateralization are (1) the Second Circuit's decision in *In re Texlon* (1979), which was decided under the Bankruptcy Act of 1898 and is generally read as (i) holding that a court cannot approve this second form of cross-collateralization without notice and hearing and (ii) reserving the question of whether a court can approve cross-collateralization with proper notice and hearing, and (2) the Eleventh Circuit's decision in *In re Saybrook Mfg. Co.* (1992), which was decided under the Bankruptcy Code and held that this second form of cross-collateralization is not permitted.

Saybrook is a case in which the appellate court took a strong stand against the second form of cross-collateralization. The debtor in possession (Saybrook) entered into postpetition financing under section 364 with Manufacturer's Hanover Bank (MHB, sometimes known in the trade as "Manny Hanny"). MHB was already a creditor to the tune of some $34 million, only $10 million of which was secured. So at filing, it had a secured claim of $10 million and an unsecured claim of $24 million.

Under the terms of the DIP financing, MHB was to lend Saybrook an additional $3 million. For that additional loan, MHB demanded and received "cross-collateralization" of its debt; that is, not only was the $3 million of new money secured by postpetition assets, but MHB's entire $34 million prepetition debt was to be secured by estate assets. This would have resulted in an increase in collateral to MHB of some $24 million (and would certainly have increased their ultimate recovery).

Two unsecured creditors complained, and appealed. They did not obtain a stay pending appeal. The first procedural skirmish was MHB's contention that it was protected by section 364(e) as a good faith lender; in the absence of a stay pending appeal, this would have doomed the unsecured creditors' appeal.

The court ultimately disapproves of cross-collateralization (at least of collateralizing old debt with new estate assets) on two grounds. First, the court notes that the Code does not specifically allow the practice. This creates a presumption against the practice. This presumption is not overcome by resort to section 105, in part because of the second ground: the effect of cross-collateralization is to force distributions that are in direct conflict with the Code's distribution scheme. As such, cross-collateralization is not permitted, and orders incorporating it are not protected by section 364(e).

§ 9.6 Preparing the Plan: Who—Exclusivity

Section 1121 answers the question, "who can file a plan." In answering questions your professor might ask about who can file a plan you need to know.

(1) in any Chapter 11 case, the debtor can, at any time, file a plan;

(2) only the debtor can file a plan unless EITHER a trustee has been appointed OR a time deadline in section 1121 has expired;

(3) Section 1121 sets out two different time deadlines: first, a deadline for filing a plan and second, a deadline for obtaining creditor approval of the plan;

(4) the period during which only the debtor can file a Chapter 11 plan is generally referred to as "exclusivity" [although the word "exclusivity" does not appear in the Bankruptcy Code].

Exclusivity can be a very significant advantage to a debtor. So long as the debtor has exclusivity, creditors have the limited options of (i) accepting what the debtor proposes or (ii) moving to convert the case to Chapter 7 and liquidating all of the assets or (iii) moving to end the debtor's exclusivity.

Section 1121(b) grants the debtor exclusivity for the first 120 days of the case. If the debtor files its plan within that 120 day period, no other plan may be filed during the first 180 days of the case while the debtor tries to obtain creditor acceptance of its plan, section 1121(c)(3).

Note the relationship between the 120–day and the 180–day periods. Both begin running at the same time—the date of the order for relief. If, for example, the debtor files a plan 30 days after the order for relief, it will have 150 more days of exclusivity to obtain creditor acceptance.

Section 1121(d) empowers the bankruptcy court to extend or reduce the 120–day and 180–day periods. It has been very unusual for courts to reduce the exclusivity periods. It has been very common for courts to extend the exclusivity period, especially in cases involving larger businesses.

BAPCPA limits the power of courts to extend the exclusivity periods. The 120–day period to file a plan and disclosure statement may not be extended beyond 18 months, and the 180–day period to obtain acceptances may not be extended beyond 20 months, section 1122(d)(2).

§ 9.7 Preparing the Plan: Overview of Who Gets What, When

The most important questions in bankruptcy are "who gets paid," "what do they get paid," and "when do they get paid." Recall that in Chapter 7 cases, the Bankruptcy Code answers these questions.

Section 726(a) provides for the distribution of "property of the estate" and, in numbered paragraphs, sets out the order of distribution; section 726(b) then mandates that if there is not sufficient property of the estate to pay all of the claims in one of the section 726(a) kinds of clams, then "payment ... shall be made pro rata among claims of the kind specified in each such particular paragraph of section 726(a)." Section 704 backs this up by requiring distributions to creditors to be made "as expeditiously as is compatible with the best interests of the parties in interest."

In Chapter 11 cases, it is the plan that answers the questions "who," "what," and "when." And, the answer provided by a Chapter 11 plan can be much more "creative" than section 726's answer.

First, distributions in a Chapter 11 plan are not limited to "property of the estate." Second, the "classes" of claims in a Chapter 11 plan can be very different from the kinds of claims in section 726. Third, "expeditiously" does not appear in Chapter 11 or in most descriptions of most Chapter 11 plans.

§ 9.8 Preparing the Plan: Satisfying Sections 1123 and 1126 and 1129

Section 1123 is entitled "Contents of the Plan." Subsection (a) of section 1123 ("shall") sets out the mandatory provisions of a Chapter 11 plan; subsection (b) ("may") indicates the permissive provisions.

While compliance with section 1123 is essential, it is important to remember that a plan will be effective only if it is approved by the requisite number of creditors and by the court. Accordingly, the "Contents of the Plan" are governed not only by section 1123 by also by what the requisite number of creditors will accept (section 1126) and what the court will confirm, (section 1129).

§ 9.9 Preparing the Plan: Importance of Classification

It is important that you understand classification of claims for three reasons:

(1) Section 1123(a)(1) requires that claims be classified so classification of claims can affect whether there is a plan;

(2) Classification of claims also affects the creditor acceptance process and the court confirmation process.

(3) Because of (1) and (2), classification of claims is a likely exam issue IF your exam covers the Chapter 11 plan process.

The usual exam questions about classification of claims are first, whether debtor has improperly put claims in the same class or more likely (and more difficult) second, whether debtor has improperly put claims in separate classes.

Section 1122 governs classification of claims in Chapter 11 plans. Section 1122(a) answers the first question, whether debtor has improperly put claims in the same class. Sort of.

Section 1122(a) says that the test for whether claims can be put in the same class is whether the claims are "substantially similar." It does not, however, define or explain "substantially similar."

In determining whether claims are "substantially similar" for purposes of section 1122(a), courts look primarily at legal rights. A claim with a section 507 priority has different legal rights from an unsecured claim and so priority claims and unsecured claims cannot be placed in the same class. Similarly, a secured claim has different legal rights than an unsecured claim or a priority claim and so secured claims cannot be placed in the same class with priority claims or unsecured claims. And, *B*'s first mortgage on Blackacre has different legal rights from *W*'s first mortgage on Whiteacre or *S*'s second mortgage on both Blackacre and Whiteacre. Accordingly, each secured claim is placed in a separate class in most[15] Chapter 11 plans.

Arguably, all unsecured, nonpriority claims have the same legal rights and so can all be placed in the same class. That is, however, not the usual law school exam argument. Rather you will be asked to argue the question whether all unsecured, nonpriority claims must be in the same class.

Section 1122 does not address this second question: whether the debtor has improperly put claims in separate classes. Section 1122(a) states that all claims in a class must be "substantially similar"; it does not state whether all claims that are "substantially similar" must be in the same class.

To illustrate, assume that *X*, *Y*, and *Z* are unsecured creditors of Chapter 11 debtor, *D*. If *D*'s plan places all three creditors' claims in the same class, section 1122(a) controls. It is clear from section 1122(a) that *D* cannot place the claims of *X*, *Y*, and *Z* in a single class unless all three claims are "substantially similar." The limits on *D*'s discretion in placing claims in a separate class are not clear from the Bankruptcy Code. Can *C* place *X* in a class different from *Y* and *Z* even though their claims are substantially similar?

There are both business reasons and a Bankruptcy Code reason that a debtor might want to divide its unsecured debts into various classes.

15. If a debtor has issued public debt secured by its assets, the claims of the various debenture holders are "substantially similar" and can be placed in a single class.

First, business reasons. Some creditors such as long-term lenders or large vendors that are continuing to sell to the debtor might be willing to take long-term notes or even stock while other creditors such as short-term lenders or discontinued vendors might insist on short-term notes or even cash.

Second, the Bankruptcy Code reason for classification of claims. A plan proponent will sometimes place claims that will vote for the plan in a separate class so that at least one class of claims accepts the plan. As discussed below, the Bankruptcy Code's Chapter 11 plan approval process requires that (i) creditors vote on Chapter 11 plans, (ii) the creditor vote be tabulated by classes and by number of claims and amount of claims in that class, and (iii) at least one class of claims vote for the plan by the requisite majorities in number and amount.

This Bankruptcy Code reason for classification and legal battles over separate classification often arise in cases in which the debtor's principal significant asset is a building. Assume, for example, that *D* is a limited partnership that owns an apartment complex valued at $12.2 million. *M* has a mortgage on the apartment complex to secure its $15 million claim. *M* thus has both a $12.2 million secured claim and a $2.8 million unsecured claim. *M* is not only *D*'s only secured creditor; it is also *D*'s largest unsecured creditor. *M*'s $2.8 million unsecured, deficiency claim is larger than all other unsecured debts combined. Unless *D* can classify *M*'s unsecured deficiency claim different from the claims of its other unsecured creditors, *M* can effectively veto any Chapter 11 plan.

The cases are divided on whether the deficiency claim of a single asset real estate debtor's secured creditor can be classified separately from other unsecured claims. That division of cases and other single asset real estate issues are considered later in this unit of the book.

§ 9.10 Obtaining Creditor Approval: Disclosure Statements

The process for obtaining creditor approval of a Chapter 11 plan is like federal securities laws in that it is premised on disclosure: if provided with adequate information, the creditors of a business in Chapter 11 (like the stockholders of a public corporation) can make their own decisions. Accordingly, section 1125 prohibits even soliciting creditor approval of plan until the court has approved a disclosure statement (or, if your are in Miami, "a disco statement"). The disclosure statement must contain "adequate information." There is a definition of "adequate information" in section 1125(a) [which you can probably ignore in your exam preparation]: "reasonably practicable" for this debtor to enable a "hypothetical reasonable investor" who is typical of the holders of the claims or interests to make an informed judgment on the plan. What constitutes "adequate information" thus depends on the circumstances of each case—what constitutes "adequate information" is thus a very unlikely exam issue.

§ 9.11 Obtaining Creditor Approval: Who Votes

Both creditors and shareholders vote on Chapter 11 plans. According to section 1126(a), creditors with claims "allowed under section 502" and shareholders with interests "allowed under section 502" vote on Chapter 11 plans. The statutory requirement of "allowed under section 502" is generally satisfied by the Bankruptcy Code's "double-deeming."

In a Chapter 11 case, section 1111 deems filed a claim or interest that is scheduled and is not shown as disputed, contingent, or unliquidated. And, section 502 deems allowed any claim or interest that is filed and not objected to by a party in interest.

(a) Section 1124 Deeming

Statutory "deeming" also eliminates voting by two classes of claims or interests. First, if a class is to receive nothing under the plan, it is deemed to have rejected the plan, and its vote need not be solicited, section 1126(g). Second, if a class is not "impaired" under the plan, the class is deemed to have accepted the plan and again its vote need not be solicited, section 1126(f).

(b) Section 1124 Impairment

The concept of "impairment" is unique to Chapter 11. Section 1124 is entitled "Impairment of Claims or Interests." Under section 1124 a class of claims or interests is impaired unless

(1) the legal, equitable, and contractual rights of the holder are left "unaltered"; [If the plan in any way changes the rights of the holder, it alters and thus impairs the holder. It is not necessary to determine whether the change adversely or beneficially affects the holder. For example, a plan provision that reduces the payment period from ten years to six months impairs.] *or*

(2) the only alteration of legal, equitable, or contractual rights is reversal of an acceleration on default by curing the default and reinstating the debt.

§ 9.12 Obtaining Creditor Approval: Section 1111(b) Election

Section 1111(b), like section 1124, deals with a concept that is unique to Chapter 11. Generally, a creditor whose debt is only partially secured has two claims—a secured claim measured by the value of its collateral and an unsecured claim for the remainder, section 506(a). Assume, for example, that *C*'s $100,000 claim against *D* is secured by real property owned by *D* that is valued at $70,000. Under section 506(a), *C* has a $70,000 secured claim and a $30,000 unsecured claim. Under section 1111(b), *C* can elect to have a $100,000 secured claim and no unsecured claim.[16]

Let's use the hypothetical in the previous paragraph to consider some of the advantages and the disadvantages of a section 1111(b) election:

Advantage of section 1111(b) election:

If *C* makes the section 1111(b) election, section 1129(b), considered infra, requires that *C* be paid at least the full amount of its debt, $100,000, under the plan. Section 1129(b) also requires that *C*'s collateral secure the payment of the $100,000.

Understand the difference between *C*'s section 1129(b) right to be paid $100,000 under the plan and a right to be paid $100,000 in cash. The plan can and undoubtedly will delay the payment of a part or even all of the $100,000. Section 1129(b) requires that the payments under the plan to *C* total $100,000, not that the plan payments have a present value of $100,000.

Disadvantages of section 1111(b) election:

(1) If *C* makes the section 1111(b) election, it will not be able to vote its $30,000 unsecured claim.

(2) If *C* makes the section 1111(b) election, it will not participate in the distribution to holders of unsecured claims.

§ 9.13 Obtaining Creditor Approval: How Many Votes

A class of claims has accepted a plan when more than one half in number and at least two thirds in amount of the allowed claims actually voting on the plan approve the plan, section 1126(c). The following hypothetical illustrates the application of section 1126(c):

D files a Chapter 11 petition. *D*'s schedule of creditors shows 222 different creditors and $1 million of debt. *D*'s Chapter 11 plan divides creditors into four classes. Class 3 consists of 55 creditors,

16. Note that section 1111(b) provides for election by classes of secured claims, not by individual holders of secured claims. Generally, each holder of a secured claim will be in a separate class. Note also that some classes of secured claims are not eligible to make a section 1111(b) election.

with claims totalling $650,000. Only 39 of the creditors in Class 3 vote on the plan. Their claims total $450,000. If at least 20 Class 3 creditors (more than 1/2 of 39) with claims totalling at least $300,000 (2/3 of $450,000) vote for *D*'s plan, the plan has been accepted by Class 3.

A class of interests has accepted a plan when at least two thirds in amount of the allowed interests actually voting on the plan approve the plan, section 1126(d).

§ 9.14 Obtaining Court Approval of a Plan That Has Been Accepted by Every Class

Even if the Chapter 11 plan has been approved (accepted) by every class of claims and interests, it will not be effective until it has been approved (confirmed) by the court. Section 1129(a) sets out thirteen numbered confirmation requirements for plans accepted by every class. Let's look only at the two of the thirteen that you might see on your exam: (1) best interests and (2) feasibility.

"Best interest of creditors test" is a possible multiple choice test question. Courts and commentators use the phrase "best interest of creditors test" to describe section 1129(a)(7) which requires that each dissenting claim holder—even dissenting claimholders in classes that accepted the plan—receive a least much under the plan as it would have received in a Chapter 7 liquidation.

"Feasibility test" is a more likely "policy/essay" exam question. Courts and commentators use the phrase "feasibility test" to describe section 1129(a)(11) which requires the court to determine that the debtor can meet its plan commitments—that confirmation is not likely to be followed by liquidation or the need for further financial reorganization. Courts typically have had little problem finding the feasibility test satisfied. Some law professors have had considerable problems with courts' lack of problems in applying this feasibility test. If your professor is one of these professors, then. . . .

§ 9.15 Obtaining Court Approval of a Plan That Has Been Accepted by One But Not All Classes of Claims—An Overview of "Cramdown"

Sometimes (more often on law school exams than in the "real world") a Chapter 11 plan will not be accepted by all classes of claims and interests. Plans accepted by at least one class of claims[17] can still be confirmed if the additional requirements of section 1129(b) are satisfied.

One more time—with feeling. Subsection (b) of section 1129 applies ONLY IF (1) there is at least one impaired class that did not

17. Section 1129(a)(10) requires that there be at least one consenting impaired class. Section 1129(a)(10) is confusing when read together with section

accept the plan and (2) there is at least one impaired class of claims that did accept the plan.

Confirmation of a plan, notwithstanding one or more nonassenting classes is commonly referred to as a "cram down" or "cramdown" or "cram-down." This term does not appear in section 1129(b). While section 1129(b) does not use the term "cramdown," it does use two other terms that you need to understand: (1) "not discriminate unfairly" and (2) "fair and equitable."

There are three things that you need to know about the "not discriminate unfairly" requirement of section 1129(b). First, it applies only if section 1129(b) applies. If all impaired classes accept the plan, then section 1129(b) does not apply and "unfair discrimination" is not a confirmation issue. Second, it applies only to the non-assenting class or classes. Again, there is no inquiry as to whether a plan discriminates unfairly against a class that has accepted the plan. Third, the test is whether the plan discriminates *unfairly* against that class, not whether the plan discriminates. And, whether discrimination is unfair is a fact question, not a likely exam question.

"Fair and equitable" is the more likely cram down exam question.

In order for a plan to be "crammed down" on a class, that plan must be fair and equitable as to that class. To determine whether a plan is "fair and equitable" to a nonassenting class, it is helpful to look to section 1129(b)(2), which contains a series of nonexclusive examples of fair and equitable treatment. And to apply these examples in section 1129(b)(2), it is necessary to know whether the nonassenting class is a class of secured claims or a class of unsecured claims or a class of interests.

§ 9.16 Obtaining Court Approval of a Plan That Has Been Accepted by One But Not All Classes of Claims: Cramdown of Secured Claims

We have already done cram down of secured claims in Chapter 13. And cram down of a secured claim in a Chapter 11 cases works basically the same as the cram down in a Chapter 13 case.

1129(a)(8) which requires the consent of all impaired classes. Section 1129(a)(10) is less confusing when read together with section 1129(b).

A plan can be confirmed if all of the requirements of section 1129(a) are satisfied including the section 1129(a)(8) requirement of consent of all impaired classes. Alternatively, a plan can be confirmed if all of the requirements of section 1129(a) other than section 1129(a)(8) are satisfied and the requirements of section 1129(b) are also satisfied. In other words, if section 1129(a)(10)'s requirement of one consenting impaired class is satisfied, then satisfaction of the cram down requirements of section 1129(b) can override section 1129(a)(8)'s requirement of consent of all impaired classes.

First, it is necessary to determine the amount of the secured claim. Under section 506, that is keyed to the value of the collateral. And, under the Supreme Court's decision in *Associates Commercial Corp. v. Rash* (1997), that is keyed to what it would cost the debtor to replace the encumbered property.

Second, it is necessary to determine a cram down interest rate—to determine how much more than just the replacement value the debtor must pay over the life of the plan so that the proposed plan payments have a discounted present value equal to the value of the collateral. If, for example, Chapter 11 debtor *D* owes *S* $100,000 and that debt is secured by equipment that would cost *D* $75,000 to replace, a cram down of *S*'s secured claim would require plan payments that have a discounted present value of $75,000. And, under the Supreme Court's plurality decision in *Till v. SCS Credit Corp.* (2004), the discount rate/cram down interest rate will be based on prime rate with an additional risk premium.

So far, Chapter 11 cram down of secured claims is identical to Chapter 13 cram down of secured claims. Section 1129(a)(2)(A)(II) has an additional requirement that the amount of the plan payments must be at least equal to the amount of the secured claim.

In most Chapter 11 cases, this additional requirement is meaningless. Generally, a stream of payments that have a discounted present value equal to the value of the collateral will exceed the amount of the secured claim.

This additional Chapter 11 cram down requirement will only matter if a secured creditor has made a section 1111(b) election. Recall that under Chapter 11 a secured creditor can elect to have its entire claim treated as secured, regardless of the value of its collateral. If, for example, *D* owes *S* $100,000 and the debt is secured by equipment with a value of $75,000, then under section 506, *S* has a $75,000 secured claim. But by making a section 1111(b) election, *S* can have a $100,000 secured claim. If *S* so elects, then a cram down of *S*'s secured claim would require both that the stream of payments under the plan have a discounted present value of $75,000—"the value of such holder's interest in the estate's interest in such property"—and that the face amount of the plan payments total at least $100,000.

§ 9.17 Obtaining Court Approval of a Plan That Has Been Accepted by One But Not All Classes of Claims: Cramdown of Unsecured Claims

Now, cram down of unsecured claims. Bankruptcy law professors, lawyers and judges (but not the Bankruptcy Code) use the phrase "absolute priority" to describe the standard for "fair and equitable" treatment of unsecured claims.

Section 1129(b)'s "fair and equitable" standard is satisfied with respect to a dissenting class of unsecured claims if "the holder of any claim or interest that is junior to the claims of such class will not receive or retain under the plan on account of such junior claim or interest any property." What does the quoted language mean? Who is "junior" to an unsecured creditor? Under the Bankruptcy Code, as under corporate codes, stockholders are "junior" to unsecured creditors. Accordingly, the "absolute priority" rule of section 1129(b)(2)(B) requires payment in full to creditors before distributions to shareholders. Accordingly, a Chapter 11 plan cannot be crammed down on unsecured creditors unless stockholders get nothing.

Consider the following illustration of section 1129(b)(2)(B): *D* Corp. files for Chapter 11 relief. Its Chapter 11 plan provides for 70 cents on the dollar to a class of holders of unsecured claims and also provides for its shareholders to retain their *D* Corp. stock. Can the plan be confirmed?

Yes, if accepted by the requisite majorities of all classes of claims. If *D* Corp.'s plan is accepted by all classes, then section 1129(b) does not apply.

If, however, *D* Corp.'s plan is not accepted by all classes, section 1129(b) will apply and will preclude confirmation. This plan is not "fair and equitable" under section 1129(b)(2)(B): stockholders are junior to the dissenting class and are retaining property under the plan.

Reconsider the language of section 1129(b)(2)(B) set out above, particularly the phrase "on account of such junior claim or interest." Can shareholders retain their stock notwithstanding nonassenting classes and section 1129(b)(2)(B) by making a new capital contribution to the corporation? In *Case v. Los Angeles Lumber Products Co.* (1939), the Supreme Court, in dicta, recognized a "new value" exception to the absolute priority rule: shareholders of an insolvent debtor could retain an interest in a reorganized entity if their "participation [is] based on a contribution in money or money's worth, reasonably equivalent in view of all of the circumstances to the participation of the shareholder."

It is unclear whether the *Case* case dictum is "good law" today—whether there is a "new value" exception. *Bank of America v. 203 North LaSalle Street Partnership* (1999), raised but did not resolve the issue.

In *203 North LaSalle*, *D*, a real estate investment partnership whose principal asset was 15 floors of a Chicago office building got into financial trouble and filed a Chapter 11 petition. *D* owed Bank $93,000,000 and Bank had a mortgage on the 15 floors which were valued at $54,500,000. *D*'s Chapter 11 plan placed Bank's secured claim and Bank's unsecured claim in separate classes. *D*'s plan also placed Bank's unsecured claim in a class separate from its two other unsecured creditors who were owed a total of $90,000.

Under *D*'s Chapter 11 plan, the Bank's secured claim was to be paid in full over more than seven years and the Bank's unsecured claim was to be paid only 16% of the $38,500,000. *D*'s plan also gave partners of the real estate investment partnership the exclusive right to contribute $6,125,000 over five years to obtain ownership of the post-Chapter 11 entity.

The Bank of course voted against the plan. *D* sought cram down. The Bank objected, invoking the absolute priority rule.

The bankruptcy court confirmed the plan, and the district court and court of appeals affirmed. The Supreme Court reversed, stating that section 11129(b)(2)(B)(ii) bars "old equity" from contributing new value and receiving ownership interests in the reorganized entity when that opportunity is afforded only to them, without some sort of market valuation to test the adequacy of their proposed contribution.

People still debate what the Court held. It did not bless the new value doctrine. It found, however, that the debtor's use of exclusivity—and using it to propose a plan that only allowed existing equity holders to contribute capital—was a use of property in violation of the absolute priority rule, and thus reversed confirmation. It held that "[i]t would thus be necessary for old equity to demonstrate its payment of top dollar, but this it could not satisfactorily do when it would receive or retain its property under a plan giving it exclusive rights and in the absence of a competing plan of any sort." Since the *203 North LaSalle* decision, courts have dealt with "new value" plans by terminating exclusivity, or by requiring an auction for the equity in the reorganized entity, or both.

§ 9.18 Confirmation of a Chapter 11 Plan—The End (Sort of)

After confirmation of a Chapter 11 plan, the debtor's performance obligations are governed by the terms of the plan. The provisions of a confirmed Chapter 11 plan bind not only the debtor but also the debtor's creditors and shareholders "whether or not such creditor, equity security holder, or general partner has accepted the plan," section 1141(a). Subject to limitations noted below, confirmation of a Chapter 11 plan operates as a discharge, section 1141(d).

The following chart compares Chapter 11 discharge rules with those of Chapter 7.

	Chapter 7	Chapter 11
Corporations, partnerships	Not eligible for discharge	Eligible for discharge unless plan is a liquidating plan and the debtor terminates business
Section 523	Applicable to individuals	Applicable to individuals
Bankruptcy Code grounds for withholding discharge	Section 727	Section 727 if a. liquidating plan, and b. termination of business operation

While Chapter 11 debtors generally encounter problems after confirmation, you will not encounter these problems on your exam. The problems are "business" problems and the answers are "business" answers.

§ 9.19 Special Forms of Chapter 11 Cases: "Prepacks," "Small Business," "Single Asset Real Estate" and "Individual"

(a) Prepackaged

A prepackaged plan is a bankruptcy plan of reorganization which has been negotiated and accepted by the requisite number of creditors prior to the commencement of the bankruptcy case. A prepackaged Chapter 11 involves the same legal requirements as any other Chapter 11 case; a prepackaged differs only in the sequence in which the requirements are satisfied.

The prepackaged process contemplates that creditor committee selection, debtor-committee negotiations, disclosure statement preparation, and creditor acceptance all occur before a bankruptcy petition is filed. The statutory bases for a prepackaged plan include (i) section 1102 which recognizes prepetition creditors' committees, (ii) section 1121 which permits a debtor to file a plan of reorganization together with its petition, and (iii) section 1126(b) which provides for solicitation of acceptances prior to bankruptcy.

The benefits of a prepackaged Chapter 11 are obvious. Prepackaged plans minimize the amount of time that the debtor operates in bankruptcy because the time-consuming negotiations occur prior to any bankruptcy filing. Less disruption to the debtor's business. Moreover, a debtor has more control over the process. A plan is finalized before the debtor submits to the bankruptcy court's jurisdiction.

The disadvantages of a prepackaged Chapter 11 should be equally obvious. The debtor does not have any of the protections of the Bankruptcy Code during the negotiations. No automatic stay, no ability to reject unfavorable contracts, no moratorium on the accrual of interest on unsecured debts, no ability to obtain needed funding by using the super-priority provision until the bankruptcy petition is filed. In general, prepackaged bankruptcy is better suited for a debtor looking for help with its highly leveraged capital structure rather than a debtor looking for help with its trade debt. In other words, on your exam use a prepackaged bankruptcy for a debtor with financial problems, not a debtor with operational problems.

(b) Small Business Cases

You need to be able to answer two questions about small business cases: (1) what is a small business Chapter 11 case, and (2) how is a small business Chapter 11 case different from other Chapter 11 cases.

A small business Chapter 11 case is a Chapter 11 case involving a debtor that comes within the Bankruptcy Code's definition of "small business debtor." Obviously, that is stating the obvious. Except that wasn't obvious prior to 2005. Before the 2005 legislation, debtors that came within the section 101 definition could choose whether they were "small business debtors." Now debtors that come within the statutory definition are "small business debtors."

That definition in section 101 focuses primarily on the amount of unsecured debt and not the size of the business operations. The amount of the debtor's earnings is irrelevant.

More specifically, in order to be a "small business debtor" the debtor must meet two requirements:

(1) debt not more than $2 million. [This includes both secured and unsecured debt; it does not include contingent or unliquidated debt.]

(2) person engaged in "commercial or business activities" other than simply "owning or operating real property."

There is a third requirement for being a "small business debtor" that is beyond the debtor's control: either the U.S. Trustee has not appointed a creditors' committee or the committee is "not sufficiently active and representative to provide effective oversight."

A small business debtor Chapter 11 case is different from other Chapter 11 cases in that

(1) United States Trustee has additional oversight duties, as described in section 1116 and 28 U.S.C. § 586, and

(2) a small business debtor has additional reporting requirements detailed in section 308 and other duties set out in section 1116, and

(3) the plan process can be simpler because section 1125(f) permits courts to

- determine that a plan itself provides adequate information so that no disclosure statement is necessary;
- approve a standard form disclosure statement;
- combine approval of the disclosure statement with confirmation.

(4) time periods and deadlines are different

- 180 days of debtor exclusivity, section 1121(c);
- 300–day deadline for filing plan and disclosure statement, section 1121(c);
- 45 days after filing for confirmation of the plan, section 1129(e).

(c) Single Asset Real Estate Cases

The phrase "single asset real estate case" is a part of the language of section 101 and of section 362 and part of the language of bankruptcy judges and lawyers. The phrase "single asset real estate case" is not, however, a phrase that actually appears in Chapter 11.

The definition in section 101 is straightforward:

- single property or project;
- real property;
- no substantial other business.

The stay provision for single asset real estate cases in section 362(d) needs to be read together with section 1121. Even though section 1121 provides for an initial 120–day exclusivity period, in a single asset real estate Chapter 11, the deadline is sometimes 90 days, not 120 days. In a single asset real estate case, lenders secured by the real property are entitled to stay relief 90 days after the bankruptcy filing unless the debtor has filed a plan and that plan has a reasonable possibility of being confirmed within a reasonable time or the debtor is making monthly payments to those lenders.

Even though there is no statutory basis for treating Chapter 11 cases involving a real estate debtor differently than other Chapter

11 cases, a distinct body of Chapter 11 single asset real estate case law has developed. Facts common to these cases include

- debtor's only asset is a piece of real estate, i.e., a shopping center, office building, apartment complex, raw land;
- debtor's only secured creditor and only significant creditor is the lender that holds the mortgage on the real estate;
- that lender is seriously undersecured;
- the amount of the mortgage lender's unsecured claim is substantially larger than the claims of all other unsecured creditors combined.

In sum, the typical single asset real estate case is a dispute between a debtor and one creditor over one asset. For some law professors and judges, such single asset real estate cases raise a bankruptcy policy question: should bankruptcy be used to resolve a dispute between a debtor and only one of its creditors?

(d) Individual Chapter 11 Cases

As a result of the 2005 legislation, a Chapter 11 case in which the debtor is an individual is now like a Chapter 13 case in most major respects. More specifically,

- section 1115, like section 1306, includes property acquired by an individual debtor postpetition within property of the estate;
- section 1123(a)(8) and 1129(a)(15), like section 1325(b), impose a "best efforts" kind of test, requiring commitment of "disposable income" to plan payments; and
- section 1141(d)(5), like section 1328(a), defers discharge until completion of plan payments.

There are two statutory differences between Chapter 13 cases and individual Chapter 11 cases that might be important on your exam. First, some individuals may not be eligible for Chapter 13 because of the debt ceilings in section 109(e)—no such bar to Chapter 11. Second, section 1325(a) generally precludes a Chapter 13 debtor from stripping down the amount of her car loans; there is no corresponding limitation on stripping down car loans in Chapter 11 cases.

§ 9.20 Section 363 Sales as the "New Chapter 11"

Increasingly, Chapter 11 cases involve sales of an operating business's assets under section 363, rather than a restructuring of an operating business's debts under a Chapter 11 plan. Recall that section 363(b) authorizes a nonordinary course sale of assets, after notice and hearing, and there is no limit in section 363(b) on how much of t he debtor's assets can be so sold. Accordingly, a Chapter 11 debtor can use section 363(b) to sell all (or substantially all) of its assets—not a liquidation, but a sale of an operating business.

Generally, a purchaser of an operating business prefers to buy a business under section 363 than pursuant to a Chapter 11 plan. Much quicker, much lower attorneys' fees.

The kinds of problems that arise in connection with sect ion 363 sales of operating businesses—breakup fees, "Revlon duties"—are problems covered in mergers and acquisitions courses and mergers and acquisitions exams, not bankruptcy courses and bankruptcy exams.

*

Part Four

OTHER STUFF THAT YOU WILL PROBABLY NEED TO KNOW FOR YOUR EXAM

Unit 10

QUESTION TEN: WHAT DOES A LAW STUDENT NEED TO KNOW ABOUT THE AVOIDING POWERS IN A BANKRUPTCY CASE?

Table of Sections

---

§ 10.1 Scope of the Avoiding Powers

In the absence of bankruptcy, some transfers of a debtor's property can be invalidated under state laws, such as state fraudulent conveyance laws. The Code incorporates these state laws in section 544(b) so that a transfer of a debtor's property that can be invalidated under state law in the absence of bankruptcy can be invalidated under section 544(b) in the event of bankruptcy.

Chapter 5 of the Code also contains several other "avoidance" provisions that are unique to bankruptcy. Accordingly, some payments, sales, exchanges, judicial liens, security interests, and other transfers that are valid under state law can be avoided in bankruptcy. The Code's avoidance provisions reach both "voluntary" transfers such as a debtor's making a gift to a relative or granting a mortgage to a creditor and "involuntary" transfers such as a creditor's garnishing the debtor's bank account or subjecting the debtor's real property to a judgment lien. See 101 (54) (definition of "transfer"). Note also that the Code's avoidance provisions reach both "absolute" transfers such as gifts, payments and sales, and "security transfers" such as mortgages and judgment liens.

In general, in applying these avoidance provisions you will be looking for a transfer of what would otherwise be property of the estate that either

(1) resulted in a decrease in the amount of property of the estate available to pay creditors; or

(2) resulted in a greater recovery by one or more but not all creditors; or

(3) was unrecorded even though nonbankruptcy law required recording in order for the transfer to be effective against third parties; or

(4) was not timely unrecorded.

§ 10.2 Consequences of Use of the Avoiding Powers

If you understand who loses and who wins when a transfer is avoided, you understand the consequences of the use of avoiding powers. The loser is the transferee from whom recovery is had. The winner is the property of the estate [and, in Chapter 7 cases, the creditors to whom the net proceeds from the liquidation of the estate are distributed].

(a) Increase in Property of the Estate

In the main, the consequence of avoiding a transfer is an increase in property of the estate. The avoiding powers are a part of a subchapter of the Code entitled "The Estate."

When the bankruptcy trustee avoids an absolute transfer of property, that property then becomes property of the estate. Assume that *D* owes *C* $25,000. *D* repays *C* $12,000 of that debt. *D* later files for bankruptcy. At the time of *D*'s bankruptcy filing, the $12,000 paid to *C* is not property of *D*'s estate. If the bankruptcy trustee is able to invoke one of the Code's avoidance provisions to avoid the payment and recover the $12,000, the $12,000 will then become property of *D*'s estate, sections 541(a)(3), 550.

The avoidance of an absolute transfer can also affect the amount of a creditor's claim. In the above hypothetical, *C* had a $13,000 claim at the time of *D*'s bankruptcy filing. Again, if the bankruptcy trustee is able to avoid the payment and recover the $12,000 *D* paid *C*, then *C* will have a $25,000 claim against *D*, section 502(h). If the bankruptcy trustee is able to establish a legal basis for avoiding the transfer but is unable to recover the payment, then *C*'s claim for $13,000 will be disallowed under section 502(d).

The consequences of avoiding a security transfer are similar. Assume, for example, that *D* borrows $77,000 from *C* and grants *C* a mortgage on Blackacre which is worth $120,000. *D* later files for bankruptcy. Absent the trustee's use of one of the avoidance powers, *C* has a $77,000 secured claim. Recall that under section 541, Blackacre itself is not property of the estate; rather the estate's interest in Blackacre is only *D*'s limited equity and other rights in Blackacre. If, however, the bankruptcy trustee is able to avoid the grant of the mortgage on Blackacre, then *C* will have a $77,000 unsecured claim, and Blackacre without any encumbrance will be property of the estate.

In the two examples, the consequences of avoidance were the recovery of the property interest transferred from the party to whom it had been transferred. Under section 550, the consequences of avoidance are not limited to recovery of the property transferred, or to the person to whom the transfer was made.

Under section 550(a), the court can order the recovery of the "value of the property" transferred, rather than the property. And, section 550 permits recovery not only from (i) the initial transferee but also (ii) from the later transferees or (iii) from a person who was not a transferee but benefitted from the transfer. And, section 550 provides protection for certain transferees.

Assume for example that (1) D gives Blackacre which was worth $400 to *X*, (2) *X* later sells Blackacre to *Y* for $100, (3) *D* files for bankruptcy, (4) the gift of Blackacre from *D* to *X* was an avoidable transfer under Chapter 5 of the Bankruptcy Code, and (5) Blackacre is now worth $200. Section 550 provides statutory authority for any of the following results:

—recovery of Blackacre from *Y*;

—recovery of the "value of such property" from either *X* or *Y* with no statutory guidance as to whether the value would be present value of $200 or value at the time of the transfer which would be $400.

(b) Disallowance of Claim Under Section 502(d) Because of Unavoided, Avoidable Transfer

You can probably skip this because your professor will probably skip section 502(d), but just in case . . .

Section 502(d) applies to a question with the following facts:

#1 creditor has an unsecured claim AND

#2 prior to bankruptcy, that creditor was the transferee of a transfer that could be avoided AND

#3 there has not been recovery under section 550.

Assume for example that

—*D* owes *C* $3,000.

—*D* pays *C* $400.

—*D* files for bankruptcy

—*D*'s payment of $400 to *C* is an avoidable transfer but *C* does not repay the $400

—*C* files a claim for $2,600.

Under section 502(d), *C*'s entire $2,600 claim can be disallowed.

§ 10.3 Avoidance Litigation

To understand the avoidance provisions, remember that avoidance does not occur by operation of law. Avoidance in bankruptcy of a prebankruptcy transfer requires litigation and raises all of the usual litigation questions such as:

(1) Who can initiate avoidance litigation?

(2) What are the time limitations on initiating an avoidance action?

The answer to the first question is the "Chapter 7 trustee, the Chapter 11 trustee, and the Chapter 12 and 13 trustee and. . . ." The avoidance provisions in Chapter 5 of the Bankruptcy Code generally use the phrase "the trustee may avoid." Accordingly, the trustee in a Chapter 7, 11, 12, or 13 case can initiate avoidance litigation.

Recall that in Chapter 11 cases without a trustee, the debtor has the rights of a trustee. Thus the Chapter 11 debtor in possession, and, in some instances, a Chapter 11 creditors' committee can initiate avoidance litigation. The cases are divided as to whether a Chapter 13 debtor can bring an avoidance action.

Section 546 deals with the second question of when an avoidance action must be brought—within two years after the order for relief except that if a trustee is appointed more than one year after the order for relief but within two years after the order for relief, then the trustee shall have one year.

Section 546 then is the statute of limitations for avoidance actions.

We will see different time periods in different avoidance provisions such as "90 days" in section 547 and "2 years in section 548." These time periods are not statutes of limitations in that they do not limit the time within which the litigation must be filed. Rather, such a time period is part of the substantive law of that avoidance provisions; they limit the time before bankruptcy within which the transfer must have occurred.

To illustrate, on 1/15/06, *D* pays *X* $100. If *D* files for bankruptcy on July 13, 2006, that payment cannot be avoided under section 547—transfer occurred more than 90 days before bankruptcy. If, however, *D* files for bankruptcy on April 5, 2006, then that payment can be avoided under section 547 if the avoidance complaint is filed within two years of April 5, 2006.

Most avoidance litigation is based on either section 548 (fraudulent transfers or obligations) or section 547 (preferential transfers). More important, most exams questions about avoidance involve either section 548 or section 547 or both. Accordingly, the next two units review first fraudulent transfers or obligations (Unit 11) and then preferential transfers (Unit 12).

Unit 11

QUESTION ELEVEN: WHAT DOES A LAW STUDENT NEED TO KNOW ABOUT FRAUDULENT TRANSFERS AND OBLIGATIONS?

Table of Sections

Obviously, "fraudulent" transfers and "fraudulent" obligations are not good things. If you represent *T* who acquired property from *D*, you don't want the transfer from *D* to *T* to be viewed as "fraudulent." Similarly, if you represent *C* whom *D* is obligated to pay, you don't want the obligation from *D* to *C* to be "fraudulent."

Most of the law with respect to fraudulent transfers and fraudulent obligations will be equally obvious if you remember that the law focuses on whether the creditors of the transferor or obligor have been adversely affected by the transfer or obligation. Fraudulent conveyance law avoids transfers and obligations that "hinder, delay or defraud" creditors of the transferor or obligor.

Consider the most obvious example of a fraudulent transfer: *D* is insolvent. *D* owns Blackacare. *D* gives Blackacre to *X* so that her unpaid creditors are unable to seize and sell Blackacre. Determining whether that transfer was avoidable under fraudulent transfer law would depend on the impact of the transfer or obligation on creditors of *D*, not the impact of the transfer on *D* or *X*.

§ 11.1 State Fraudulent Transfer Law

Every state has a statute that empowers creditors to avoid transfers that "hinder, delay or defraud creditors." While these various state statutes vary in detail, they are basically the same.

And, these various state fraudulent conveyance statutes are basically the same as section 548 of the Bankruptcy Code.

In bankruptcy, both section 548 of the Bankruptcy Code and state fraudulent conveyance law can be used to avoid a prebankruptcy transfer of the debtor's property or a prebankruptcy obligation of the debtor. And, in real world bankruptcy cases, both are used. In law school bankruptcy classes and, more important, on law school bankruptcy exams section 548 is what is emphasized. So let's focus first on section 548.

§ 11.2 Section 548

(a) Looking at the Language and Structure of Section 548

Bankruptcy test questions on section 548 test your ability to read and apply section 548—especially section 548(a)(1). Look at the language and structure of section 548(a)(1)

First, notice the "two years" in the prefatory language to section 548(a). This is not a statute of limitations; it is a requirement of section 548. Only transfers of the debtor's property that occurred within two years before the date of the bankruptcy petition or obligations incurred by the debtor within two years before the filing are within the scope of section 548. If, for example, *D* transfers Blackacre in January 2006 and files for bankruptcy in March 2008, that transfer is not subject to section 548 scrutiny.

Now look at the structure of section 548(a)(1). There is an (A) and (B) connected by the conjunction "or." This means that a transfer or obligation may be avoided as "fraudulent" by satisfying the requirements of either (A) or (B).

(1) Actual Fraudulent Intent and Section 548(a)(1)(A)

The key phrase in (A) is "actual intent." Section 548(a)(1)(A) only applies to transfers that are actually fraudulent, i.e., made with the actual, subjective intent of hurting creditors.

There is almost never any direct evidence of actual fraudulent intent. Establishing actual fraudulent intent is usually established through circumstantial evidence.

There are certain facts, often referred to as "badges of fraud," that courts generally treat as strong indicia of actual fraudulent intent. The three most significant badges of fraud are

—the existence of a family or other close relationship between the transferor and the transferee;

—the absence or inadequacy of consideration;

—the secrecy of the transfer.

(2) Constructive Fraud and Section 548(a)(1)(B)

Most fraudulent transfer cases and most exam questions do not involve section 548(a)(1)(A) actual fraudulent intent. Constructive fraud under section 548(a)(1)(B) is more important.

The words "constructive fraud" do not appear in section 548(a)(1)(B) but do appear in cases applying it. And the word "constructive" appears throughout law—"constructive eviction," "constructive trespass," etc. According to Bryan Garner's Black's Law Dictionary, "constructive" is an adjective meaning "legally imputed, having an effect in law though not necessarily in fact." In short, "constructive" means "let's pretend." When a transfer or meets the standards of section 548(a)(1)(B) it is constructively fraudulent, and section 548(a)(1)(B) "pretends" it is a fraudulent transfer or obligation and treats it that way even though no one intended anything fraudulent by it.

To understand the requirements of section 548(a)(1)(B), it is necessary to understand its structure. Section 548(a)(1)(B) is divided into two main parts (i) and (ii) which are connected by "and." Accordingly, it is necessary to satisfy both (i) and (ii): (i) focuses on the adequacy of what the debtor received in exchange for the debtor gave and (ii) focuses on the financial condition of the debtor at the time of the transfer.

(b) Common Exam Examples of Constructive Fraud

The two easiest examples of transfers that are constructively fraudulent under section 548(a)(1)(B) are (1) gifts by a person who is insolvent and (2) below market sales by a person who is insolvent.

(1) Gifts

Let's do gifts first. People give stuff away to friends and relatives all the time. No section 548(a)(1)(B) problem so long as the donor still has enough stuff left to pay her creditors–is not insolvent.

Your professor can make this more difficult by making the donee a "qualified religious or charitable entity or organization." Some such gifts are protected by section 548(a)(2) from avoidance as a fraudulent transfer by section 548(a)(1)(B)

(2) Sales at Unreasonably Low Prices

Now sales. Your common sense (and your reading the language of section 548(a)(1)(B)) should tell you that an insolvent person's selling her stuff at an unreasonably low price should be treated similarly to her giving away the stuff. If *D* can't give Blackacre to her sister to keep her creditors from seizing and selling it, then *D* should not be able to "sell" Blackacre to a relative or friend for a fraction of its value to keep her creditors from seizing and selling it.

Again, your professor can make this more difficult by making the sale a foreclosure sale that completely complied with state law.

Assume, for example, that *D* borrowed $180,000 from *M*. The debt was secured by a deed of trust. *D* defaulted. *M* foreclosed on the realty and sold the property for $115,400, the amount of *D*'s outstanding debt. *M*'s foreclosure and sale completely complied with state law. A few days later, *D* filed for bankruptcy.

Do you see any possible fraudulent conveyance argument? What if *D* found an appraiser who was willing to testify that the value of the realty at the time of the foreclosure sale was $200,000? Can it be argued that the foreclosure sale was a fraudulent conveyance since it was a transfer for less than reasonably equivalent value while the debtor was insolvent? Such an argument was made in various cases with varying degrees of success until the Supreme Court decision in *BFP v. RTC* (1994). In a 5–4 decision, the Court held that " 'reasonably equivalent value' is the price received at the foreclosure sale so long as all the requirements of the state's foreclosure law have been complied with."

(3) Guarantees

Guarantees are more challenging examples of constructive fraud. An unsecured guarantee by a person who is "insolvent" can result in a fraudulent obligation. A secured guarantee by such a person can result in both a fraudulent obligation and a fraudulent transfer.

The key to applying section 548(a)(1)(B) to debt guarantees that the debtor made before filing for bankruptcy is remembering that the noun "debtor" precedes the verb phrase "received less than reasonably equivalent value in exchange" in section 548(b)(1)(B)(I). The standard is not whether someone in the world received "reasonably equivalent value in exchange" but rather whether the debtor received reasonably equivalent value.

In a personal debt guarantee or an intercorporate debt guarantee, the creditor generally is providing an appropriate amount of consideration, but is providing the consideration to a person other than the guarantor. Assume, for example, that *C* lends $900,000 to *X*, Inc., *D* Corp., a subsidiary of *X*, Inc., guarantees repayment. A few months later *D* Corp. files for bankruptcy. Can the trustee use section 548(a)(1)(B) to avoid *D* Corp.'s guarantee to *C* as a constructively fraudulent obligation?

Note that *C* provided a sufficient amount of consideration–*C* is trying to collect $900,000 from *D* Corp. because it loaned $900,000.

to *X*, Inc. Note also that *C* provided that consideration to someone other than *D* Corp.—someone other than the transferor/debtor in this bankruptcy case. And, note that section 548(a)(1)(B) does not ask whether the creditor/transferee *gave* reasonably equivalent consideration to someone but rather whether the debtor "*received*" reasonably equivalent value.

Do you now understand why a bankruptcy trustee for the guarantor can challenge an intercorporate guarantee as a fraudulent obligation under section 548(a)(1)(B)? Do you also understand why such challenges will not always be successful?

Recall that section 548(a)(1)(B) inquires not only into the adequacy of consideration to the debtor but also the financial condition of the debtor. If *D* Corp. was clearly solvent at the time of the guarantee, there is no section 548 transaction.

Additionally, a loan to one corporation can benefit related entities. Conceivably, *C*'s loan to *X*, Inc., *D* Corp.'s parent, did indirectly benefit *D* Corp. Accordingly, the point is to compare the value of what *D* Corp. gave up by guarantee to *C* and the value of what *D* Corp. got from *C*'s loan to *X*, Inc. That was the point of *Rubin v. Manufacturers Hanover Trust* (1981).

(c) Applying Section 548(a)(1)(B) to Leveraged Buyouts

Leveraged buyouts can be approached similarly. In essence, a leveraged buyout (LBO) involves a person buying a business and then using the assets of that business to secure its financing. Assume, for example, that *C* makes a loan to *X* to enable her to buy all of the stock of *D* Corp. from its shareholders. Once *X* has all the *D* Corp. stock, *X* causes *D* Corp. to grant *C* a lien on the assets of *D* Corp., as collateral for the loan from *C* to *X*. Shortly after the LBO is completed, *D* Corp. files for bankruptcy.

Do you see the trustee's possible section 548(a)(1)(B) argument to avoid the lien on *D* Corp.'s assets? *D* Corp. made a security transfer of its assets to *C*. Was *D* Corp. solvent? If not, what value did *D* Corp. receive for the transfer? *C* gave value to someone; it made the loan to *X* that made the LBO possible. Value to someone, value to *X*, is not the question. Did the LBO result in reasonably equivalent value to the debtor/transferor, *D* Corp.? Was the change in ownership of value to *D* Corp.? Was it of a value reasonably equivalent to what *D* Corp. transferred while insolvent?

(d) Remembering Insolvency or . . .

As the above LBO hypothetical reminds us, proof of a constructive fraudulent transfer under section 548(a)(1)(B) requires not only proof of the absence of reasonably equivalent value but also proof of the existence of insolvency or one of the other forms of financial distress described in section 548(a)(B)(ii). Remember that.

§ 11.3 Remembering "Two Years"

And, remember, the "within two years" requirement of section 548. If the transfer occurred or the obligation was incurred more than two years before bankruptcy, section 548 does not apply. Instead, do state fraudulent conveyance law which generally looks back four or more years and is made a part of bankruptcy law by section 544(b), discussed below.

(a) And Remembering Section 548(d) When You Remember the "Two Years Requirement"

The purpose of section 548(d) is to prevent sales of real estate, mortgages on real estate, and security interests on personal property from escaping invalidation as fraudulent transfers by being kept secret, Because of (1) nonbankruptcy requirements of recording real estate transfers and perfecting Article 9 security interests and (2) language in section 548(d)(1), a sale or mortgage of real estate or a grant of an Article 9 security interest does not occur for purposes of the requirements of section 548 until the required recordation or other perfection.

For example, on January 10, 2006, *D* gives Redacre to *X* who does not record the deed until November 11, 2009. On December 12, 2010, *D* files a bankruptcy petition.

Remember section 548 has a two-year look back period. *D*'s transfer of Redacre was actually made more than two years before the bankruptcy filing. The transfer, however, was not effective against a subsequent bona fide purchaser until it was recorded on November 11, 2009. Accordingly, under sect ion 548(d), the transfer is deemed made on November 11, 2009. Accordingly, section 548's two-year requirement and all of the other requirements under section 548 focus on November 11, 2009.

November 11, 2009, is not only the relevant date for applying the "within 2 years" requirement but also the relevant date for determining whether *D* was insolvent. Note the prefatory language of section 548(d)(1) "For purposes of THIS section," not merely for purposes of the "within 2 years" requirement of this section.

(b) And Remembering Section 544(b) When You Remember the "Two Years" Requirement

While section 548 is limited to transfers made or deemed made within two years of the bankruptcy filing, state fraudulent conveyance law generally is not so limited. The Uniform Fraudulent Transfer Act, for example, looks back four years.

And, state fraudulent conveyance can become a part of bankruptcy law by reason of section 544(b) Section 544(b) does not specifically provide for the avoidance of fraudulent conveyances. Rather, it empowers the bankruptcy trustee to avoid any prebankruptcy transfer that is "voidable under applicable law by a creditor holding an unsecured claim that is allowable."

While the existence of the trustee's section 544(b)'s avoiding power depends upon the existence of a nonbankruptcy law avoiding right held by an actual creditor, the extent of the trustee's section 544(b)'s avoidance power is greater than the power of the actual creditor. Under the Supreme Court's decision in *Moore v. Bay* (1931), the trustee is not limited in her recovery to the amount of the claim of the actual creditor. A transfer by the debtor before bankruptcy which is avoidable by a single creditor under state law may be avoided entirely by the trustee, regardless of the size of the actual creditor's claim.

Use the following hypothetical to review: *D* sells Blackacre which has a value of at least 2000 to *X* for 100. *X* immediately records the deed. At the time of the sale, *D* was insolvent and one of *D*'s creditors was *Y* who was owed 7. Two and one-half years later, *D* files for bankruptcy and still owes *Y* 3.

Section 548(a)(1) is not applicable–not within two years. Section 544(b) is applicable (if applicable state fraudulent conveyance law had a look-back period of more than two and one-half years), and the entire transfer of Blackacre can be avoided.

§ 11.4 Not Applying Section 548 or 544 to Payments to Creditors

Assume that *D* has $100,000 of assets and has the following debts: $50,000 to *A*, $60,000 to *B* and $70,000 to *C*. (*D* is "insolvent.") While insolvent, *D* transfers $40,000.

If *D* transferred the $40,000 of assets to someone other than one of its three creditors and then filed for bankruptcy, the transfer will be scrutinized as a fraudulent transfer under section 544 and 548. The issue will be whether *D* received reasonably equivalent value.

On the other hand, if *D* transferred the $40,000 to one of its three creditors—*A*, *B*, or *C*, then there is no issue of whether the transfer is fraudulent under section 548 or 544—no issue of reasonably equivalent value. Satisfying a debt satisfies the statutory "value" requirement, cf section 548(d)(2)(A). Transfers to one or more but not all of the creditors raise preference issues not fraudulent transfer issues. The next Unit addresses these preference issues.

Unit 12

QUESTION TWELVE: WHAT DOES A LAW STUDENT NEED TO KNOW ABOUT PREFERENCES?

Table of Sections

Law professors love preference law. The question is not whether preference law will be on your exam but how much of your exam will be on preference law.

§ 12.1 Differences Between Fraudulent Transfers and Preferences

Looking back at the material on fraudulent transfers, the essence of an argument that a transfer is a fraudulent transfer avoidable under section 548 or section 544(b) is that stuff that but for the transfer would be property of the estate was transferred before bankruptcy (1) to someone who was not a creditor (2) for less than reasonably equivalent value so that ALL creditors got less.

Looking ahead to the material on preferential transfers, the essence of an argument that a transfer is avoidable under section 547 is that stuff that but for the transfer would be property of the estate was transferred before bankruptcy (1) to someone who was a creditor (2) for a prior debt so that all OTHER creditors got less.

Again, in looking for a fraudulent transfer, we looked for what the debtor/transferor received—we were concerned that a transferee who was not a creditor benefitted from the transfer to the disadvantage of creditors generally. In looking for a preference, we will look at to whom the transfer was made rather than what the debtor/transferor received for the transfer, and we will be concerned about whether one creditor transferee benefitted from a transfer to the disadvantage of other similar creditors.

There is no state law counterpart to the Code's preference provisions. State creditor's rights law does not "condemn" a preference. Outside of bankruptcy, a debtor, even an insolvent debtor, can treat some creditors more favorably than other similar creditors. Although *D* owes *X*, *Y*, and *Z* $1,000 each, *D* can pay *X* in full before paying *Y* or *Z* anything.

Bankruptcy law *does* "condemn" *certain* preferences. A House report that accompanied a draft of the Code explained the rationale for such a bankruptcy policy as follows:

> The purpose of the preference section is two-fold. First, by permitting the trustee to avoid prebankruptcy transfers that occur within a short period before bankruptcy, creditors are discouraged from racing to the courthouse to dismember the debtor during his slide into bankruptcy. The protection thus afforded the debtor often enables him to work his way out of a difficult financial situation through cooperation with all of his creditors. Second, and more important, the preference provisions facilitate the prime bankruptcy policy of equality of distribution among creditors of the debtor. Any creditor that received a greater payment than others of his class is required to disgorge so that all may share equally.

H. REP. NO. 595, 95TH CONG., 1ST SESS. 117–18 (1977).

§ 12.2 Structure of Section 547

Look to paragraph (b) of section 547 to determine whether a transfer is a preference. If, and only if, the requirements of ALL of the numbered paragraphs of section 547(b) are met, then look to section 547(c) to determine whether the preference qualifies for an exception, i.e., is a preference that may not be avoided. If the requirements of ANY of the of the numbered paragraphs are met, there is an exception. Again, ALL for section 547(b); ANY for section 547(c).

§ 12.3 Requirements for (a/k/a "Elements of") a Preference in Section 547(b)

Section 547(b) sets out the elements of a preference. Section 547(b) is kind of tricky. There are five numbered requirement, and the tendency is to start with (1). You need to catch the unnumbered requirement in the prefatory clause–transfer of an interest of the debtor in property.

Under section 547(b), the trustee may avoid a prebankruptcy transfer of an interest of the debtor in property if she can establish ALL of the following:

(1) the transfer was "to or for the benefit of a creditor"; and

(2) the transfer was made for or on account of an "antecedent debt," i.e., a debt owed prior to the time of the transfer; and

(3) the debtor was insolvent at the time of the transfer; and

(4) the transfer was made within 90 days before the date of the filing of the bankruptcy petition, or, was made between 90 days and 1 year before the date of the filing of the petition to an "insider";[18] and

(5) the transfer has the effect of increasing the amount that the transferee would receive in a Chapter 7 case.

Again, don't miss the first element of a preference which comes before any of the numbered elements: "transfer of an interest of the debtor in property." Payments and other transfers by people other than the person who is later the debtor in the bankruptcy case are never section 547 preferences.

Assume for example, *D* owes $100 to *A*, *B*, and *C*. *M*, *D*'s momma, pays *A* but not *B* and *C*. *D* later files for bankruptcy. In a real sense, *M*'s payment of *A* but not *B* or *C* treated *A* more favorably than *B* or *C*—preferred *A* over *B* or *C*. In a bankruptcy sense, *M*'s payment is not a preference because it was not a "transfer of an interest of the debtor in property," not a diminution of property of *D*'s estate—*A* of course benefitted from being paid by *M*, but not to the detriment of *D*'s other creditors.

Now assume *M* gave the $100 to *D* who then used that $100 to pay *A*. Is *D*'s payment to *A* a "transfer of interest an interest of the debtor in property"? In answering that question, most courts would look to the "earmarking doctrine." Under this court-created concept, if an insolvent debtor pays one of her creditors with funds from a third party that were clearly earmarked to pay a specific antecedent debt, there is no section 547 preference. Again, *A* benefitted, but not to the detriment of other creditors. Generally, the pivotal questions in cases in which the earmarking doctrine is an issue is whether the debtor had any control over how the funds from the third party could be used.

18. "Insider" is defined in section 101. An insider includes relatives of an individual debtor and directors of a corporate debtor.

The first three numbered requirements of section 547(b) will usually be easy to apply. To illustrate the first requirement—"to or for the benefit of a creditor"–a true gift is not a preference—not to or for the benefit of a creditor. A mortgage to secure a new loan is not a preferential transfer because of section 547(b)'s second requirement—not for or on account of antecedent debt. The third requirement—insolvency of the debtor at the time of transfer—is made easy by section 547(f)'s creation of a rebuttable presumption of insolvency for the 90 days immediately preceding the filing of the bankruptcy petition.

In applying the fourth requirement of section 547(b), within the statutory preference period, it may be necessary to look to section 547(e) and section 101. If under state law, a transfer is not fully effective against third parties until recordation or other public notice of the transfer has been timely given and the transfer was not timely recorded, then section 547(e) [considered later in this chapter] deems the transfer to have occurred at the time of recordation.

To illustrate, assume that on January 15, *D* borrows $100,000 from *S* and grants *S* a security interest on a piece of equipment. Under relevant nonbankruptcy state law, *S*'s security interest is not effective against other creditors who might claim a lien on that same equipment unless a financing statement was filed. *S* delays filing its financing statement until April 5. *D* then files for bankruptcy on July 1. By reason of section 547(e), the transfer from *D* to *S* creating *S*'s security interest is regarded as occurring on April 5, not January 15. And since the debt was incurred on January 15 and the transfer is not deemed to have occurred until April 5, the security interest was a transfer for an antecedent debt within 90 days of the July 1 bankruptcy.

Section 101's definition of "insider" becomes a part of the fourth requirement of section 547(b) in determining whether the transfer was made to an "insider" so that the relevant period is one year, rather than 90 days. Remember that the presumption of insolvency is limited to the 90 days immediately preceding the bankruptcy petition. Accordingly, in order to invalidate a transfer that occurred more than 90 days before the filing of the bankruptcy petition the trustee must establish that (i) the transferee was an "insider"; and (ii) the debtor was insolvent at the time of the transfer.

The fifth element essentially tests whether the transfer enabled the creditor/transferee to get *more* than she would have received if (a) the transfer had not taken place and (b) the case was a Chapter 7 case. This fifth element is satisfied unless (i) the transferee has a claim secured by property worth more than the amount of its claim or (ii) the transferee has a secured claim and all that is transferred to her is part or all of the collateral that secured the claim or (iii) the estate is sufficiently large to pay all unsecured claims in full. In (i), (ii), and (iii), a prebankruptcy transfer does not result in the creditor's receiving more than what she would receive in a Chapter 7 case if the transfer had not been made; she is simply receiving earlier all or part of what she would have ultimately received in the Chapter 7 case.

Assume, for example, that *D* makes a $1,000 payment to *C*, a creditor with a $10,000 unsecured claim, on January 10. On February 20, *D* files a bankruptcy petition. The property of the estate is sufficient to pay each unsecured creditor 50% of its claim. An unsecured creditor with a $10,000 claim will thus receive $5,000. *S*, however, will receive a total of $5,500 from *D* and *D*'s bankruptcy unless the January 10th transfer is avoided. ($1,000 + 50% × ($10,000 − $1,000)). Accordingly, the bankruptcy trustee can avoid the January 10th transfer.

Again, except for the situations described in (i), (ii), and (iii), a prebankruptcy transfer that satisfies section 547(b)(1)–(4) will result in the transferee receiving more, i.e., will also satisfy section 547(b)(5).

The favorite exam question on section 547(b)(5) involves a prebankruptcy payment to a creditor who was partly secured. Assume that *D* owes *C* $100 and *C* is secured by Blackacre which is worth $40. *D* pays *C* $30 and files for bankruptcy the next month. Also assume that *D*'s creditors would not be paid in full in a Chapter 7 case.

You need to be able to explain to your professor why the payment of $30 was preferential, i.e., enabled *C* to receive more. Before the payment, *C* had a $60 unsecured claim and a $40 secured claim. After the $30 payment, *C* has a total claim of only $70. Nothing in the facts indicate that *C* released its mortgage and so *C* still has its lien on Blackacre and so *C* still has a secured claim of $40. Accordingly, *C* now has an unsecured claim of $30—accordingly, the economic effect of the payment was to reduce *C*'s unsecured claim, i.e., to enable *C* to receive more.

§ 12.4 Review of Section 547(b)

We are so certain that your test will include section 547(b) fact patterns that we include the following section 547(b) fact patterns for your review:

In each of the following, assume that (1) *D* cannot rebut the section 547(f) presumption of insolvency and (2) *D*'s creditors would not be paid in full in a Chapter 7 case.

#1 On January 10, *D* borrows $10,000 from *C*. On February 2, *D* pays *C* $7,000. On March 3, *D* files for bankruptcy.

The trustee can recover the $7,000.

#2 On February 2, *D* borrows $10,000 from *C*. On March 3, *D* grants *C* a mortgage on Blackacre worth $7,000. On April 4, *D* files for bankruptcy.

The trustee can avoid the mortgage on Blackacre so that Blackacre is again unencumbered property of the estate. The mortgage is a "transfer." That transfer, if not avoided, would result in *C*'s having a $7,000 secured claim that would be paid in full, and a $3,000 unsecured claim. If the transfer had not been made, *C* would have a $10,000 unsecured claim.

[Watch for this on your exam. Section 547(b) invalidates liens to secure past debts.]

#3 On March 3, *D* borrows $100,000 from *C* and grants *C* a mortgage on Blackacre worth $70,000. On April 4, *D* files for bankruptcy.

The trustee CANNOT avoid the mortgage on Blackacre. The mortgage was NOT "for or on account of an antecedent debt."

#4 On April 4, *D* borrows $10,000 from *C*. On May 5, *D* pays *C* $70,000. On December 12, *D* files a bankruptcy petition.

The trustee cannot the May 5 payment UNLESS *C* was an insider AND the trustee can prove that *D* was insolvent on May 5th. Remember (1) 90–day preference period unless the transferee is an insider AND (2) the section 547(e) presumption of insolvency only applies for the 90 days prior to bankruptcy

§ 12.5 Applying the Requirements of Section 547(b) to Three Party Transactions

Thus far, we have dealt with two-party preferences. *D* makes a transfer to *C* that prefers *C*. These two-party preferences are also known as direct preferences.

In class and on your exam, you will have to deal with three-party, indirect preferences. Section 547(b) introduces this possibility with the phrase "to or for the benefit of a creditor." *D* makes a transfer to *C* that is for the benefit of *X* and results in a preference to *X*.

There are three different "exam-important" three-party, indirect preferences fact patterns: (1) guarantees, (2) two or more liens on the same property, and (3) letters of credit. Guarantees are the easiest to understand (and the most likely to be tested).

Assume, for example, that *C* makes a loan to *D*, and *X* guarantees payment of the loan. It is obvious from reading the hypothetical that *C* is a creditor of *D*. And, it should be obvious from reading the definitions of "creditor" and "claim" in section 101 that *X* is also a creditor of *D* for purposes of section 547.

What if *D* pays *C* on January 15 and then files for bankruptcy on January 17? *D*'s payment to *C* is a transfer "TO a creditor." The payment is also "FOR THE BENEFIT OF a creditor." As explained above, *X* is a creditor. *X* benefits from *D*'s payment to *C*: *D*'s payment to *C* frees *X* from her obligations under the guarantee. Accordingly, the payment to one creditor, *C*, can be an indirect preference to another creditor, *X*, if the other elements of section 547(b) are satisfied.

Finding such an indirect preference can be important to *D*'s bankruptcy trustee where the transferee, *C*, is also insolvent. Recovering from *X* is possible because section 550 allows the trustee to recover a preference from either the actual transferee or "the entity for whose benefit the transfer was made."

Finding such an indirect preference can also be important where the transfer is not avoidable as to the actual transferee. Assume, for example, that *D* pays *C* on January 15 and then files for bankruptcy on July 13. *C* is not an "insider," but *X* is. The payment to *C* is not a preference as to *C*. Since *C* is not an insider, the relevant section 547(b) time period is 90 days. The payment of *C* is a preference as to *X*. Since *X* (like most guarantors) is an insider, the relevant time period is one year. Obviously, the trustee could recover from *X*. And until a 1994 amendment, every circuit court that considered these facts held that the trustee could also recover from *C*.

Levit v. Ingersoll Rand Financial Corp. (1989) (more commonly referred as the *Deprizio* case) was the first circuit court case to hold that a payment to a noninsider creditor where there was an insider guarantor could be recovered from that noninsider creditor even though it occurred more than 90 days before the bankruptcy filing. In so holding, the court relied primarily on the language of section 547 and 550.

The *Levit* decision and the several other circuit court decisions following it look at section 547 and 550 as independent, unrelated provisions. The methodology of these decisions can be outlined as follows. First, look at section 547(b) and determine if there has been a preference as to anyone. Second, if there is a preference as to anyone under section 547(b), look at section 550 and determine the possible responsible parties. The party responsible under section 550 does not have to be the same party as to whom the transfer was preferential. In application, even though the payment to *C* was only preferential as to *X* under section 547, the trustee can still recover from *C* since section 550 permits recovery from the actual transferee.

A 1994 amendment to section 550 and a 2005 amendment to 547(i) change the result in *Levit*. Section 550 now precludes recovery from a creditor that is not an insider for preferences made more than 90 days before the bankruptcy filing.

While this amendment changes the *Levit* result, it does not change the *Levit* reasoning. The significance of the *Levit* approach to sections 547 and 550 is not limited to guaranteed loans.

Assume, for example, that both *F* and *S* are creditors of *D* with a lien on Blackacre. *F* is owed $100,000 and has a first lien. *S* is owed $200,000 and has a second lien. The value of Blackacre is $150,000. Consider the consequences of *D*'s paying *F* $30,000. If you remember what you have read, you will remember that a payment to a fully secured creditor is not preferential, section 547(b)(5). Accordingly, the payment to *F* cannot be a section 547 preference as to *F*. And, if you understand what you have read, you will understand that this payment to *F* is preferential as to *S*. By paying *F* $30,000 and reducing *F*'s secured claim on Blackacre to $70,000, *D* has indirectly benefited *S* by increasing *S*'s secured claim on Blackacre to $80,000. Accordingly, the payment to *F* can be a section 547 preference as to *S*. And, under *Levit* and its progeny, the trustee arguably can use section 550 to recover from either *S* or *F*.

Letter of credit deals are more complicated. The letter of credit deal that you may have to deal with on your exam as an indirect preference looks like this. *D* owes *C* $1,000; *D*'s debt is unsecured. *D* does not pay *C*—that would be a section 547(b) preference. *C* does not get a mortgage on *D*'s real estate—that would be a section 547(b) preference. Instead, *D* obtains a letter of credit from *X* Bank for the benefit of *C*. In order to obtain that letter of credit, *D* grants *X* Bank a mortgage on its real estate. *C* draws on the letter of credit, i.e., *C* is paid $1,000 by *X* Bank. *D* then files for bankruptcy.

Remember the elements of section 547(b), staring with "transfer of an interest of the debtor in property." That's the mortgage granted to *X* Bank. While that transfer was not for an antecedent debt owed by *D* to *X* Bank, it was "on account of" an antecedent debt owed by *D* to *C* and it did enable *C* who would have been an unsecured creditor in *D*'s bankruptcy but for the transfer and the letter of credit and the draw to "receive more...." Accordingly, if *D*'s bankruptcy occurred within 90 days of the mortgage, there is a voidable transfer under section 547(b). And under *Deprizio* and section 550, there can be recovery from either *C* or *X* Bank.

§ 12.6 Knowing the Two Preference Exceptions That Might Come Up on Your Exam

Recall that section 547(b) sets out the elements of a preference. In order to avoid a transfer as a preference, the trustee must allege and establish each of the elements of section 547(b).

Even if the trustee proves her entire case under section 547(b), she may not be able to avoid the transfer. Section 547(c) contains nine, numbered exceptions from section 547(b): a creditor/transferee can prevent avoidance of the transfer by proving that the transfer is covered by one of the section 547(c) exceptions.

Remember the relationship between paragraphs (b) and (c) of section 547(b). "B" not only comes before "C" in the alphabet but also in section 547 of the Code. And, there is a reason that the elements of a preference are set out in section 547(b) before the exceptions are set out in section 547(c). Do section 547(b) first.

Section 547(c) protects transfers that would otherwise be avoidable by the trustee under section 547(b). Section 547(c) applies only in concert with section 547(b). If the trustee fails to establish a preference under section 547(b), it is not necessary to look to section 547(c). It is only after the trustee has proved her entire case under section 547(b) that it becomes necessary to determine whether section 547(c) protects all or part of the transfer from avoidance.

Although section 547(c) has nine numbered exceptions, you are likely to need to know only two of the nine for your exam: (2) and (4).

(a) 547(c)(2) "Ordinary Course"

Routine. Section 547(c)(2) is about routine. Where you see the phrase "ordinary course," think routine. Section 547(c)(2) protects a debtor's routine payments on its routine debts.

For example, *D* receives her water bill for January on February 5th and pays it the same day. That payment was a transfer for an antecedent debt. If *D* files for bankruptcy within 90 days of February 5th, that payment probably meets the preference requirements of section 547(b). And, that payment also meets the exception requirements of section 547(c)(2).

Section 547(c)(2) has two requirements. First, the first requirement looks at the nature of the debt and requires that the debt be routine. More specifically, the debt must be "routine" for both the debtor and the creditor: i.e., in the ordinary course of business if the debtor is a business debtor or in the ordinary course of financial affairs if the debtor is a consumer debtor.

Second, the second requirement looks to the nature of the payment and requires that the payment be routine. In looking to the "routineness" of a payment look primarily to the form of payment (cash, wire transfer, check, etc.) and the timeliness of the payment (five days late, two months late, etc.). The form and time of payment must be routine, i.e., "ordinary." The "routineness" or "ordinariness" of the payment can be established EITHER by looking at what has been routine in the past in payments by this debtor to this creditor (a subjective test) OR by showing what has been routine in payments by similar parties on similar debts (an objective test).

To illustrate, *D* Stores routinely buys merchandise on credit from *S*. Invoices provide "net 7 days" meaning that payment is due within seven days. *D* Stores makes three payments to *S* within the 90 days before *D* Stores bankruptcy filing. Each of the three payments was made between 12 and 32 days after receipt of the invoice. *D*'s late payments will be treated as "ordinary" for purposes of section 547(c)(2) if either *D* Stores routinely paid *S* 12 to 32 days after invoice or if such late payments were ordinary in that type of merchandise sale.

(b) 547(c)(4) Subsequent Advances

You need to think of section 547(c)(4) as a SUBSEQUENT advance rule, NOT a NET RESULT rule. That will likely be the key to your answering an exam question on section 547(c)(4) correctly.

The key words in section 547(c)(4) are "after such transfer."

Section 547(c)(4) provides a measure of protection for a creditor who receives a preference and "after such transfer" extends further unsecured credit. For example, on June 6, *C* lends *D* $6,000. On July 7, *D* repays $4,000. On August 8, *C* lends *D* an additional $3,000. On September 9, *D* files a bankruptcy petition. The bankruptcy trustee can recover only $1,000. The July 7 payment of $4,000 was a preference under section 547(b). The trustee's recovery, however, is reduced by the amount of the August 8 unsecured advance of $3,000, section 547(c)(4).

Note that under section 547(c)(4), the sequence of events is of critical significance. The additional extension of credit must occur after the preferential transfer. If on June 6, *C* lends *D* $6,000; on July 7, *C* lends *D* an additional $3,000; on August 8, *D* repays $4,000, and on September 9, *D* files a bankruptcy petition, the trustee could recover $4,000 under section 547. No new unsecured credit "after such transfer."

Section 547(c)(4) contains two additional requirements beyond the creditor/transferee's giving new value after the transfer. First, the new value must be unsecured, i.e., "not secured by an otherwise unavoidable security interest," section 547(c)(4)(A). Second, the new value must go "unpaid," i.e., "on account of which new value the debtor did not make an otherwise avoidable transfer to or for the benefit of such creditor," section 547(c)(4)(B).

§ 12.7 Two Other Preference Exceptions Much Less Likely to Be on Your Exam

(a) 547(c)(1) Substantially Contemporaneous Transfers

The most important thing to know about section 547(c)(1) is that it is not important. More specifically, in the real world, it is very unusual for a preference to be protected by section 547(c)(1), and on a law school exam, it is very unusual for a fact pattern to meet the requirements of section 547(c)(1),

Section 547(c)(1) has two requirements

(1) the transfer was intended to be for new value, not an antecedent debt

(2) the transfer did in fact occur at a time "substantially contemporaneous" with the time that the debt arose.

For example, *D* borrows $5,000 from *C* on April 5. Both parties then intend the loan to be a secured loan, secured by a pledge of *D*'s *X* Corp. stock. On April 6, *D* pledges her *X* Corp. stock by delivering the certificates to *C*. On May 6, *D* files a bankruptcy petition. The bankruptcy trustee will not be able to void the April 6 pledge under section 547 even though it is a transfer for an antecedent unsecured debt within 90 days of bankruptcy. The transfer is protected by section 547(c)(1).

Note that section 547(c)(1) requires both that the transfer actually be a "substantially contemporaneous exchange" and that the parties so intended. Assume that *C* makes a loan to *D* that both *C* and *D* intend to be a 180–day loan. Later that same day *C* first learns that *D* is in financial difficulty and so demands and obtains repayment. Section 547(c)(1) could not apply to the repayment. While the transfer actually was a "substantially contemporaneous exchange," it was not so intended. If bankruptcy occurs within 90 days, the trustee can avoid the payment under section 547(b).

(b) Section 547(c)(5) Floating Liens

Section 547(c)(5) is really hard to understand, really hard to explain, and really unimportant in the real world. Nonetheless, it is covered in most bankruptcy casebooks. We hope that your professor skipped that part of the casebook so that you can skip this part of our book.

Section 547(c)(5) creates a limited exception from preference attack for certain Article 9 floating liens. Article 9 provides a mechanism for establishing a "floating lien." Such liens are most commonly used in financing accounts or inventory which normally "turnover" in the ordinary course of the debtor's business. For example, on January 10 Credit Co., *C*, lends Department Store, *D*, $800,000 and takes a security interest in the store's inventory. Obviously, *C* wants *D* to sell its inventory so that it can repay the loan. It is equally obvious that as inventory is sold, the collateral securing *C* loan decreases unless *C*'s lien "floats" to cover the proceeds from the sale of the inventory and/or cover new inventory that *D* later acquires. Accordingly, the security agreement that *D* signs on January 10 will probably contain an after-acquired property clause—will probably grant *C* a security interest not only in the inventory that *D* now owns but also in the inventory that *D* later acquires.

Even though *D* only signs this one security agreement, section 547 views *D* as making numerous different transfers of security interests. Under section 547(e)(3), "For purposes of this section, a transfer is not made until the debtor has acquired rights in the property transferred." This means that every time *D* acquires additional inventory there is a new transfer for purposes of section 547. Thus, if *D* acquires new inventory on March 3 and files for bankruptcy within the next 90 days, it would *seem* that the trustee can invalidate *C*'s security interest in the March 3 inventory because there was

1. a transfer of property of the debtor to a creditor
2. for an antecedent debt

   [The debt was incurred on January 10. As noted above, section 547(e)(3) dates the transfer of the security interest in the March 3 inventory as March 3.]

3. presumption of insolvency

   [Remember section 547(f)]

4. transfer made within 90 days of the bankruptcy petition
5. transfer increased bankruptcy distribution to *C* (unless *C* was already fully secured.)

Section 547(c)(5), however, will usually protect *C*. Under this provision, a creditor with a security interest in inventory or accounts receivable is subject to a preference attack only to the extent that it improves its position during the 90–day period before bankruptcy. The test is a two-point test and requires a comparison of the secured creditor's position 90 days before the petition and on the date of the petition. [If new value was first given after 90 days before the case, the date on which it was first given substitutes for the 90–day point.]

There are seven steps involved in applying section 547(c)(5)'s "two-step" test:

1. Determine the amount of debt on the date of the bankruptcy petition;
2. Determine the value of the debtor's accounts and/or inventory encumbered by the secured creditor's lien on the date of the petition;
3. Subtract #2 from #1;
4. Determine the amount of debt 90 days before the petition;
5. Determine the value of the debtor's accounts and/or inventory encumbered by the secured creditor's lien 90 days before the petition;
6. Subtract #5 from #4;
7. Subtract the answer in #3 from the answer in #6.

This is the amount of the preference.

The following hypotheticals illustrate the application of section 547(c)(5).

(1) At the time of its bankruptcy petition, *D* owes *C* $100,000 and has inventory with a value of $60,000. *C* has a security interest in all of *D*'s inventory. Ninety days before bankruptcy, *D* owed *C* $90,000 and had inventory with a value of $70,000. All of *D*'s inventory was acquired within the last 90 days. Under these facts, *C* has not improved its position. Under these facts, *C*'s security interest will be protected by section 547(c)(5).

(2) At the time of its bankruptcy petition, *D* owes *C* $100,000 and has inventory with a value of $75,000. *C* has a security interest in all of *D*'s inventory. Ninety days before bankruptcy, *D* owed *C* $90,000 and had inventory with a value of $30,000. All of *D*'s inventory was acquired within the last 90 days. Under these facts, the bankruptcy trustee may reduce *C*'s secured claim from $75,000 to $40,000.[19]

Compare the facts of (1) with (2). Which fact situation is more common? How often in the "real world" will a debtor in financial difficulty acquire additional inventory or generate an increased amount of accounts? It is submitted that in the usual situation section 547(c)(5) completely protects a security interest in after-acquired inventory or accounts—that in the usual situation the "except" language of section 547(c)(5) is inapplicable.

19. There was a $35,000 reduction in the amount by which the claim exceeded the collateral. (90–30)–(100–75). The $75,000 secured claim is thus reduced by this $35,000 improvement in position.

(3) *D* files a bankruptcy petition on April 22. At the time of the bankruptcy petition, *D* owes *S* $200,000. *S* has a security interest in *D*'s inventory of Oriental rugs which then have a value of $200,000. On January 22, 90 days before the bankruptcy petition was filed, *D* owed *S* $200,000, and the rugs had a fair market value of $150,000. *D* did not acquire any additional rugs after January 22; the value of *D*'s rugs increased because of market considerations. The trustee has no section 547 rights against *S*. There is no transfer to invalidate. *S*'s improvement in position was not "to the prejudice of other creditors holding an unsecured claim."

(4) *D* Manufacturing Co., *D*, files a bankruptcy petition on April 4. At the time of the filing of the bankruptcy, *D* owes *C* Credit Corp., *C*, $40,000. *C* has a valid in bankruptcy security interest in all of *D*'s equipment. The *D-C* security agreement has an after-acquired property clause. On the date of the filing of the petition, *D*'s equipment has a fair market value of $31,000. On January 4, 90 days before the filing of the bankruptcy petition, *D* owed *C* $40,000 and *D*'s equipment had a fair market value of $32,000. On February 2, *D* sold a piece of equipment for $6,000. (*D* used the $6,000 to pay taxes.) On March 3, *D* bought other equipment for $5,000. The trustee can limit *C*'s security interest to the equipment owned on January 4. The March 3 "transfer" is a preference under section 547(b).[20] The March 3 "transfer" of a security interest in equipment is not protected by section 547(c)(5) because the section 547(c)(5) exception only applies to security interests in inventory or accounts.

20. Remember, that March 3 is the date that the transfer is deemed made for purposes of section 547, section 547(e)(3).

Unit 13

QUESTION THIRTEEN: WHAT DOES A LAW STUDENT NEED TO KNOW ABOUT THE OTHER AVOIDING POWERS?

Table of Sections

The short answer is "maybe nothing." Many basic bankruptcy courses cover only fraudulent transfers and preferences and do not cover 553 or other avoiding powers. In case your teacher does cover other avoiding powers, you need to cover this Unit.

§ 13.1 Avoiding Prebankruptcy Setoffs[21] (and Not Recoupment)

(a) Explanation of Setoff (and Not Recoupment)

"The right of setoff (also called 'offset') allows entities that owe each other money to apply their mutual debts against each other, thereby avoiding the absurdity of making *A* pay *B* when *B* owes *A*." *Citizens Bank of Maryland v. Strumpf* (1995).

Historically, the most common use of setoff has been by banks against borrowers who are also depositors. Many states have codified the right of a bank or other financial institution in situations such as the following: *D* owes B Bank $100,000; *D* has an account in Bank with $40,000. When *D* defaults on her debt to *B* Bank, B

21. The Bankruptcy Code uses the term "setoff" and "offset" interchangeably. Some professors instead use the term "set-off" or the words "set off." If that is what your professor does, then....

Bank can exercise its right of setoff by taking the funds in *D*'s bank account to reduce *D*'s loan balance. After setoff, *D*'s debt balance is $60,000 and her deposit account balance is zero.

Changes in Article 9 of the Uniform Commercial Code in 2001 will probably reduce the importance of setoffs by banks. Banks now can (and do) obtain security interests in their debtor's deposit accounts. These security interests give the banks' claims to the funds in the deposit accounts priority over the claims of other creditors.

Setoff is not limited to banks and depositors. Assume, for example, that *S* from time to time sold goods on credit to *B*. *B* owes *S* $20,000 for December deliveries, and *S* owes *B* $30,000 for damages caused by defects in the October and November deliveries. *S* could exercise its common law right of setoff, reduce its $30,000 debt to *B* by *B*'s $20,000 debt to it, and pay *B* $10,000.

In a setoff, the mutual debts arise from different transactions—*S* owes *B* because of the October and November transactions while *B* owes *S* because of the December transaction or *D* owes *B* Bank because of loans while *B* Bank owes *D* because of deposits. The doctrine of recoupment is similar to but distinct from common law or statutory setoff. In recoupment, both debts must arise out of a single integrated transaction so that it would be inequitable for the debtor to enjoy the benefits of that transaction without also meeting its obligations. For example, *B* owes *S* $20,000 for December delivery and *B* claims that *S* owes its $12,000 for damages caused by problems with that same December delivery. *B* can exercise its right of recoupment to reduce its $20,000 to *S* by *S*'s $12,000 liability to it arising from that same transaction.

The word "recoupment" does not appear in the Bankruptcy Code. The word "setoff" does. The Bankruptcy Code, however, does not create any rights of setoff. Instead, the Code, with limited (but important) exceptions recognizes whatever right of setoff a creditor would have outside of bankruptcy.

(b) Overview of Bankruptcy Law of Setoff

The bankruptcy law of setoff does NOT include sections 548, 544 or 547. NEVER, NEVER on an exam describe a prebankruptcy setoff as a fraudulent transfer or a preference.[22] Again, do not apply section 544, 547, or 548 to a prebankruptcy exercise of a right of set-off.

The bankruptcy law of setoff is primarily sections 506(a), 362(a)(7), and 553.

22. The statutory basis for this statement is in section 553(a): "this title (title 11, including sections 544, 547, and 548 of title 11) does not affect. . . ."

First, the secured claim status of setoff under section 506. As section 506(a) states, bankruptcy law equates the right of setoff with a lien. *S* Bank, the creditor with a $200,000 right of setoff gets the same recovery in bankruptcy as *Z*, the creditor with a $200,000 lien.

Second, the stay of setoff under section 362(a)(7). A creditor who did not do its setoff prior to the debtor's filing for bankruptcy cannot exercise the right of setoff after the bankruptcy filing without first obtaining relief from the stay from the bankruptcy court.

Third, the recognition of and limitations on a nonbankruptcy right of setoff in section 553. Again, neither section 553 nor any other provision of the Code creates a right of setoff. Instead, section 553 does three things:

- it generally recognizes a nonbankruptcy right of setoff;
- it protects any prebankruptcy setoff from avoidance under sections 544–548 and any postbankruptcy setoff from avoidance under section 549;
- it provides a basis in section 553(b) for avoiding a prebankruptcy setoff in which the creditor improved its position within 90 days of bankruptcy and provides bases in section 553(a) for limiting the amount that can be setoff prepetition or postpetition.

(c) Using Section 553 to Avoid Prebankruptcy Setoff

Section 553 contains a number of limitations on setoffs [and the number is (6)]:

(1) "Mutual Debt"

The debts must be between the same parties in the same right or capacity. For example, a claim against a "bankrupt"[23] as an administratrix cannot be set off against a debt owed to the "bankrupt" as an individual.

(2) "Arose Before the Commencement of the Case"

Both the debt owed to the "bankrupt" and the claim against the "bankrupt" must have preceded the filing of the bankruptcy petition. A creditor cannot setoff its prepetition claim against a "bankrupt" against its postpetition obligation to the "bankrupt."

23. The Bankruptcy Code uses the term "debtor," not the term "bankrupt." Nevertheless, in discussing setoffs in which each party is the debtor of the other, it seems less confusing to use the term "bankrupt" to identify the party that filed a voluntary bankruptcy petition (or the party whose creditors filed an involuntary bankruptcy petition).

(3) "Disallowed," Section 553(a)(1)

Certain claims against a "bankrupt" are disallowed. See section 502 considered in Unit 15. A claim that is disallowed under section 502 may not be used as the basis for a setoff. To illustrate, *A* owes *B* $4,000. *B* files a bankruptcy petition. The debt from *A* to *B* is property of the estate. The trustee attempts to collect the $4,000 from *A*. *A* only pays the trustee $3,000. *A* alleges that it had set off a $1,000 claim it had against *B* prior to the bankruptcy filing. If that $1,000 claim would be barred by the statute of limitations in a state collection action, that $1,000 claim would be disallowed under section 502(b)(1) and the setoff would be disallowed under 553(a)(1).

(4) "Acquired" Claims, Section 553(a)(2)

Certain acquired claims cannot be setoff. Assume for example, that *B* is insolvent; *A* owes *B* $4,000; *B* owes *C* $1,000. Because *B* is insolvent, *C*'s $1,000 claim against *B* is of little value to *C*. *C* would be willing to sell its claim against *B* to *A* for less than $1,000. *A* would be willing to buy *C*'s claim for less than $1,000 if it could then assert that claim as a setoff to reduce its debt to *B* from $4,000 to $3,000.

Under section 553(a)(2) claims against the "bankrupt" acquired from a third party may *not* be set off against a debt owed to the "bankrupt" if:

a. the claim was acquired within 90 days before the bankruptcy petition or after the bankruptcy petition, *and*

b. the "bankrupt" was insolvent when the claim was acquired. [Section 553(c) creates a rebuttable presumption of insolvency.]

(5) Build–Ups, Section 553(a)(3)

Section 553(a)(3) precludes a setoff by a bank[24] if:

a. money was deposited by the "bankrupt" within 90 days of the bankruptcy petition,[25] and

b. the "bankrupt" was insolvent at the time of the setoff (remember section 553(c)'s presumption of insolvency), and

c. the purpose of the deposit was to create or increase the right of setoff.

For example, *X* Bank makes a loan to *D* Corp. Payment of the loan is guaranteed by *P*, the president of *D* Corp. *D* Corp. suffers

24. Again, section 553(a)(3) is not limited to bank setoffs.

25. A bank deposit is the most common example of a "debt owed to the debtor by such creditor" for purposes of section 553(a)(3).

financial reverses. *X* Bank pressures *D* Corp. and *P* to increase the balance of the *D* Corp.'s general bank account. *D* Corp. moves $100,000 from other banks to its *X* Bank account before filing its bankruptcy petition. Section 553(a)(3) would preclude *X* Bank from taking the $100,000 by way of setoff.

(6) Improvement in Position, Section 553(b)

Section 553(b) is designed to prevent an improvement in position within 90 days of bankruptcy. Application of section 553(b) requires a lot of computations: [we hope that your professor does not do math so that you don't have to do the next couple of pages]

1. Determine amount of claim against the debtor 90 days before the date of the filing of the petition;[26]
2. Determine the "mutual debt" owing to the "bankrupt" by the holder of such claim 90 days before the filing of the petition;
3. Subtract #2 from #1 to determine the "insufficiency.";
4. Determine the amount of the debt on the date that the right of setoff was asserted;
5. Determine the amount of the setoff;
6. Subtract #5 from #4 to determine the insufficiency;
7. Subtract the answer in #6 from the answer in #3, to determine what part, if any, of the amount of setoff the trustee may recover.

The following problems illustrate the application of section 553(b):

(1) *D* files a bankruptcy petition.

90 days before the petition, *D* owes *B* Bank $100,000 and has $40,000 on deposit.

10 days before the petition, *B* exercises its right of setoff. At that time, *D* owes *B* Bank $70,000 and the account has $60,000 balance.

The trustee may recover $50,000 from *B* Bank.[27]

(2) *D* files a bankruptcy petition.

26. If there is no "insufficiency" (as defined in section 553(b)(2)) 90 days before the petition, examine the 89th day, then the 88th day, etc. until a day is found that has an "insufficiency."

27. There was a $60,000 ($100,000 – $40,000) "insufficiency" 90 days before the bankruptcy petition was filed. At the time of the setoff, the "insufficiency" was only $10,000 ($70,000 – $60,000). There was a $50,000 improvement in position ($60,000 – $10,000). The bankruptcy trustee may recover $50,000 of the amount of offset under section 553(b).

> 90 days before the petition, *D* owes $200,000 to *B* Bank and has $200,000 on deposit at *B* Bank.
>
> 88 days before the petition, *D* withdraws $80,000 from the account; 5 days before the petition, *B* exercises its right of setoff. At that time, *D* owes *B* $70,000 and has $60,000 on deposit in *B* Bank.

The trustee may recover $60,000 from *B* Bank.[28]

In summary, a bankruptcy trustee will apply the above six tests to any setoff that has occurred prior to the filing of the bankruptcy petition.

(d) Setoff and Bankruptcy—Review and Overview

If a creditor exercises its right of setoff before bankruptcy, it runs the legal risks that section 553 may result in the recovery of all or some of the funds it obtained from the setoff. On the other hand, if a creditor delays in the exercise of its right of setoff it runs the business risk that it will lose the setoff (e.g., the debtor moves its funds from banks to which it is indebted to other banks) as well the costs of the delay in setoff resulting from the automatic stay.

(e) Bankruptcy Law of Recoupment

Again, there is no bankruptcy law of recoupment. The Bankruptcy Code does not use the word "recoupment," and the cases consistently hold that the Bankruptcy Code provisions affecting the exercise of a right of setoff do not affect the exercise of a right of recoupment. More specifically,

(1) the automatic stay does not bar a creditor from exercising a right of recoupment after the filing of a bankruptcy petition, and

(2) recoupment is not limited to debts and claims that arose before the commencement of the case.

For example, prepetition Medicare overpayments made to a nursing home debtor in one fiscal year before bankruptcy and Medicare payment obligations for a nursing home debtor's post-petition services made in a later fiscal year have been held to be part of the same "transaction" for purposes of equitable recoupment. Thus Medicare could, on grounds of equitable recoupment, deduct prepetition over-payments from the sums that the government owed to the nursing home debtor for postpetition services, without violating section 553 (or the automatic stay).

28. On the first date within the 90 day period that there was an "insufficiency," it was an insufficiency of $80,000. At the time of the setoff, the "insufficiency" was only $10,000 ($70,000 − $60,000). There was an improvement in position of $70,000 ($80,000 − $10,000). Nevertheless, the trustee may recover only $60,000 under section 553(b). "The amount so offset" establishes the ceiling for recovery under section 553(b).

§ 13.2 Avoiding Unrecorded Deeds and Mortgages and Unperfected Security Interests Under Section 544(a) (a/k/a the "Strong–Arm Clause")

Section 544(a) is one of the least "transparent" Bankruptcy Code provisions. In reading section 544(a), you don't find the terms "record" or "perfect" or "mortgage" or "deed" or "security interest" or "hypothetical." Nonetheless, on your exam, you will use section 544(a) ONLY to avoid a mortgage or deed that is not recorded as of the date of the bankruptcy petition or a security interest that is not perfected as of the date of the bankruptcy petition. And, the basis of such avoidance will be the trustee's rights as a hypothetical lien creditor and bona fide purchaser under section 544(a).

The above paragraph should be more than you need to know about section 544(a). If, however, your professor spent more class time on section 544(a), then you probably should take the time to read the following paragraphs.

Section 544(a) focuses on the rights of hypothetical lien creditors and bona fide purchasers of real property. Section 544(a) empowers the bankruptcy trustee to invalidate any transfer that under non-bankruptcy law is voidable as to a creditor who extended credit and obtained a lien on the date of the filing of the bankruptcy petition or is voidable as to a bona fide purchaser of real property whether or not such a creditor or purchaser actually exists. In applying section 544(a), it is thus necessary to determine whether:

(1) nonbankruptcy law public notice requirements have been satisfied as of date of the filing of the bankruptcy petition;

(2) a creditor who extended credit and obtained a lien on the date that the bankruptcy petition was filed or a bona fide purchaser of real property on the date of the bankruptcy petition comes within the class of persons protected by such state law.

The following hypotheticals illustrate the application of section 544(a):

#1 On January 10, *D* borrows $10,000 from *M* and gives *M* a mortgage on Redacre. On February 2, *D* files a bankruptcy petition. As of the date of the petition, *M* had not recorded its mortgage.

In #1, the bankruptcy trustee may invalidate *M*'s mortgage under section 544(a).

The public notice requirements of the state real property recording statutes were not satisfied. Real property recording statutes typically protect bona fide purchasers. Since the mortgage was unrecorded on the date that the bankruptcy petition was filed, M's mortgage would be ineffective as against a bona fide purchaser of Redacre on the date that the petition was filed. Section 544(a) gives the bankruptcy trustee the same powers as a person who was a bona fide purchaser on the date that the bankruptcy petition was filed.

#2 On January 10, *D* borrows $10,000 from *S* and gives *S* a security interest in equipment. On February 22, *D* files a bankruptcy petition. *S* fails to perfect its security interest prior to February 22.

In #2, the bankruptcy trustee will be able to invalidate *S*'s security interest under section 544(a).

Again, the applicable public notice requirement was not satisfied. Article 9 of the Uniform Commercial Code requires that a security interest be perfected in order to be effective against a lien creditor, section 9–317(a)(2). Since the security interest was unperfected on the date that the bankruptcy petition was filed, *S*'s security interest would be subordinate[29] to the claim of a creditor who obtained a judicial lien on the date that the petition was filed. Section 544(a) gives *S* the same invalidation powers as a person who extended credit and obtained a judicial lien on the date that the bankruptcy petition was filed.

#3 On January 10, *D* borrows $10,000 from *S*[30] to buy equipment and gives *S* a purchase money security interest in the equipment. On January 28, *D* files a bankruptcy petition. On January 29, *S* perfects its security interest.[31]

In #3, the bankruptcy trustee may not invalidate *S*'s security interest.

Section 544(a) empowers the bankruptcy trustee to invalidate security interests that would be subordinate to the claims of a creditor who obtained a judicial lien on the date that the petition was filed, January 28. *S* did not perfect its security interest until January 29. Recall the general rule of section 9–317(a)(2), that an

29. Even though the Uniform Commercial Code uses the term "subordinate" instead of "voidable," a security that would be "subordinate" to a creditor that obtained a judicial lien on the date of the filing of the bankruptcy petition is "voidable" by the bankruptcy trustee.

30. *S*'s security interest is "purchase money" since this extension of credit enabled *D* to obtain the property that is the collateral for the extension of credit. See section 9–103.

31. The filing of a bankruptcy petition stays or stops most creditor collection efforts. Section 362(a), considered infra, defines the scope of the stay, by listing the acts that are stayed by the commencement of the bankruptcy case. Section 362(a)(4) stays lien perfection. Section 362(b) lists exceptions to the automatic stay. Section 362(b)(3) read together with section 546(b) excepts perfection of purchase money security interests.

unperfected security interest is subordinate to a lien creditor. This general rule is subject to section 9–317(e)'s exception for purchase money security interests. Purchase money security interest perfected within 20 days prevails over a gap lien creditor. By reason of section 9–317(e),[32] *S*'s *purchase* money security interest perfected on January 28 (within the requisite 20 days) would be effective as against a creditor who obtained a lien on January 28, the date that the bankruptcy petition was filed. Accordingly, *S*'s *purchase* money security interest is effective against the bankruptcy trustee.

The above hypotheticals suggest three general rules for the use of section 544(a) in invalidating transfers:

(1) If the transfer has been recorded or otherwise perfected prior to the date that the bankruptcy petition was filed, the trustee will not be able to invalidate the transfer under section 544(a).

(2) Except as noted in (3) below, if the transfer was not recorded or otherwise perfected by the date that the bankruptcy petition was filed, the bankruptcy trustee will be able to invalidate the transfer under section 544(a).

(3) The bankruptcy trustee will not be able to invalidate a purchase money security interest perfected within 20 days after the delivery of the collateral to the debtor even if the debtor files a bankruptcy petition in the gap between the creation of the security interest and perfection.

§ 13.3 Avoiding Recorded Deeds and Mortgages and Perfected Security Interests Under Section 547 Because of a More Than 30–Day Delay in Recording or Perfecting

If a transfer of an interest in land is recorded before bankruptcy, that transfer cannot avoided under section 544(a). Even if there was a more than 30–day delay in recording. Similarly, if a security interest in personal property is perfected before bankruptcy, it cannot be avoided under section 544(a). Even if there was an more than 30–day delay in perfecting. A more than 30–day delay in recording or perfecting, however, can result in the avoidance of the land transfer or security interest under section 547.

Long delays in recording a real estate transfer or in perfecting a security interest can have the same effect on other creditors as a failure to record. Unaware of the "secret" not yet recorded or perfected transfer, other creditors might extend credit that they

32. Section 9–317(e) provides: "[I]f a person files a financing statement with respect to a purchase money security interest before or within 20 days after the debtor receives delivery of the collateral, the security interest takes priority over the rights of a ... lien creditor which arise between the time the security interest attaches and the time of filing."

would not have extended if aware of the transfer or might delay in collecting a delinquent debt that they would have tried to collect if aware of the transfer.

Although it is easy to see the reason for invalidating liens that are not timely perfected, it is difficult to understand why section 547 should be the mechanism for invalidating such liens. The easy way to invalidate such liens would be to add a section to the Bankruptcy Code to the effect that any lien that can be recorded or otherwise perfected under state law must be recorded within 30 days after it is obtained in order to be valid in bankruptcy. While that is the "easy way," it is not the way of the Bankruptcy Code. Basically, the Bankruptcy Code's method is to "deem" that for purposes of applying the requirements of section 547(b) the date of transfers not timely recorded is the date of perfection, not the actual date of transfer.

The following hypothetical illustrates the practical significance of the statutory delay of the effective date of the transfer until public notice of the transfer has been given. *D* borrowed $10,000 from *S* on January 10 and gave *S* a security interest in equipment which *S* perfected on December 29. *D* filed a bankruptcy petition on December 30. At first, it might seem that section 547 is not applicable—that the security transfer from *D* to *S* was not for an antecedent indebtedness and did not occur within 90 days of the bankruptcy petition. For purposes of section 547, however, the transfer will be *deemed made on December 29, not* January 10. [Under section 9–317, *S*'s security interest would not be effective as against subsequent judicial lien creditors until that date. Accordingly, by reason of section 547(e), the transfer will not be deemed made until that date.] Thus, the "December 29 transfer" would be within 90 days of the bankruptcy petition. Thus, the "December 29 transfer" would be for an antecedent indebtedness, i.e., the $10,000 loaned on January 10. Thus, the trustee would be able to invalidate S's security interest under section 547 if *D* was insolvent on December 29. [Remember section 547(f) creates a rebuttable presumption of insolvency.]

The above hypothetical illustrates that a delay in perfection can result in a security interest actually given for present consideration being deemed made for an antecedent indebtedness and thus a section 547 preference.

In the hypothetical, over 11 months elapsed between the granting of the security interest and the perfecting of the security interest. What if the delay was eleven weeks? Eleven days? Eleven hours? Is there some sort of "grace period" in section 547?

Section 547(e) does not require immediate perfection. It provides a general 30–day "grace period" for perfection.

§ 13.4 Avoiding Postbankruptcy Transfers

(a) Not 544, Not 547, Not 548

Sections 544, 547, and 548 apply only to a prebankruptcy transfer. Never use the phrase "fraudulent transfer" or the term "preference" in discussing something that happened after bankruptcy. Sections 549 and 542 and 546(c) apply to postbankruptcy transfers.

(b) And Primarily Chapter 7 Cases, and Primarily in Law School Exam Chapter 7s

Since section 549 is a part of Chapter 5, it is a part of a bankruptcy case under any chapter—7, 11, 12, or 13. Nonetheless, do section 549 primarily in law school exam problems involving debtors who filed for Chapter 7 relief.

Postbankruptcy transfers of property of the estate present problems primarily in Chapter 7 cases. Only in Chapter 7 cases does the right of possession of property of the estate pass to the trustee; only in Chapter 7 cases are the proceeds from the trustee's liquidation of property of the estate what is distributed to creditors. In Chapter 11 and Chapter 13 cases, the debtor continues to possess property of the estate postpetition and creditors are paid under a plan that is generally based on the debtor's future earnings. And, in Chapter 11 and Chapter 13 cases, most postpetition transfers of property of the estate are permitted by section 363.

Accordingly, section 549 is much more important to Chapter 7 cases than to Chapter 11 cases or Chapter 13 cases. And, section 549 is much more important to Chapter 7 cases in law school than to Chapter 7 cases in the "real world." Most Chapter 7 debtors do not have significant assets to transfer postbankruptcy; and most Chapter 7 debtors do not make improper postbankruptcy transfers; and most Chapter 7 trustees are able to recover property of the estate that was transferred postbankruptcy without litigation.

(c) Recovery From Debtor/Transferor or Transferee Under a Conversion Theory

Again, if a Chapter 7 debtor sells property of the estate postpetition, that is conversion. Property of the estate no longer belongs to the debtor—it is property of the estate. As a representative of the estate, the trustee can use conversion law to recover the value of the property transferred from the debtor/transferor's postpetition assets. Or the trustee can recover the transferred property of the estate from the transferee. Unless the transferee is protected by section 549.

(d) 549 Protection for Transferees

Generally, the trustee can recover from the transferee property transferred by a Chapter 7 debtor after the filing of the petition unless the transferee is protected by section 549. Again section 549 only protects the transferee—not the debtor/transferor.

And, generally section 549 does not protect the transferee. The three subsections to section 549 describe three situations in which a postbankruptcy transferee is protected. The first of the three, section 549(a), is generally applicable only to Chapter 11 cases. The second of the three, section 549(b), is applicable only to involuntary cases—approximately 1% of the cases. And, the third, section 549(c) covers only postbankruptcy transfers of real estate.

If your exam covers section 549, it is almost certain to cover only section 549(c). We will cover section 549(a) then section 549(b) then section 549(c) but you have our permissions to skip to section 549(c) below.

Section 549(a) states the obvious.

Obviously, a postbankruptcy transfer will be effective against the bankruptcy trustee if the transfer was authorized by the Bankruptcy Code or the bankruptcy court. See section 549(a)(2)(B). Most of the postbankruptcy transfers by a Chapter 11 debtor will be authorized under section 363.

Section 549(b) validates transfers by the debtor that occur after the filing of an *involuntary* bankruptcy petition and before the order for relief to the extent that the transferee gave value to the debtor after the filing of the bankruptcy petition. To illustrate,

(1) On February 22, *D*'s creditors file an involuntary petition. On February 25, *D* sells her boat to *X* for $30,000. The trustee may *not* recover the boat from *X*. *X* is protected by section 549(b).

(2) Same facts as #1 except that *X* knew of the involuntary petition. Same result. Section 549(b) protects postpetition transfers "notwithstanding any notice or knowledge of the case that the transferee has."

Section 549(c) protects postpetition transfers of *realty* from trustee avoidance. A transfer of real property by the debtor after the filing of a voluntary petition or after an order for relief in an involuntary case will be effective against the bankruptcy trustee if:

(1) the transfer occurs and is properly recorded before a copy of the bankruptcy petition is filed in the real estate records for the county where the land is located, and

(2) the transferee is a buyer or lienor for fair equivalent value without knowledge of the petition.

Consider the following hypothetical illustrating the operation of section 549(c):

On February 2, *B* files a voluntary petition. On February 3, *B* sells land in White County to *Y* for $10,000, the "fair equivalent value" of the land. *Y* has no "knowledge of the commencement of the case." *Y* properly files the transfer in the White County real estate records on February 4. A copy of the bankruptcy petition is filed in the real estate records for White County on February 5. The trustee *cannot* avoid the transfer. *Y* is protected by section 549(c).

There is no personal property counterpart of section 549(c). Personal property of the debtor transferred by the debtor after the filing of a voluntary petition can be recovered from the transferee unless the transfer was authorized by the Bankruptcy Code or by the bankruptcy court.

(e) Rights of Unpaid Seller of Goods

When a buyer fails to pay for goods it accepts, the seller has a legal right to recover the contract price, U.C.C. § 2–709. This legal right to be paid is of limited practical significance if the buyer is insolvent. Accordingly, the Uniform Commercial Code grants certain unpaid sellers a right to recover the goods. Section 2–702 of the Uniform Commercial Code empowers a seller to "reclaim" (recover) the goods if:

(1) credit sale, *and*

(2) buyer insolvent when goods received, *and*

(3) written misrepresentation of solvency within 3 months before delivery or the demand for reclamation is made within 10 days of the buyer's receipt of the goods.

Case law has created a similar right of reclamation for sellers paid with bad checks.

Legally, the seller's right of reclamation outside of bankruptcy turns on the seller's satisfaction of the various requirements in section 2–702 discussed above. Practically, the seller's right of reclamation also turns on what the debtor has and has not done prior to the seller's reclamation demand. If the debtor has disposed of the goods prior to the seller's reclamation demand, then there is nothing to reclaim—the reclamation remedy is an *in rem* remedy, limited to the goods that the seller delivered.

Similarly, if the debtor has granted another creditor a security interest that covers all of its inventory, there is nothing to reclaim—under the UCC, a security interest has priority over a right of reclamation. To illustrate, if *D* is indebted to *B* Bank which has a security interest in *D*'s inventory and *D*'s inventory includes goods sold by *C* on credit, all of *D*'s inventory, including the goods delivered by *C*, must be used to satisfy *B* Bank's security interest before *C* is able to reclaim anything under section 546(c).

In bankruptcy, section 546(c) governs the right of reclamation. Section 546(c) was significantly amended by BAPCPA, and there are a lot of yet unanswered questions about section 546(c). To answer any possible exams you might get, you need to know that

(1) section 546(c), unlike section 2–702, requires that the reclamation demand be in writing and

(2) section 546(c) has a 45–day period, not a 10–day period,

Again, the right of reclamation—in or out of bankruptcy (in the real world or on your exam)—is not likely to be of any practical significance. What is likely is that the buyer/debtor has granted a security interest that covers that goods; the rights of the secured party will have priority over the reclamation rights of an unsecured seller.

Section 546(c) needs to be read together with section 503(b)(9). BAPCPA added section 503(b)(9) which creates a new administrative priority for unpaid sellers measured by the "value" of goods received by the debtor within 20 days before the filing of the bankruptcy petition. You need to notice four differences between section 546(c) and section 503(b)(9):

1. Most obvious (and least important), relevant time: 20 days for 503(b)(9) v. 45 days for 546(c)

2. More important, what is at stake: recovery of the goods that the debtor still has under section 546(c) v. payment of the value of the goods delivered as an administrative expense priority under section 503(b)(9). [The importance of administrative expense priorities is discussed in Unit 15.]

3. Possibly important, whether buyer/debtor still has goods: essential to reclamation under section 546(c) v. irrelevant to administrative expense priority under section 503(b)(9)

4. Likely important, whether goods are covered by security interest: defeats right of reclamation v. no effect on administrative expense priority.

Unit 14

QUESTION FOURTEEN: WHAT DOES A LAW STUDENT NEED TO KNOW ABOUT LEASES AND "EXECUTORY CONTRACTS"?

Table of Sections

Every business debtor and most individual debtors have leases and unperformed contracts. Every bankruptcy exam has questions about these leases and unperformed contracts.

§ 14.1 Basic Bankruptcy Concepts and Leases and "Executory Contracts"

You need to think about both the basic bankruptcy concept of "property of the estate" and the basic bankruptcy concept of "claim" when you think about leases and "executory contracts".

Generally, the Bankruptcy Code's provisions dealing with the debtor's assets are separate from the Bankruptcy Code's provisions dealing with the debtor's obligations and the estate's obligations: property of the estate in section 541, allowable claims and administrative expenses in sections 502 and 503. A lease or executory contract involves potentially both property of the estate and a claim against the debtor or the estate.

This hybrid nature of a lease or executory contract is most apparent in lease situations in which the debtor is the lessee. Assume, for example, that *D* Store, Inc. (*D*) leases its store in the mall from *L*. *D* later files for bankruptcy. *D*'s rights to the use of the space in the mall is an asset of the estate. *D*'s lease, however, involves burdens as well as benefits. *D* has performance obligations under the lease such as paying rent. *D*'s obligation to pay rent to *L* is a claim for *L*.

§ 14.2 Overview of Section 365 Treatment of Leases and "Executory Contracts"

The Bankruptcy Code deals with leases and executory contracts primarily in section 365. And, this book deals with section 365.

[Sections 1110, 113, and 1114 also deal with special kinds of contracts involving Chapter 11 debtors. Generally, basic bankruptcy courses do not deal with these provisions. If your professor has dealt with one of those provisions, then. . . .]

Section 365 mentions three possible consequences of bankruptcy on a lease on executory contract:

(1) rejection (think "breaching," think "giving up" the lease or contract)

(2) assumption (think "performing," think "keeping" the lease or contract)

(3) assignment (think "selling" the lease or contract).

In comparing rejection, assumption and assignment, it is important to keep in mind that the lease or contract involves potentially both property of the estate and a claim against the estate. The following chart provides a general view of the effect of rejection, assumption and assignment on property of the estate and claims against the estate.

	Rejection	**Assumption**	**Assignment**
Property of the estate	No property of the estate.	Debtor's rights under contract or lease.	Proceeds, if any, from assignment of debtor's rights under contract or lease.
Claims	Unsecured claim for (i) prepetition defaults and (ii) breach resulting from rejection; administrative expense priority claim for postpetition obligations, if any.	Administrative expense priority claim for all obligations under contract or lease, postpetition or prepetition.	No claim against the estate. Non-debtor party to an assigned contract or lease looks solely to the assignee.

An understanding of the bankruptcy law of leases and executory contracts requires an understanding not only of rejection, assumption and assignment, the three different elections available to the debtor under the Bankruptcy Code, but also an understanding of the election that is not available to the debtor under the

Bankruptcy Code. A debtor does not have a legal right under the Bankruptcy Code to modify or change the terms of an unexpired lease or an executory contract.

To illustrate, assume that *D* Store, Inc. (*D*) leases space in a mall from *L* for $20,000 a year. *D* owes $600,000 to unsecured trade creditors and $3 million to secured lenders. *D* files a Chapter 11 petition. *D* wants to continue operating in the mall, wants to retain the leasehold. Under the language of the Bankruptcy Code, *D* will have to assume the lease to retain the leasehold, will have to assume the lease payment as is: $20,000 a year, no change. In its Chapter 11 plan, *D* will be able to alter its payment obligations to lenders and trade creditors, secured and unsecured. Under the language of the Bankruptcy Code, *D* cannot, however, use bankruptcy to effect a modification in its obligations under its leases or executory contracts. Rejection, assumption or assignment. Not modification.

[The previous statement in the previous paragraph is both correct and misleading. There are only the three possible choices under the Bankruptcy Code. A debtor does not have a right under the Bankruptcy Code to change the terms of an unexpired lease or executory contract. Nonetheless, a debtor is often able to use its bargaining power and other legal rights under the Bankruptcy Code to "persuade" the other party to the lease or contract to "agree" to modifications in the lease or contract. For example, *D* is leasing a building from *L*. *D* files for bankruptcy. *D* wants *L* to reduce her rent. *D* presents *L* with the choice that either *D* will reject the lease which will leave *L* with an empty building and a general claim in *D*'s bankruptcy case or *L* will agree to modifications in the lease. *L* will often choose to "agree" to modify the lease.]

To review, look primarily to section 365 to determine the effect of bankruptcy on a debtor's leases and executory contracts. Under section 365, a bankruptcy trustee can either:

1. reject a lease or executory contract;
2. assume a lease or executory contract;
3. assign a lease or executory contract.

§ 14.3 Nine Section 365 Issues Most Likely to Appear on Your Exam

Your teacher is most likely to test your understanding of these three options by an exam question which raises one of more of the following 9 issues: (a) Effects of rejection, assumption, and assignment decisions; (b) Roles of the debtor and the bankruptcy court in the decision; (c) Time period for making decision (a/k/a gap period); (d) Performance during the gap period; (e) Limitations on effect rejection; (f) Contract limitations on assumption or assignment; (g) Requirements for assumption or assignment; (h) Contracts that cannot be assumed or assigned; and (i) Scope of executory contract.

(a) Effects of Rejection, Assumption, and Assignment Decisions

One way of comparing the effects of rejection, assumption, and assignment is by a chart. As luck would have it, there is a chart comparing rejection, assumption, and assignment a page back that you skipped.

An easier way of comparing rejection, assumption, and assignment is by writing an episode of the Andy Griffith show.

Floyd Lawson, *F*, leases a building for his barbershop from Mayberry Realty Corp., *M*. The lease agreement provides for a 10–year term and monthly rentals of $250. *F* files a bankruptcy petition. What is the effect of the bankruptcy trustee or debtor in possession rejecting the lease? Assuming the lease? Assigning the lease?

If the lease is rejected, *F* has no further right to use the building for his barbershop. If the lease is rejected, *F* has no further personal liability on the lease. The rejection of the lease is, of course, a breach of the lease, section 365(g). *M* will have an allowable unsecured claim against the bankrupt estate for back rent and future rentals, section 502(g), 502(b)(7). The amount that *M* will receive on this unsecured claim will depend on the property of the estate in a Chapter 7 case and will depend on the provisions of the plan in a Chapter 11 or Chapter 13 case.

If the lease is assumed, the leasehold continues to be an asset of the estate. *F* can continue to operate his barbershop in the building. Assumption covers the burdens of the lease as well as the benefits. By assuming the lease, the trustee or debtor in possession is obligating the estate to make all payments under the lease. This obligation is a first priority administrative expense. For example *D*, a Haircutters franchisee, files for Chapter 11 relief owing suppliers, Haircutters and his landlords. If *D* assumes his leases and his Haircutters' licensing agreement, the landlords and Haircutters have an administrative expense priority and will be paid in full before the suppliers are paid at all.

What if, in Floyd Lawson's bankruptcy, the trustee or debtor in possession sells the lease to Aunt Bea Taylor who wants to open an adult bookstore in the building? Such an assignment "relieves the trustee and the estate from any liability for any breach of such contract or lease occurring after such assignment," section 365(k). After the assignment, *M* can look only to Aunt Bea for the payment of the postassignment obligations under the lease.

(b) Roles of the Debtor and of the Bankruptcy Court in the Decision

Section 365(a) provides, "The trustee ... may assume or reject." And section 1107 gives a Chapter 11 debtor in possession a trustee's powers.

Section 365(a) also requires court approval of assumption or rejection of leases or executory contracts. Section 365(a) does not indicate what standard the bankruptcy court should apply in determining whether to approve the assumption or rejection of a lease or executory contract. Bankruptcy judges generally apply a business judgment test and give great weight to the business judgment of the debtor.

(c) Time Period for Making Decision (a/k/a Gap Period)

It takes time for debtors to decide whether to reject, assume or assign leases or contracts. And, it takes time for court approval of that decision.

The time between the debtor's filing a bankruptcy petition and a bankruptcy court's approving that decision is commonly called the "gap period." Without using that phrase, subsection (d) of section 365 sets out the rules for how long the gap period can be. Three sets of rules: (1) first, a rule for Chapter 7 cases applicable to all contracts and leases, other than nonresidential real property leases, (2) second, a rule for Chapter 11 and 13 cases, applicable to all contracts and leases, other than nonresidential real property leases and (3) third, a rule for nonresidential real property leases in all cases.

(1) Chapter 7 (Other Than Nonresidential [Business] Real Property Leases)

In Chapter 7, there is a general rule that executory contracts and leases that are not assumed by the Chapter 7 trustee within 60 days after the order for relief are deemed rejected, section 365(d)(1). You should know three exceptions to this general rule. First, section 365(d)(1) provides that the court can extend the 60 days. Second, section 365(d)(1) does not apply to nonresidential real property leases. Third, section 365(p) provides a three-step process by which an individual debtor can herself assume a personal property lease. The first step is for the debtor to make a written request; the second step is for the lessor to notify the debtor of its willingness to have the lease assumed by the debtor; the third step is for the debtor to notify the lessor that the lease is assumed. When a lease is assumed by the debtor under section 365(p), the debtor individually (and not the estate) has both the benefits and the burdens of the lease.

(2) Chapters 11 and 13 (Other Than Nonresidential Real Property Leases)

In cases under Chapter 11 or Chapter 13, the general rule is that executory contracts and leases can be assumed or rejected any time before the confirmation of the plan, section 365(d)(2). Again, you should know two exceptions to this general rule. First, section 365(d)(2) provides that the court can order an earlier determination of whether the contract or lease is to be assumed or rejected. Second, section 365(d)(2) does not apply to nonresidential real property leases.

(3) Nonresidential Real Property Leases in Chapters 7, 11, and 13 Cases

The general rule is that a lease of nonresidential real property is deemed rejected unless it has been assumed within 120 days after the order for relief, section 365(d)(4). And, this general rule is also subject to two exceptions. First, if a plan is confirmed earlier, then the deadline becomes the date of the entry of the order confirming the plan. Second, the court can extend the 120 period by 90 days. The lessor must agree to any additional extension.

(d) Performance During the Gap Period

There is always going to be some gap period between the filing of a bankruptcy petition and action on a contract or lease. Accordingly, it is necessary to consider the rights and responsibilities of the debtor and nondebtor party during the interim between the commencement of the bankruptcy case and the assumption or rejection decision.

(1) Nondebtor's Performance

Section 365 does not expressly deal with the performance obligations of the nondebtor party to a lease or executory during this gap period. The few cases that have expressly dealt with the question have held that the nondebtor party is obligated to perform. Most courts seem simply to assume that the nondebtor party is so obligated. For example, if *L* is leasing a building or machinery to *D*, *L*'s performance (providing the building or machinery) continues after *D*'s bankruptcy filing.

(2) Debtor's Performance

Section 365(d)(3) expressly deals with the performance obligations of the debtor party to a nonresidential real property lease: it requires a debtor/lessee to "timely perform" all obligations under a nonresidential real property lease. Assume that dentist *D* files for Chapter 13 relief. *D* leases her office from *L*; the unexpired lease provides for rent of $2,000 per month. While it is clear that section

365(d)(3) requires that within 60 days of the filing, *D* will be making all postpetition rent payments to *L*, including lease payments that arise within the first 60 days, it is not clear from the cases under section 365(d)(3) what happens if *D* is unable to perform during the gap period.

Section 365(d)(5) deals with the gap period performance obligations of the debtor on its equipment leases. Section 365(d)(5) needs to be read together with and compared to section 365(d)(3). While section 365(d)(3) requires that a debtor will make all postpetition rent payments on commercial real estate and will start making such payments within 60 days, section 365(d)(5) requires that the debtor make equipment lease payments that first arise after 60 days. And, the court can excuse equipment payments that first arise after 60 days "based on the equities of the case."

Section 365(d)(5) also needs to be read together with section 363(e). Under section 363(e), a lessor of personal property can request that the court prohibit or restrict the debtors use of its property. Unlike section 365(d)(5), section 363(e) applies to consumer leases.

(e) Limitations on the Effect of Rejection of a Lease or Executory Contract

Nothing in section 365 limits the availability of rejection. Section 365 does, however, set out four situations in which the effect of rejection is limited:

1. Section 365(h) limits the effect of rejection of a lease of real property when the debtor is the landlord. A trustee for a debtor who owns rental real property may not use section 365 to evict tenants. Even, if the trustee decides to reject the debtor/lessor's leases, the tenant has a right to remain in possession. Assume, for example, that Epstein uses some of his concise hornbook royalties to build an office building; your law firm rents an office in Epstein's building. If Epstein later files for bankruptcy and rejects the lease, your firm can still remain in possession of the leasehold.

The trustee for the debtor/lessor may, however, use rejection to terminate some of the services required by the lease such as maintenance. The lessee may then offset any damages caused by such termination against its rent obligation.

2. Sections 365(h) and (i) provide similar limitations on a debtor/seller's rejection of a timeshare contract.

3. Section 365(i) provides similar limitations on the debtor/seller's rejection of an installment land sales contract.

4. Section 365(n) provides similar limitations on the debtor licensor's rejection of a license of a patent, copyright, or other "intellectual property."

In other words, a debtor who owns and licenses a copyright or patent cannot use bankruptcy to deprive its licensees of the right to use that copyright or patent. Assume, for example, that *D* holds a patent on for Eppielater machines and has licensed that patent to *X* who makes Eppielater machines. *D* later files for bankruptcy. While *D* can reject that patent license under section 365, that rejection will not deprive *X* of his right to use the patent as it existed as of the time of *D*'s bankruptcy. The primary practical effect of *D*'s rejection will be to deprive *X* of any right to postbankruptcy improvements in the patent technology.

Congress added two sections to Chapter 11 to protect employee contracts. Section 1113 limits the rejection of collective bargaining contracts in Chapter 11 cases. Because of class time limits, these sections are not generally covered in bankruptcy classes or bankruptcy exams.

(f) Contract Limitations on Assumption and Assignment

Contract clauses that prohibit or limit the assumption and assignment of leases and executory contracts will not be effective in bankruptcy, section 365(e), (f). The trustee or debtor in possession can assume a lease even though the lease agreement provides in the lease for automatic termination or a right of termination because of bankruptcy or insolvency, section 365(e). Similarly, the trustee or debtor in possession can sell or otherwise assign a lease even though the lease agreement provides it is not assignable, section 365(f).

Assume, for example, that in 2005, *D* leases a building from *L* for ten years. The lease provides that it cannot be assigned without *L*'s written approval and that the lease terminates *ipso facto* on *D*'s bankruptcy. In 2007, *D* files for bankruptcy. Her one valuable asset is the lease. Because of the desirability of the location and the favorable rental rate, third parties are willing to pay substantial sums to acquire the lease from *D*. Notwithstanding the language in the lease, *D*'s trustee can sell the lease by meeting the requirements for assignment set out in section 365(f).

What happens to the "substantial sums" that the trustee receives when he sells the "nonassignable lease"? Recall that the debtor's interest in the lease was section 541(a)(1) property of the estate and that proceeds from the sale of property of the estate are property of the estate, section 541(a)(6). Accordingly, it would seem that the answer to this question is that the"substantial sums" from the sale of the "nonassignable lease" would, like the rest of the property of the estate, be available for distribution to unsecured creditors in a Chapter 7 case and be available for the debtor's plan performance in a Chapter 11 or 13 case.

By changing two facts, I can change this answer significantly. First, change the real property lease to a cable franchise contract and second add, a security interest in the contract. Assume (1) that *D* has rights under a cable franchise contract that prohibits assignments and (2) notwithstanding this contractual prohibition, *D* has granted *S* a security interest in the cable franchise contract. If *D* files for bankruptcy, section 365(f) will still operate to make the contract prohibition against assignments ineffective. But now the practical effect of the operation of section 365(f) will be different; *S* will now get the "substantial sums" because

1. Section 9–408 of the 2001 version of Article 9 enables a creditor to obtain a security interest in a franchise contract or other "general intangible"[33] even though the contract itself expressly prohibits such assignments and

2. Under section 552(b) of the Bankruptcy Code, *S*'s security interest would reach the proceeds from the sale of the franchise contract. See section 9–408, Official Comment 7.

(g) Requirements for Assumption and Assignment

Paragraph (b) of section 365 sets out the requirements for assumption of a lease or executory contract. Note that paragraph 365(b) only applies to an assumption if there has been a default other than breach of a provision relating to bankruptcy filing or insolvency. Assume, for example, that *D* rents a building from *L*. *D* files a bankruptcy petition. At the time of the bankruptcy petition, *D* is current on all of its obligations under the lease. If *D* decides to assume the lease, section 365(b) does not apply.

If there has been a default, section 365(b) imposes requirements with respect to the past failures to perform and requirements with respect to the future performance obligations. As to past defaults, section 365(b)(1) requires

(A) cure of past defaults or "adequate assurance"[34] of prompt cure;

33. Section 9–408 only applies to "promissory notes, health-care insurance receivables and certain general intangibles." A real property lease is none of these. Indeed, Article 9 does not apply to a lien on a real estate lease. See 9–109(d)(11).

34. This standard sounds similar to but is different from the standard applied in stay litigation. Section 362(d) protects the holder of secured claims by requiring "adequate protection" of the creditors interest in the collateral. Section 362(d) thus protects a creditor's property rights. Section 365(b) protects the lessor of property by requiring "adequate assurance" of the lease obligations. Section 365(b) thus protects a creditor's contract rights.

(B) compensation for "actual pecuniary loss" resulting from the default or "adequate assurance" of prompt compensation.

Obviously, some prebankruptcy defaults cannot be cured. Assume, for example, that *D* Tavern's lease required that it not be closed for more than 72 consecutive hours and that in the week prior to its bankruptcy filing, *D* Tavern was closed for 75 hours. In 2005, section 365(b) was amended to "clarify" that *D* Tavern can assume this lease even though it is impossible to cure an earlier nonmonetary default. (If your professor points out that section 365(b) is still not clear and makes a point of this, you might want to make a point of carefully comparing 365(b)(1)(A) with section 365(b)(2)(D).)

As to future performance, section 365(b)(1)(C) requires "adequate assurance" of future performance. The term "adequate assurance" is not statutorily defined. Section 365(b)(3) indicates what constitutes "adequate assurance" if the lease covers real property that is a part of a "shopping center."[35]

"Adequate assurance" of future performance is always a condition precedent to assignment of a lease or executory contract. Even if no default. Remember that after an assignment, the other party to the lease or executory contract can look only to the assignee for the performance of the debtor's postassignment obligations under the lease or contract. To protect the nonbankrupt party, section 365(f)(2) requires that the assignee provide "adequate assurance" of future performance as a condition to any assignment.

(h) Leases and Executory Contracts That Cannot Be Assumed or Assigned

There are some leases and executory contracts that cannot be assumed and assigned. A lease or contract that has terminated before bankruptcy cannot be assumed. *D* leases Blackacre from *L*. *D* defaults. *L* takes the steps required by state law to evict *D* and terminate the lease. *D* later files for bankruptcy. *D* cannot assume the lease. Regardless of religious views, there is no such thing as a born-again lease.

A loan commitment or other financing arrangement cannot be assumed, section 365(c)(2). *C* agrees to provide *D* with a $250,000 line of credit. *D* files a bankruptcy petition before drawing on this line of credit. *D* cannot assume this executory contract and compel *C* to loan the $250,000.

Contracts that are not assignable under "applicable law" are not assignable in bankruptcy, section 365(c)(1). "Applicable law"

35. The term "shopping center" is not statutorily defined. Because of section 365(b)(3), a lessor of a shopping center enjoys greater protection than a lessor of other real property.

can be the common law of contracts. Under such law, for example, personal services contracts cannot be assigned and delegated. Batman contracts to patrol the streets of Gotham City. Batman later files a bankruptcy petition, Batman cannot assign this personal services contract to Madonna.

"Applicable law" for purposes of section 365(c) can also be a statute so long as it is a statute other than the Bankruptcy Code. Assume, for example, that state law prohibits the assignment of a car dealer franchise contract without the approval of the franchisor. *D* Ford dealer could not file for bankruptcy and then assign his franchise without the approval of the franchisor because of "applicable law."

Read literally (and most courts have read section 365(c)(1) literally), a debtor cannot assume a lease or executory contract in its bankruptcy case if, outside of bankruptcy, there would be legal bar (other than a contract provision) to assigning it. In other words, section 365(c)(1), by its terms, bars a debtor in a bankruptcy case from even assuming (i.e., keeping) a lease or executory contract where applicable nonbankruptcy law bars assignment (i.e., selling) the contract to a third party.

Most case books include the Ninth Circuit decision *In re Catapult Entertainment, Inc.* (1999). There a Chapter 11 producer of video games was not able to assume essential but nonexclusive patent licenses since patent law makes nonexclusive patent licenses nontransferable.

(i) Scope of Executory Contract

Section 365 applies to leases and executory contracts. The Bankruptcy Code does not define the term "lease." There is probably no need for a definition. When there is a problem as to whether a "lease" of personal property is a disguised credit sale, bankruptcy courts look to a large body of case law under the Uniform Commercial Code.

Similarly, the Bankruptcy Code does not define the phrase "executory contract." The most frequently cited and most thorough discussion of executory contracts in bankruptcy is a two-part, 142–page article written prior to the enactment of the Bankruptcy Code by Professor Vern Countryman. Professor Countryman concludes that an executory contract for purposes of bankruptcy is one that is so far unperformed on both sides that the failure of either party to complete her performance would be a material breach excusing further performance from the other party. See Countryman, *Executory Contracts In Bankruptcy*, 57 MINN. L. REV. 439 (1973); 58 MINN. L. REV. 479 (1974).

Most reported cases seem to follow the Countryman definition. There are, however, bankruptcy judges who have written opinions and law professors who have written articles calling for a different definition of "executory contract." If your bankruptcy teacher is one of these judges or professors, then you need to read her opinions or articles.

Unit 15

QUESTION FIFTEEN: WHAT DOES A LAW STUDENT NEED TO KNOW ABOUT THE BANKRUPTCY CLAIMS PROCESS: A REVIEW AND OVERVIEW

Table of Sections

Every bankruptcy case is about claims. Every Unit of this book is about claims. Every bankruptcy exam question has claims issues. This Unit collects what you need to know about the bankruptcy claims process.

§ 15.1 Overview of Proof of Claim

In all bankruptcy cases, the debtor is required to file a list of its creditors. The bankruptcy court will then send a notice of the bankruptcy to the listed creditors.

Creditors that want to participate in the distribution of the proceeds of a Chapter 7 liquidation must file a "proof of claim." In Chapter 11 cases, creditors generally are not required to file proofs of claims. Section 1111(a) "deems" (i.e., pretends) that listed creditors have filed proofs of claim.

A creditor can participate in bankruptcy distributions (i.e., get paid) only if it has actually filed a proof of claim or is deemed to have filed a proof of claim. Regardless of whether it has filed a proof of claim and participates in bankruptcy payments, a creditor is barred by the automatic stay from trying to get paid by the debtor during the bankruptcy case and barred by a discharge from trying to collect from the debtor personally after the bankruptcy case.

§ 15.2 Overview of Claims Allowance Process

Sometimes people claim that they have a right to be paid but they are wrong. Some claims are not valid.

The process of determining which claims are valid in bankruptcy is described as "allowance" (or, if you see a glass as half empty instead of half full, "disallowance"). Once a proof of claim is actually filed or deemed filed, the claim is deemed allowed. And, the claim is allowed (i.e., valid in bankruptcy as filed) "unless a party in interest objects."

Who is "a party in interest"? Who cares whether a claim is disallowed in whole or in part?

We know that you don't care. You need to know why other creditors care whether a creditor's claim is allowed.

In a sense, bankruptcy is a "zero-sum" game. In Chapter 7 cases, creditors are limited to the proceeds from the liquidation of the property of the estate. In Chapter 12 and 13 cases, creditors' recoveries are limited to the debtor's disposable income. In Chapter 11, the creditors are limited to payments as provided in the proposed plan.

The larger the claims that are made against the Chapter 7 liquidation proceeds or the Chapter 11, 12, or 13 plan payments, the smaller the distribution to a particular claim. To mix metaphors, the size of the pie is finite—a claimant gets a bigger share of the pie by reducing the other claims on that pie. And a claimant can reduce the other claims to the bankruptcy pie—win the zero sum game—by successfully objecting to the allowance of other claims. Grounds for objection to the allowance of a claim are set out in section 502(b), (d), (e), and (k).

§ 15.3 Claims Allowance Issue Most Likely to Arise in a Real Case

The most frequently invoked ground for disallowance of a claim is section 502(b)(1): "The claim is unenforceable ... under any agreement or applicable law for a reason other than because such claim is contingent or unmatured." In other words, a defense that the debtor would have had to the enforceability of the claim outside of bankruptcy is a defense to the allowance of the claim in bankruptcy. Statute of limitations and failure of consideration are examples of such defenses.

Reread the last part of section 502(b) ("other than because such claim is contingent or unmatured"). Notice: the fact that a claim is speculative or contingent or that its amount is difficult to ascertain is not a basis for disallowance. In these circumstances, the court can either estimate the amount of the claim under section 502(c) or delay distribution and closing of the bankruptcy case until the amount of the claim has been determined.

§ 15.4 Three Claims Allowance Issues Most Likely to Arise on Your Exam (If There Are Questions on Allowance of Claims on Your Exam)

(a) Disallowance of Postpetition Interest

D borrows $100,000 from *C*; the loan agreement provides for 9% interest. *D* later files for bankruptcy. At the time of *D*'s bankruptcy filing, *D* owes *C* $119,000 in principal and accrued interest. *C*'s allowable claim will be limited to $119,000, regardless of how long *D*'s bankruptcy lasts.

The general rule is that interest stops accruing when a bankruptcy petition is filed. Saying the same thing another way, claims for "unmatured interest" are disallowed. That is what section 502(b)(2) says.

(b) Limited Allowance of Landlord's Claim for Future Rents

Section 502(b)(6) says that there is a cap on a landlord's claim for future rents: the greater of one year's payments or 15% of the balance of the lease, not to exceed three years' payments in total. Don't worry about having to do the math. Law professors know that if you could "crunch numbers" you would be in an MBA program.

Here, what is more important to understand is what section 502(b)(6) does not say. It does not say that there is any limit on a a landlord's claim for back rent. And, section 502(b)(6) does not say that a landlord always has an allowable claim for future rent.

Assume for example, *D* rents a building from *L* for 10 years for $100,000 a year. At the time *D* files its bankruptcy petition, it owes $100,000 in back rent. If after filing for bankruptcy, *D* breaches (i.e., rejects) the lease and *L* is able to relet the building for $120,000 a year, *L*'s allowable claim is limited to the $100,000 in back rent. No claim for future rent.

(c) Contingent Contribution Claims

Section 502(e) provides for the disallowance of a claim for contribution or indemnity that is still contingent. Assume, for example, that *C* loans *D* $20,000 and *G* provides a guarantee—*G* agrees that it will pay *C* if *D* does not. *D* later files for bankruptcy. At the time of *D*'s bankruptcy, *C* has not been paid by either *D* or *G*. Obviously, *C* has a claim. Since under nonbankruptcy law, *G*, as a guarantor has a right of reimbursement against the primary obligor *D* if *G* has to pay *C*, *G* also a right of payment, albeit a contingent right of payment. Accordingly, under the section 101 definition of claim, *G* also has claim.

And under section 502(e) disallowance of contingent contribution claim rule, *G*'s claim will be disallowed. The rationale is that since *C*'s claim obviously should be allowed, then *G*'s claim should be disallowed since the allowance of both *C*'s claim and *G*'s claim could result in the estate paying twice for a single debt—paying $40,000 for a $20,000 obligation.

Section 502(e) is an exception to the general rule that contingent claims are allowed–that the fact that a claim is contingent does not affect its allowance. Only claims for contribution or indemnity are disallowed because they are still contingent.

§ 15.5 Priority

In bankruptcy, some claims—secured claims—are treated differently from others because, pursuant to nonbankruptcy law, the holder of the claim has obtained a lien. And, in bankruptcy, some unsecured claims are treated differently from others because the unsecured claims—priority claims—meet the section 507 priorities requirements.

(a) Significance of Priority

In virtually all bankruptcy cases, the amount of claims exceeds the amount available to be distributed to claims. It is kind of like that first Phish concert after the "hiatus" in Madison Square Garden on December 31, 2002. More people wanting seats than seats.

Some people got seats for the Madison Square Garden Phish concert because of a past relationship with Trey or some other Phish members. *Cf.* 11 U.S.C. § 507(a)(1). Other people got seats (albeit less desirable seats because they worked on making the concert happen.) *Cf.* 11 U.S.C. § 507(a)(2). In "bankruptcy talk," these were people with priorities.

There are a number of statements in reported cases, books, and articles about equality of distribution to creditors in bankruptcy cases. Such statements must be using the term "equality" in the Phish concert (or perhaps *Animal Farm*) sense.

In bankruptcy cases, some claims are more equal than others. Secured claims are more equal than unsecured claims. And, priority unsecured claims are more equal than other unsecured claims.

In a bankruptcy case, certain allowed unsecured claims are entitled to priority in distribution over other unsecured claims. Section 507(a) sets out the levels of priorities. Creditors apply section 507 in preparing proofs of claim. In its proof of claim form, a creditor can assert a priority and state the amount and basis therefor.

Chapter 7 requires that the various priority classes are paid in the order in which they are listed in section 507, section 726(a)(1). In other words, each first priority claim is to be paid in full before any second priority claim is paid at all. If there are not sufficient funds to pay all claims within a particular class, then generally all claims entitled to that priority are paid pro rata.

Chapter 11, Chapter 12, and Chapter 13 require the plan to provide for payment in full of all priority claims, although the payments of claims within certain priority classes may be stretched over a period of time, sections 1129(a)(9), 1222(a)(2), 1322(a)(2).

(b) "Most Exam–Important" Grounds for Priority

Most exam questions on priority claims involve administrative expense priority issues under section 507(b)(2) which incorporates section 503(b). In looking for such issues, look for (1) professional fees or (2) postpetition costs of maintaining, operating. selling property of the estate (including the business of a Chapter 11 business debtor) or (3) the two new BAPCPA administrative expenses.

Recall that as a result of BAPCPA, there is a new administrative expense priority for the value of goods sold on credit to the debtor in the ordinary course of business and received by the debtor within 20 days before the commencement of the case. And as a result of BAPCPA, when a nonresidential real estate lease is assumed and later rejected, then up to two years of post-rejection lease payments can be an administrative expense.

If you have an exam question involving an individual debtor you might also watch for an issue relating to his or her alimony or child support payment obligations. A debtor's "domestic support obligations" as defined in section 101 now have a first priority under section 507(b)(1).

§ 15.6 Subordination

Section 507, the priority provision, has the effect of moving certain, specified claims to the head of the line. Section 510, the subordination provision, has the effect of moving some claims to the end of the line.

Think again about that Phish Madison Square Garden concert. If you are a Phish fan, you don't want to be at the end of the line—even if you have a ticket (think allowable claim). If you are at the end of the line, there probably will not be any seats left.

How can a person wind up at the end of the line at a Phish concert? It might be because of an agreement. Epstein agrees to buy the tickets if Nickles will get in line a day earlier and then yield that spot in line to Epstein 15 minutes before the doors open. *Cf.* 11 U.S.C. § 510(a). Or, it might be because of bad behavior. Epstein and Nickles get in line earlier than anyone else but because of their bad behavior, the New York security guards move them to the end of the line. *Cf.* 11 U.S.C. § 510(c).

If your bankruptcy class covered section 510, you covered section 510(c) which is generally referred to as "equitable subordination". The Bankruptcy Code does not define or even describe the principles of by which equitable subordination is to be applied.

The reported cases on equitable subordination emphasize facts. The facts most emphasized are (1) whether the claimant engaged in some type of inequitable conduct and (2) whether that conduct injured other creditors and (3) whether the claimant was an insider or fiduciary.

*

Part Five

UNDERSTANDING WHAT HAPPENS IN YOUR BANKRUPTCY COURSE BY UNDERSTANDING WHAT HAPPENS IN REALISTIC, CONSUMER BANKRUPTCY CASES*

* Units 16 and 17 illustrate, respectively, fairly typical Chapter 7 and 13 cases involving individual debtors with primarily consumer debts. Why? We have had students who best understand legal concepts by seeing how those concepts apply in a "real world" context. (And these students seem to turn out to be the best lawyers.) Accordingly, Unit 16 uses a realistic, Chapter 7 consumer debtor case and Unit 17 uses a realistic Chapter 13 to show you how the legal concepts discussed in your law school course and in the earlier units of this book apply in real cases.

We have not included a unit on a typical business case because (i) real world business bankruptcy cases are much more about "business" than about bankruptcy; (ii) business cases are typically atypical (e.g., cases involving family-owned businesses are dramatically different from cases involving public corporations; cases involving manufacturing businesses with products liability problems are dramatically different from cases involving high tech businesses with cash-flow problems, and so on); (iii) this book is principally designed for law students, and the typical law school bankruptcy course focuses mostly on consumer cases under Chapters 7 and 13; and (iv) we are "pitching" our unit on business bankruptcy to David Milch as his next HBO series. In this series, we see Ian McShane as chair of the creditors' committee; Keone Young as the DIP lender; Epstein as the CEO; Nickles as the White, Black, or Green Knight (He can't decide.); and, well, you complete the cast and send us your ideas.

Unit 16

A TYPICAL CHAPTER 7 CASE

Table of Sections

---

§ 16.1 Meet the Kaddours[1]

Ahmed and Irshad Kaddour are married with two sons whose ages are three and seven. The family's home is Winston–Salem, North Carolina, where they have lived for several years.

1. A large part of the story we tell here is true. It's based on an actual case; and the information we report about the petition, accompanying schedules and other forms, and the docket is taken from court records. The names of the parties and their lawyer are changed; and personal and official identifying numbers are deleted or changed.

The case involved no adversary proceeding, and nothing about the case is reported on Westlaw. Even if disputes had arisen during the case that required a hearing before and decision by the judge, it's typical that the judge's opinion would not be published on Westlaw. So, the jillions of reported bankruptcy decisions you can find on Westlaw represent only a very, very small percentage of the mega-jillions of decisions bankruptcy judges are asked and required to make in bankruptcy cases.

We believe the Kaddours' case is a typical Chapter 7 case, by which we mean a case involving natural people whose debts are primarily consumer debts incurred for personal, family, or household purposes. We also believe, based on the record, that the actual debtors in this case, whom we call the Kaddours, are typical in the sense they are good, hardworking people who experienced some financial trouble and, as a last resort, turned to Chapter 7 bank-

Ahmed is an electrical engineer. Irshad is an insurance clerk. They work for different health care companies.

The Kaddours have really tried to keep up with their bills but can no longer make all the monthly payments they owe. The total of these payments for their mobile home, cars, and credit cards exceeds their net, monthly income.

Some of their creditors are very persistent in their collection efforts. The Kaddours are tired of the "harassment;" very worried about being sued; embarrassed by their financial situation and what people may think; and, even more, about how to get back on track toward their family and professional goals.

§ 16.2 The Kaddours Meet Larry, a Bankruptcy Lawyer

Lawrence (Larry) Freidman (no relation to Kinky) is a local attorney who practices with two other lawyers in a loose partnership specializing in consumer bankruptcy. The firm employs several paralegals who handle almost all of the routine client "in-take" and "paperwork."

Actually, the in-take is computer automated and the paperwork is largely digital. The lawyers and paralegals heavily rely on computer software programs in opening, processing, and managing cases.

The lawyers need the paralegals, and the paralegals need the software, to cut the costs of practicing consumer bankruptcy law. The market and the bankruptcy courts limit a lawyer's fee to somewhere between $750 and $1500 for the typical Chapter 7 case. To make decent money, the lawyer must handle lots of cases, i.e., volume. To handle lots of cases, the lawyer hires paralegals (who are paid less than lawyers) for the routine (though hugely important) "non-legal" legal work. To enable the paralegals to work more efficiently, they use computer programs to input the information that is necessary for analyzing and filing the case.

The Kaddours found Larry's name in the Yellow Pages under the heading, "Attorneys–Bankruptcy–Consumer." On the same page, and close to Larry's individual listing, Larry's firm has a nice-looking ad with a bold, easy-to-remember phone number and this declaration:

> ***We're real proud to work for our clients as a debt relief agency. We help people use the Bankruptcy Laws to get much needed, legal relief from burdensome debts and***

ruptcy for relief. They acted to take legitimate advantage of bankruptcy protection in good faith and without any hint of an attempt to abuse the bankruptcy system. It's true of most Chapter 7 debtors.

tiresome creditors. Let us help you get all of the relief from debts and creditors the law entitles you to get! We can do it!

The Kaddours called the number. The receptionist who answered their call made an appointment for them to see Larry. She also told them the kinds of information and "papers" they should bring to the meeting.

When the Kaddours arrived at Larry's office for the appointment, they filled out a very basic information form and then visited for a few minutes with Larry. They explained their basic situation; he asked some basic questions; and he briefly explained three basic options. He told them that depending on what he learns when he gets all the stuff he needs to know, he could recommend trying to work out their problems outside of bankruptcy through a credit counselor or the like; liquidating their property and getting a discharge under Chapter 7; or getting a discharge after repaying some of their debts under a three- to five-year Chapter 13 plan.

They spent most of the time, however, with Jane, a paralegal. Using her computer, Jane opened a new "file" and began to ask the Kaddours lots of questions. Jane needed the information to satisfy the "data entries" or "data points" the software program requires for a consumer bankruptcy case.

The front end of the software program sits on top of a database that collects and stores data (information) about the client and the client's financial and other situations. The information this system seeks, through Jane, is primarily based on the information required by the Bankruptcy Code and Official Forms and Rules to file, alternatively, a Chapter 7 or 13 case.

This intake session takes lots of time. Typically, the client cannot answer (with the necessary certainty and detail) many of the questions Jane asks. It happened to the Kaddours. So, as usual, Jane printed a list of the unanswered questions and a list of the documents Larry would need. Jane asked them to return with (or fax) the information necessary to complete the file. Jane also gave them a brochure explaining how to provide the necessary information Jane needs to complete the file and Larry needs for deciding what advice to give them. It also explained that within 180 days before their case is filed, they must have been briefed (in person, by phone, or on the Internet) by an approved, nonprofit budget and credit counseling agency about the opportunities for available credit counseling and also about performing a related budget analysis. The brochure explains how to identify and contact such agencies and even offers to have Larry's office electronically "register" the debtor for briefing by an appropriate agency.

Jane also gave the Kaddours certain, standard-form notices. The law requires giving these notices to consumer debtors within three business days after the debtors receive bankruptcy assistance. For example, the debtor must receive a written notice that warns:

- all information that the assisted person is required to provide with a petition and thereafter during a case under this title is required to be complete, accurate, and truthful;
- all assets and all liabilities are required to be completely and accurately disclosed in the documents filed to commence the case, and the replacement value of each asset as defined in section 506 must be stated in those documents where requested after reasonable inquiry to establish such value;
- current monthly income, the amounts specified in section 707(b)(2), and, in a case under chapter 13 of this title, disposable income (determined in accordance with section 707(b)(2)), are required to be stated after reasonable inquiry; and
- information that an assisted person provides during their case may be audited pursuant to this title, and that failure to provide such information may result in dismissal of the case under this title or other sanction, including a criminal sanction.

Another required notice must provide:

> "IMPORTANT INFORMATION ABOUT BANKRUPTCY ASSISTANCE SERVICES FROM AN ATTORNEY OR BANKRUPTCY PETITION PREPARER.
>
> "If you decide to seek bankruptcy relief, you can represent yourself, you can hire an attorney to represent you, or you can get help in some localities from a bankruptcy petition preparer who is not an attorney. THE LAW REQUIRES AN ATTORNEY OR BANKRUPTCY PETITION PREPARER TO GIVE YOU A WRITTEN CONTRACT SPECIFYING WHAT THE ATTORNEY OR BANKRUPTCY PETITION PREPARER WILL DO FOR YOU AND HOW MUCH IT WILL COST. Ask to see the contract before you hire anyone.
>
> "The following information helps you understand what must be done in a routine bankruptcy case to help you evaluate how much service you need. Although bankruptcy can be complex, many cases are routine.
>
> "Before filing a bankruptcy case, either you or your attorney should analyze your eligibility for different forms of debt relief available under the Bankruptcy Code and which form of relief is most likely to be beneficial for you. Be sure you understand the relief you can obtain and its limitations. To file a bankrupt-

cy case, documents called a Petition, Schedules and Statement of Financial Affairs, as well as in some cases a Statement of Intention need to be prepared correctly and filed with the bankruptcy court. You will have to pay a filing fee to the bankruptcy court. Once your case starts, you will have to attend the required first meeting of creditors where you may be questioned by a court official called a 'trustee' and by creditors.

"If you choose to file a chapter 7 case, you may be asked by a creditor to reaffirm a debt. You may want help deciding whether to do so. A creditor is not permitted to coerce you into reaffirming your debts.

"If you choose to file a chapter 13 case in which you repay your creditors what you can afford over 3 to 5 years, you may also want help with preparing your chapter 13 plan and with the confirmation hearing on your plan which will be before a bankruptcy judge.

"If you select another type of relief under the Bankruptcy Code other than chapter 7 or chapter 13, you will want to find out what should be done from someone familiar with that type of relief.

"Your bankruptcy case may also involve litigation. You are generally permitted to represent yourself in litigation in bankruptcy court, but only attorneys, not bankruptcy petition preparers, can give you legal advice."

The Kaddours left Larry's office but quickly returned with the stuff Jane asked for. Jane then produced a computer file that consolidated all of the information in electronic versions of the many forms, required by law, which Larry will need to file the Kaddours' case. The system also performs certain mathematical calculations required by the Bankruptcy Code, Official Rules, and Forms. The system may also produce a summary of key data that Larry can use in advising the clients on such big matters as: whether or not to file bankruptcy; if both husband and wife should file or only one of them; whether or not their cases should be consolidated if they both file; and the kind of case to file.

(a) Larry Advises the Kaddours

Larry reviewed the Kaddours' file the next day. He quickly decided to advise the Kaddours to file a joint, Chapter 7 case because they jointly own all of their property and are jointly liable on all of their debts.

The Kaddours got this advice during a second visit with Larry. He told them lots of stuff; but they heard most clearly that the fee for him handling the case is $1500, which they must pay in advance of the filing.

The Kaddours asked Larry where he thinks they can get $1500. Larry carefully avoids advising them either to incur more debt or rob a bank to pay his fee.

To change the subject, Larry further explained that this fee is determined by the market and, in effect, by the bankruptcy judge and that the fee assumes the case produces no extraordinary issues or problems. In other words, the fee is based on the cost of a typical case, which means that Larry files the case and basically is required to do very little else and certainly nothing that requires him to appear and argue in court or appeal something.

Larry adds, however, that if this case is typical, nothing much beyond the filing is required. They'll "meet" a Chapter 7 trustee and answer a few more questions about their assets and income. The trustee probably (almost surely) will decide there is no property to sell and distribute to unsecured creditors, which is the trustee's job, and will report this conclusion to the court. The bankruptcy judge will accept the report, issue a discharge, and close the case. It's a pro forma routine that transpires quietly, through "paperwork," over several months.

The Kaddours learn, too, that they must pay other costs up front. First, the total of filing and other fees they must pay the court for a joint case is $274. Additionally, they must get and pay for a *briefing* from an approved, nonprofit budget and credit counsel agency within 180 days before the bankruptcy filing. And, before the court grants a discharge, they must complete a financial management instructional *course*.

The Kaddours asked Larry whether or not, if they file Chapter 7, they can keep their mobile home, cars, and some other stuff important to them. Larry responded that he could probably "take care of that" if and when they decided to hire him and file Chapter 7.

Before the Kaddours left Larry's office, he and Jane gave them some paperwork to read and think about. The Kaddours also got a refrigerator magnet that looks exactly like the firm's Yellow Pages ad.

(b) The Kaddours Decide to File and Larry Gets to Work

Within two days, the Kaddours are back in Larry's office. They had decided to take Larry's advice and file a joint, Chapter 7 case. They bring with them $1500 in cash. Nobody asks where they got the money. Everybody notices that the cash is not splashed with any brightly colored dye.

Then, or maybe a little later, the Kaddours signed a written contract for legal services that includes provisions explaining the services Larry will provide; the fees and charges for the services; and the terms of payment, which is payment in full before the case is filed. With Jane's help, Larry thereafter prepared the bankruptcy petition and other, necessary schedules and forms that would be filed with the petition.

On January 16, the Kaddours signed the petition and certain of the other forms Larry would file to commence the case. Among these forms is a certification that the debtors were timely briefed by an approved, nonprofit budget and credit counseling agency that explained the opportunities for available credit counseling and assisted the debtors in performing a related budget analysis. Immediately after their first visit to Larry's office, the Kaddours received such a 45–minute briefing by phone for a $50 fee; and the agency emailed a "certificate of completion" to them and Larry.

Several days later, on January 21, Larry filed the petition accompanied by a bunch of other, completed forms including:

- Summary of Schedules
- Statistical Summary of Certain Liabilities
- Schedule A Real Property
- Schedule B Personal Property
- Schedule D Creditors Holding Secured Claims
- Schedule E Creditors Holding Unsecured Priority Claims
- Schedule F Creditors Holding Unsecured Nonpriority Claims
- Schedule G Executory Contracts and Unexpired Leases
- Schedule H Codebtors
- Schedule I Current Income of Individual Debtor(s)
- Schedule J Current Expenditures of Individual Debtor(s)
- Declaration (under Penalty of Perjury) Concerning Debtor's Schedules
- Statement of Financial Affairs
- Chapter 7 Individual Debtor's Statement of Intention
- Disclosure of Compensation of Attorney for Debtor(s)
- Notice to Individual Consumer Debtor under § 342(b)
- Matrix of Creditors' Addresses and Debtor(s) Verification
- Statement of Current Monthly Income and Means Test Calculation
- Certification of Completing Credit Counseling

- Statement of Social Security Numbers
- Debtor's Claim for Property Exemptions (Ahmed Kaddour)
- Debtor's Claim for Property Exemptions (Irshad Kaddour)

Larry may have filed everything in hard copy form at the bankruptcy courthouse; or he may have filed everything electronically with the court. Even if he filed hard copy, he may have been required to provide some e-form of the entire filing that the court will post in its online, case management system.

Significantly, Larry also signed the Kaddours' bankruptcy petition. In so doing and filing the petition, Larry certified that to the best of his knowledge, information, and belief, formed after an inquiry reasonable under the circumstances:

- It is not being presented for any improper purpose, such as to harass or to cause unnecessary delay or needless increase in the cost of litigation;
- The claims, defenses, and other legal contentions therein are warranted by existing law or by a non-frivolous argument for the extension, modification, or reversal of existing law or the establishment of new law;
- The allegations and other factual contentions have evidentiary support or, if specifically so identified, are likely to have evidentiary support after a reasonable opportunity for further investigation or discovery; and
- The denials of factual contentions are warranted on the evidence or, if specifically so identified, are reasonably based on a lack of information or belief.

In effect, Larry is also certifying that the case fits Chapter 7 and will not be dismissed for the reason that the debtors have sufficient, future income to fund a Chapter 13 plan. Larry is risking liability for damages and even his license to practice law if these assurances are later proved wrong.

(c) Substance of the Petition and Some of the Forms Larry Filed

The petition and all of the other forms that Larry filed to commence the Kaddours' case are standard forms. You can see the official versions of these forms on the Web site of the U.S. Courts.*

Larry's computer system spits out completed forms that are exact duplicates of the official forms. The information used to complete the forms is the information Larry and his paralegals get from clients and enter into their computer system.

* http://www.uscourts.gov/bkforms/bankruptcy_forms.html#official.

In the Kaddours' case (as in every typical Chapter 7 case), a few of the forms Larry filed are blank or mostly blank. The official forms allow for complicated cases with lots of information, but the typical case is uncomplicated. For example, the typical Chapter 7 debtor has no executory contracts or leases. Nevertheless, Larry must file all the forms the Bankruptcy Code and Official Rules and Forms require.

Here is the essential substance of the principal forms that Larry filed in the Kaddours' case:

(1) Petition

A bankruptcy petition, by itself, is very simple for every kind of bankruptcy case. Larry fills in some basic information about the debtors and answers some basic, multiple-choice questions about them and the nature of the case. The Kaddours' petition essentially contains the following information:

- Ahmed's full name and address;
- Irshad's full name, address, and indication that she is Ahmed's spouse and joint debtor;
- Type of debtor: individual;
- Chapter under which petition is filed: Chapter 7;
- Nature of debts: consumer/non-business;
- Filing fee attached;
- Box checked whereby debtor estimates that, after exemptions and administrative expenses, no funds will remain for unsecured creditors;
- Estimated number of creditors: somewhere between 1 and 49;
- Estimated assets: somewhere between $100,001 and $500,000;
- Estimated debts: somewhere between $100,001 and $500,000;
- No prior bankruptcy case filed within the last eight years;
- No pending bankruptcy case filed by spouse, partner, or affiliate;
- Larry's signed declaration that he explained to the debtors the options for them under the different chapters of the Bankruptcy Code;
- Indication that debtor doesn't own or possess any property that poses a threat of imminent harm to public health or safety;

- Certification that the debtors received approved budget and credit counseling during the 180–day period preceding the filing of their petition;
- Statement that debtors have lived within the federal, judicial district of the bankruptcy court for 180 days immediately preceding the date of their petition;
- Ahmed's dated signature;
- Irshad's dated signature; and
- Larry's dated signature, address, phone number, and email address.

(2) Summary of Schedules

	ASSETS	LIABILITIES	OTHER
Real Property	81,500.00		
Personal Property	42,831.00		
Creditors Holding Secured Claims		126,917.07	
Creditors Holding Unsecured Priority Claims		0.00	
Creditors Holding Unsecured Nonpriority Claims		43,770.88	
Current Income of Individual Debtors			3,656.55
Current Expenditures of Individual Debtors			4,054.54
Total Assets	**124,331.00**		
Total Liabilities		**170,687.95**	

(3) Schedule A Real Property

The debtors list only a "doublewide mobile home and 2 acres of land" which they own jointly in fee simple. The value of the property is $81,500.00, subject to secured claims (two mortgages) totaling $78,764.23.

(4) Schedule B Personal Property

This standard form lists 35 categories or types of personal property, and the debtor is required to fit descriptions of all of her personal property within these categories. Here are the categories the Kaddours used and the descriptions they provided:

Type of Property	Description and Location of Property	Owner[2]	Current Value[3]
Checking, savings or	LSB checking account	J	100.00

2. Actually, the form asks if the owner is "Husband, Wife, Joint, or Community."

3. The form asks for the "Current Value of Debtor's Interest without Deducting any Secured Claim or Exemption."

Type of Property	Description and Location of Property	Owner[2]	Current Value[3]
other financial accounts[4]	LSB savings account—jointly owned by debtors and male debtor's mother—value $400; portion—$266.	J	266.00
Household goods and furnishings[5]	Assorted household goods	J	1,500.00
Wearing apparel	Assorted clothing	J	750.00
Furs and jewelry	Assorted miscellaneous jewelry	J	750.00
Firearms and sports equipment[6]	Hunting equipment	H	750.00
Pension or profit sharing plans[7]	401K 401K 529 college savings plan	W H W	1,200.00 400.00 40.00
Stock and interests in businesses[8]	22 shares of Sara Lee	W	400.00
Automobiles, trucks, trailers, and other vehicles and accessories	2004 Chrysler Pacifica 2003 Dodge Truck 1967 Ford Truck 6 x 12 utility trailer 6 x 14 utility trailer	W H H H H	16,475.00 15,700.00 400.00 500.00 500.00
Farming equipment and implements	1952 Ford Tractor	J	1,500.00
Other personal property of any kind not already listed. Itemize.	Golf cart	J	1,600.00
TOTAL			**42,831.00**

(5) Schedule D Creditors Holding Secured Claims[9]

Creditor's Name and Mailing Address[10]	H W J C	Date Claim Was Incurred, Nature of Lien, and Description and Value of Property Subject to Lien	Amount of Claim Without Deducting Value of Collateral	Unsecured Portion, if Any
LSB Bank	J	Second Mortgage Doublewide mobile home Dand 2 acres land Value: $81,500.00	1,778.38	0.00
M & I	H	Lien on motor vehicle 2003 Dodge Truck Value: $15,700.00	22,839.48	7,139.48
Select Portfolio	J	First Deed of Trust		

4. This category also includes: "certificates of deposit, or shares in banks, savings and loan, thrift, building and loan, and homestead associations, or credit unions, brokerage houses, or cooperatives."

5. It also includes: "audio, video, and computer equipment."

6. This category also includes: "photographic and other hobby equipment."

7. In full, this category covers: "Interests in IRA, ERISA, Keogh, or other pension or profit sharing plans. Give particulars."

8. "Businesses" include "incorporated and unincorporated."

9. This schedule also requires showing, as to each claim, an account number; if there is a codebtor; and whether the claim is contingent, unliquidated, or disputed.

10. We deleted the creditors' mailing addresses.

Servicing Customer Support Unit		Doublewide mobile home and 2 acres land Value: $81,500.00	76,985.85	0.00
Wells Fargo	W	Lien on motor vehicle 2004 Chrysler Pacifica Value: $16,475.00	25,313.36	8,838.36
TOTAL			**126,917.07**	

(6) Schedule F Creditors Holding Unsecured Nonpriority Claims[11]

Creditor's Name and Mailing Address	H W J C	Date Claim Was Incurred and Consideration for Claim. State if Claim is Subject to Setoff.	Amount of Claim
Capital One	J	Credit card purchases	510.06
Chase	J	Credit card account	439.37
Circuit City	J	Credit card purchases	500.00
Credit Bureau	J	Informational purposes only	0.00
Dell	W	Credit account	1,053.11
Discover	H	Credit card account	7,604.63
Discover Card	W	Credit card purchases	8,772.87
GE Money Bank	J	Credit account	1,880.00
GEMB/JC Penney's	W	Credit card purchases-JC Penney	2,917.40
Lowes	J	Credit card purchases	4,400.00
LSB MasterCard	J	Credit card account	1,508.43
MBNA America	H	Credit card purchases	14,185.01
TOTAL			**43,770.88**

(7) Schedule I Current Income of Individual Debtor(s)

The very top of this form reports the debtors are married; the ages of their two sons who are listed as dependents; the debtors' occupations and names and addresses of their employers. Following this information is a table reporting the debtors' income:

INCOME: (Estimate of average monthly income)	DEBTOR	SPOUSE
1. Current monthly gross wages, salary, and commissions	2,426.67	3,182.40
2. Estimate monthly overtime	0.00	0.00
3. SUBTOTAL	2,426.67	3,182.40
4. LESS PAYROLL DEDUCTIONS		
a. Payroll taxes and social security	514.39	593.95
b. Insurance	0.00	498.03
c. Union Dues	0.00	0.00
d. Other (specify): 403(k)/401(k)	87.97	0.00
401k		258.18
5. SUBTOTAL OF PAYROLL DEDUCTIONS	602.36	1,350.16
6. TOTAL NET MONTHLY TAKE HOME PAY	1,824.31	1,832.24
7. Regular income from operation of business or profession or farm	0.00	0.00

11. This schedule also requires showing, as to each claim, an account number; if there is a codebtor; and whether the claim is contingent, unliquidated, or disputed; and we deleted the creditors' mailing addresses.

INCOME: (Estimate of average monthly income)	DEBTOR	SPOUSE
8. Income from real property	0.00	0.00
9. Interest and dividends	0.00	0.00
10. Alimony, maintenance or support payments payable to the debtor for the debtor's use or that of dependents listed above	0.00	0.00
11. Social security or other government assistance	0.00	0.00
12. Pension or retirement income	0.00	0.00
13. Other monthly income (specify)	0.00	0.00
14. SUBTOTAL OF LINES 7 THROUGH 13	0.00	0.00
15. TOTAL MONTHLY INCOME (Add amounts shown on lines 6 and 14)	1,824.31	1,832.24
TOTAL COMBINED MONTHLY INCOME		$3,656.55
Describe any increase or decrease in income reasonably anticipated to occur within the year following the filing of this document:		

(8) Schedule J Current Expenditures of Individual Debtor(s)

This form is completed by estimating the average monthly expenses of the debtor and the debtor's family. Any expenses paid bi-weekly, quarterly, semi-annually, or annually are prorated to estimate the monthly cost.

1. Rent or home mortgage payment (include lot rented for mobile home) a. Are real estate taxes included? NO b. Is property insurance included? NO	499.95
2. Utilities	
a. Electricity and heating fuel	100.00
b. Water and sewer	25.00
c. Telephone	45.00
d. Other:	
Cell phone	56.72
Cable	81.00
3. Home maintenance (repairs and upkeep)	25.00
4. Food	516.00
5. Clothing	83.33
6. Laundry and dry cleaning	0.00
7. Medical and dental expenses	166.67
8. Transportation (not including car payments)	480.00
9. Recreation, clubs and entertainment, newspapers, magazines, etc.	25.00
10. Charitable contributions	20.00
11. Insurance (not deducted from wages or included in home mortgage payments)	
a. Homeowner's or renter's	136.57
b. Life	0.00
c. Health	0.00
d. Auto	117.00
e. Other:	0.00
12. Taxes (not deducted from wages or included in home mortgage payments) Specify: property taxes	70.30

13.	Installment payments (In Chapter 11, 12 and 13 cases, do not list payments to be included in the plan.)	
	a. Auto	561.00
	b. Other: Truck	428.00
	c. Other: Second mortgage	100.00
14.	Alimony, maintenance, and support paid to others	0.00
15.	Payments for support of additional dependents not living at your home	0.00
16.	Regular expenses from operation of business, profession, or farm (attach detailed statement)	25.00
17.	Other:	
	Misc.	100.00
	Child care	404.00
18.	TOTAL MONTHLY EXPENSES	4,065.54
19.	Describe any increase or decrease in expenditures reasonably anticipated to occur within the year following the filing of this document:	
20.	STATEMENT OF MONHTLY NET INCOME	
	a. Total monthly income from Line 16 of Schedule I	3656.55
	b. Total monthly expenses from Line 18 above	4,065.54
	c. **Monthly net income**	**-408.99**

(9) Statement of Financial Affairs

This form asks lots and lots of questions. Only two of the questions, however, were relevant to (or answered by) the Kaddours and their bankruptcy case:

- Income from employment or operation of business. State gross amount of income the debtor has received from employment, trade, or profession, or from operation of the debtor's business, including part-time activities either as an employee or in independent trade or business, from the beginning of this calendar year to the date this case was commenced. State also the gross amounts received during the two years immediately preceding this calendar year.

AMOUNT	SOURCE
$ 2,000.00	Income—2006 ytd
$56,000.00	Income—2005
$61,294.00	Income—2004

- Payments related to debt counseling or bankruptcy. List all payments made or property transferred by or on behalf of the debtor to any persons, including attorneys, for consultation concerning debt consolidation, relief under the bankruptcy law or preparation of the petition in bankruptcy within one year immediately preceding the commencement of this case.

Name and Address of Payee	**Date of Payment**	**Amount of Money or Description and Value of Property**
Larry Friedman	January 16, 2006	$1,500.00

(10) Chapter 7 Individual Debtor's Statement of Intention

On this form, the debtors report that they "have filed a schedule of assets and liabilities which includes debts secured by property of the estate" and that they "intend to do the following with respect to property of the estate which secures those debtors . . . ."

Description of Secured Property	**Creditor's Name**	**Property will be Surrendered**	**Property is claimed as exempt**	**Property to be redeemed pursuant to § 722**	**Debt to be reaffirmed pursuant to § 524(c)**
2003 Dodge Truck	M & I		X (avoid lien)		
2004 Chrysler Pacifica	Wells Fargo		X (avoid lien)		
Doublewide mobile home and 2 acres land	Select Portfolio Servicing	Debtor will retain collateral and continue to make regular payments.			

(11) Statement of Current Monthly Income and Means Test Calculation

The purpose of this form is to calculate, according to a complex, statutory formula, whether or not the debtors have sufficient monthly income, i.e., "means," to fund a Chapter 13 case. If the calculations show a monthly income that equals or exceeds certain benchmarks the Bankruptcy Code provides, the court "shall presume" that filing a Chapter 7 case is an "abuse" and must dismiss the case unless the debtors elect to convert their case to Chapter 13.

	According to the calculations required by this statement [or form]: ☐ **The presumption arises.** ☑ **The presumption does not arise.** (Check the box as directed in Parts I, III, and VI of this statement.)		
	PART I. EXCLUSION FOR DISABLED VETERANS		
1			
	PART II. CALCULATION OF MONTHLY INCOME FOR § 707(b)(7) EXCLUSION		
2	Marital/filing status [This space contains a set of boxes to check, and the Kaddours check the box, "Married, filing jointly," which then requires completing Columns A and B for Lines 3–11 below.]	**Col A Debtor's Income**	**Col B Spouse's Income**
3	Gross wages, salary, tips, bonuses, overtime, commissions	2,426.67	3,182.40
4	Income from the operation of a business, profession or farm	0.00	0.00
5	Rents and other real property income	0.00	0.00
6	Interest, dividends, and royalties	0.00	0.00
7	Pension and retirement income	0.00	0.00
8	Regular contributions [from anyone] to the household expenses of the debtor or the debtor's dependents	0.00	0.00
9	Unemployment compensation	0.00	0.00
10	Income from all other sources	0.00	0.00
11	Subtotal of Current Monthly Income [for each debtor] (add lines 3 through 10)	2,426.67	3,182.40
12	Total Current Monthly Income [both debtors]		5,609.07
	PART III. APPLICATION OF § 707(b)(7) EXCLUSION		

13	Annualized Current Monthly Income for § 707(b)(7). Multiply the amount from Line 12 by the number 12 and enter the result.	67,308.84
14	Applicable Median Family Income. Enter the median family income for the applicable state and household size.[12]	55,117.00[13]
15	Application of Section 707(b)(7). Check the applicable box and proceed as directed. ☐ The amount on Line 13 is less than or equal to the amount on Line 14.[14] ☐ The amount on Line 13 is more than the amount on Line 14. Complete the remaining parts of this form.[15]	
	PART IV. CALCULATION OF CURRENT MONTHLY INCOME FOR § 707(b)(2)	
16	Enter the amount from Line 12.	5,609.07
17	Marital adjustment.	0.00
18	Current monthly income for § 707(b)(2). Subtract Line 17 from Line 16 and enter the result.	5,609.07
	PART V. CALCULATION OF DEDUCTIONS UNDER § 707(b)(2) **SUBPART A: DEDUCTIONS UNDER STANDARDS OF THE INTERNAL REVENUE SERVICE (IRS)**	
19	National Standards: food, clothing, household supplies, personal care, and miscellaneous	1,298.00
20A	Local Standards: housing and utilities; non-mortgage expenses	418.00
20B	Local Standards: housing and utilities; mortgage/rent expense Enter in Line a below the amount of [the IRS allowance for] mortgage/rent expense for your county and family size; enter on line b the total of the Average Monthly Payments for any debts secured by your home; subtract line b from line a and enter the amount. a. [Amount of IRS allowance] 829.00 b. [Less] average monthly payment for any debts secured by your home 1312.73 c. Net mortgage/ rental expenses 0.00	0.00
21	Local Standards: housing and utilities; adjustment	0.00
22	Local Standards: transportation; vehicle operation/public transportation expense Check the number of vehicles for which you pay operating expenses ☐ 0 ☐ 1 ☑ 2 or more Enter the amount [the IRS allows] for the applicable number of vehicles	336.00
23	Local Standards: transportation ownership/lease expense; Vehicle 1 Check the number of vehicles for which you claim an ownership/lease expense ☐ 1 ☑ 2 or more Enter in Line a below the [IRS allowance for your] First Car; enter in Line b the total of the Average Monthly Payments for any debts secured by Vehicle 1; subtract Line b from Line a and enter the result in Line 23. a. [Amount of IRS First Car allowance] 475.00	

12. In the Kaddours' case, the applicable state is North Carolina and the family size is four.

13. This amount was the applicable median at the time the petition was filed.

14. Essentially, if this box is checked, the debtor stops here and (if the numbers are correct) can proceed with the Chapter 7 case. She lacks the means to fund a Chapter 13 case.

15. In this event, more calculations are necessary to decide whether or not the debtor can stay in Chapter 7, i.e., whether or not the debtor has the "means" to fund a Chapter 7 case. The Kaddours checked this box.

<table>
<tr><td></td><td>b. [Less] average monthly payment for any debts secured by Vehicle 1, as stated in Line 42 — 421.00
c. Net ownership/lease expense Vehicle 1 — 54.00</td><td>54.00</td></tr>
<tr><td>24</td><td>Local Standards: transportation ownership/lease expense; Vehicle 2
Enter in Line a below the [IRS allowance for your] Second Car; enter in Line b the total of the Average Monthly Payments for any debts secured by Vehicle 2; subtract Line b from Line a and enter the result in Line 24.
a. [Amount of IRS Second Car allowance] — 338.00
b. [Less] average monthly payment for any debts secured by Vehicle 2, as stated in Line 42 — 380.00
c. Net ownership/lease expense Vehicle 2 — 0.00</td><td>0.00</td></tr>
<tr><td>25</td><td>Other necessary expenses: taxes</td><td>898.00</td></tr>
<tr><td>26</td><td>Other necessary expenses: mandatory payroll deductions</td><td>346.15</td></tr>
<tr><td>27</td><td>Other necessary expenses: life insurance</td><td>0.00</td></tr>
<tr><td>28</td><td>Other necessary expenses: court-ordered payments</td><td>0.00</td></tr>
<tr><td>29</td><td>Other necessary expenses: education for employment or for a physically or mentally challenged child</td><td>0.00</td></tr>
<tr><td>30</td><td>Other necessary expenses: childcare</td><td>404.00</td></tr>
<tr><td>31</td><td>Other necessary expenses: health care</td><td>166.67</td></tr>
<tr><td>32</td><td>Other necessary expenses: telecommunication services</td><td>56.72</td></tr>
<tr><td>33</td><td>Total Expenses Allowed under IRS Standards (Lines 19–32)</td><td>3977.54</td></tr>
<tr><td colspan="3">SUBPART B. ADDITIONAL EXPENSE DEDUCTIONS UNDER § 707(b)
Note: Do not include any expenses that you have listed in Lines 19–32</td></tr>
<tr><td>34</td><td>Health Insurance, Disability Insurance and Health Savings Account Expenses</td><td>498.03</td></tr>
<tr><td>35</td><td>Continued contributions to the care of household or family members</td><td>0.00</td></tr>
<tr><td>36</td><td>Protection against family violence</td><td>0.00</td></tr>
<tr><td>37</td><td>Home energy costs in excess of the allowance specified by the IRS Local Standards</td><td>0.00</td></tr>
<tr><td>38</td><td>Education expenses for dependent child less than 18</td><td>0.00</td></tr>
<tr><td>39</td><td>Additional food and clothing expense</td><td>47.00</td></tr>
<tr><td>40</td><td>Continued charitable contributions</td><td>20.00</td></tr>
<tr><td>41</td><td>Total Additional Expense Deductions under § 707(b)</td><td>565.03</td></tr>
<tr><td></td><td>SUBPART C: DEDUCTIONS FOR DEBT PAYMENT</td><td></td></tr>
<tr><td>42</td><td>Future payments on secured claims. For each of your debts that is secured by an interest in property that you own, list the name of the creditor, identify the property securing the debt, and state the Average Monthly Payment. The Average Monthly payment is the total of all amounts contractually due to each Secured Creditor in the 60 months following the filing of the bankruptcy case divided by 60.
<table>
<tr><td>LSB Bank</td><td>Second mortgage; doublewide mobile home and 2 acres land</td><td>29.64</td></tr>
<tr><td>Select Portfolio</td><td>First deed of trust; doublewide mobile home and 2 acres land</td><td>1283.09</td></tr>
<tr><td>M & I</td><td>Lien on motor vehicle; 2003 Dodge truck</td><td>380.66</td></tr>
<tr><td>Wells Fargo</td><td>Lien on motor vehicle; 2004 Chrysler Pacifica</td><td>421.89</td></tr>
</table></td><td>2115.28</td></tr>
<tr><td>43</td><td>Past due payments on secured claims</td><td>0.00</td></tr>
<tr><td>44</td><td>Payments on priority claims</td><td>0.00</td></tr>
<tr><td>45</td><td>Chapter 13 administrative expenses. If you are eligible to file a case under Chapter 13, complete [a chart following in</td><td></td></tr>
</table>

	this space to calculate the average monthly administrative expense of a Chapter 13 case based on your circumstances].	0.0016
46	Total Deductions for Debt Payment (Lines 42–45)	0.00
SUBPART D: TOTAL DEDUCTIONS ALLOWED UNDER § 707(b)(2)		
47	Total of all deductions allowed under § 707(b)(2). Enter the total of Lines 33, 41, and 46	7057.85
PART VI. DETERMINATION OF § 707(b)(2) PRESUMPTION		
48	Enter the amount from Line 18 (Current monthly income for § 707(b)(2))	5,609.07
49	Enter the amount from Line 47 (Total of all deductions allowed under § 707(b)(2))	6657.85
50	Monthly disposable income under § 707(b)(2). Subtract Line 49 from Line 48 and enter the result.	-1,048.78
51	60–month disposable income under § 707(b)(2)	–62926.80
52	Initial presumption determination. Check the applicable box and proceed as directed. ☑ The amount on Line 51 is less than $6,000. Check the box for "The presumption does not arise" at the top of page 1 of this [form], and complete the verification in Part VIII. Do not complete the remainder of Part VI. ☐ The amount set forth on Line 51 is more than $10,000. Check the box for "The presumption arises" at the top of page of this [form], and complete the verification in Part VIII. You may also complete Part VII. Do not complete the remainder of Part VI. ☐ The amount on Line 51 is at least $6,000, but no more than $10,000. Complete the remainder of Part VI (Lines 53 through 55).	
53	Enter the amount of your total non-priority unsecured debt	
54	Threshold debt payment amount. Multiply the amount in Line 53 by the number 0.25 and enter the result.	
55	Secondary presumption determination. Check the applicable box and proceed as directed. ☐ The amount on Line 51 is less than the amount on Line 54. Check the box for "The presumption does not arise" at the top of page 1 of this [form], and complete the verification in Part VIII. ☐ The amount on Line 51 is equal to or greater than the amount on Line 54. Check the box for "The presumption arises" at the top of page 1 of this [form], and complete the verification in Part VIII. You may also complete Part VII.	
PART VII. ADDITIONAL EXPENSE CLAIMS		
56	Other Expenses. List and describe any monthly expenses, not otherwise stated in this form, that are required for the health and welfare of you and your family and that you contend should be an additional deduction from your current monthly income under § 707(b)(2)(A)(ii)(I). All figures should reflect your average monthly expense for each item. Total the expenses.	
PART VIII. VERIFICATION		
57	I declare under penalty of perjury that the information provided in this statement [form] is true and correct. (If this is a joint case, both debtors must sign.) [The Kaddours both added dated signatures.]	

(12) Debtor's Claims for Property Exemptions

A very, very important filing that accompanies a Chapter 7 bankruptcy petition is the debtor's claim of exemptions. In a joint

16. The Kaddours were eligible to file under Chapter 13, but their monthly disposable income is a negative number. For purposes of line 45, the hypothetical Chapter 13 administrative expenses are based on "projected average monthly Chapter 13 plan payment," which generally (in theory) is monthly disposable income. Arguably, inasmuch as the Kaddours had no disposable income, line 45 is zero.

Again, though, it really didn't matter in the Kaddours' case. They passed the means test despite what could or should have been an amount for line 45.

case, each debtor files a claim of exemptions, as happened in the Kaddours' case.

Section 522 provides that an individual debtor may exempt property from the estate; and Rule 4003 requires the debtor to "list the property claimed as exempt under § 522 of the Code on the schedule of assets required to be filed ...." Usually, in practice, the claim of exemptions is filed as a separate, standard form designed in line with the exemptions allowed under the applicable, exemptions law. The form details the law's allowable exemptions, and the debtor completes the form by describing property she owns that matches property the law exempts.

Usually, the applicable exemptions law is state law. Usually, the debtor claims everything she owns [or most everything] as exempt. In the Kaddours' case, the debtors together exempted virtually everything listed in their Schedules A and B. Their claims of exemptions are discussed later as part of the review of what happens to their case after the petition is filed.

(d) Where Larry Files the Petition, Schedules, and Other Forms

Technically, federal district courts have jurisdiction of bankruptcy cases. However, "[e]ach district court may provide that any or all cases under title 11 [i.e., the Bankruptcy Code] and any or all proceedings arising under ... or arising in or related to a case under title 11 shall be referred to the bankruptcy judges for the district."[17] As a result of this authority, every district court in the country has issued a standing order referring all bankruptcy cases to the bankruptcy court in the district.

So, Larry filed the case with the bankruptcy court in the district where venue was proper. The proper venue for a case involving an individual debtor is the federal judicial district "in which the domicile [or] residence ... of the [debtor] [has] been located for the [180] days immediately preceding [the filing] ...or for a longer portion of such [180–day] period ...."[18]

The Kaddours have lived in Winston–Salem, North Carolina, for years. Therefore, Larry filed their case in the United States Bankruptcy Court for the Middle District of North Carolina, which has several bankruptcy judges sitting [most of the time] in federal court buildings in Winston–Salem and nearby Greensboro. Larry filed the Kaddours' case with the bankruptcy court in Winston–Salem.

17. 28 U.S.C.A. § 157(a).

18. Id. § 1408.

§ 16.3 What Happens to the Kaddours' Case after Filing

The bankruptcy court assigns every Chapter 7 case to a Chapter 7 trustee. Chapter 7 trustees are officers of the court but are not employees of the court. Accountants and other professionals can serve as Chapter 7 trustees; but, typically, they are practicing lawyers who have applied and been selected by the Office of the United States Trustee[19] to form a local "panel" of Chapter 7 trustees. Very often, a panel trustee works only part time in this role and simultaneously maintains a private practice, which may include representing bankruptcy debtors in cases where the trustee is somebody else. Therefore, after Larry filed the Kaddours case, the bankruptcy court (which includes the clerk's office) assigned the case to one of the local Chapter 7 trustees according to a blind rotation system that divides the work among the panel of trustees.

The main job of a Chapter 7 panel trustee (who is called a case trustee with respect to a case assigned to her) is to "collect and reduce to money the property of the estate ...." The purpose, of course, is to distribute this money to unsecured creditors. Remember: the property the trustee liquidates is property of the estate which consists of the debtor's interest in property. If the debtor owns a car that is secured by an Article 9 security interest, the property of the estate is the debtor's title *subject to the lien.* Effectively, then, the estate gets only the debtor's equity; and, typically, the debtor can exempt from the estate some or all of this equity.

Therefore, most commonly in Chapter 7 cases, the estate contains no equity to "collect and reduce to money" for distribution to unsecured creditors or so little equity that liquidating the property is not worth the effort. This kind of case is called a "no-asset" case.

The trustee is paid a small, flat fee for every no-asset case. She makes money with these cases based on volume. Most Chapter 7 cases are no-asset cases, but the number of these cases is every-

19. The Office of the United States Trustee is a component of the Department of Justice. The Executive Office (a/k/a EOUST) is located in Washington and is headed by a director whom the Attorney General appoints. The Attorney General also appoints 21 regional U.S. Trustees who are spread (almost) throughout the country in local offices and who are aided by Assistant U.S. Trustees. The entire U.S. Trustee system, including its programs and people, mainly serves in a national role to supervise and support the administration of the bankruptcy system (and therefore let bankruptcy judges focus on judging cases instead of managing them) and also to help ensure compliance with applicable laws and procedures.

For reasons not important or explainable here, the jurisdiction of the U.S. Trustee program excludes Alabama and North Carolina, which are administratively served otherwise by bankruptcy administrators through the Administrative Office of the United States Courts.

where very large every year. As a result, the total of small, flat fees is not so small.

In the rare case with more than nominal equity, the trustee makes money in a different way: she is paid a percentage of the proceeds she collects by selling property—liquidating it—to reduce the debtor's interest, i.e., equity, to money. It's called an incentive or recovery commission. The trustee is therefore incented to evaluate each case assigned to her in terms of the existence and value of the debtor's equity in property of the estate.

The trustee cannot afford to investigate cases. In evaluating them, the trustee relies on the truthfulness of the schedules and other forms filed with their petition.[20] In addition to the many forms we've already described above, the debtor is required to file other information that is helpful to the trustee's evaluation, such as evidence of payments from employers received by the debtor within 60 days before the filing of the petition. Later in the case, and at least seven days before the 341(a) meeting described below, the debtor must provide to the trustee (and to any creditor making a timely request) a copy of the debtor's federal income tax return (or transcript of the return) for the preceding tax period.[21]

The trustee also relies on information she learns at the 341(a) meeting. Section 341(a) requires a "meeting of creditors" in every case. The meeting is held within a reasonable time after the case is filed and is, according to the Code, convened and run by a local United States Trustee. Typically, however, this job is delegated to the Chapter 7 case trustee. In any event, the Chapter 7 case trustee attends even if she doesn't run the meeting; the debtor and the co-debtor in a joint case are required to attend; and creditors are allowed to attend (but they rarely do in an individual Chapter 7 case).

The main purposes of the 341(a) meeting are to ensure the debtor knows what she's doing in filing bankruptcy and also to

20. Truthfulness is encouraged by debtors' morality and, just as backup, by a set of legal disincentives to lie or be incomplete in filling out bankruptcy forms. To begin with, as the debtor is warned from the beginning of the bankruptcy process, she risks criminal liability for perjury if the information she provides is not true and correct. This risk is emphasized by the debtor's bankruptcy lawyer who herself, to some extent, certifies the accuracy of the petition and pleadings. The risk is increased because every United States Attorney's office is required to designate a prosecutor and every FBI field office an agent who will assume primary responsibility for bankruptcy fraud cases; and the Office of the United States Trustee maintains a Criminal Enforcement Unit in cooperation with federal investigators and prosecutors in field offices through the country.

Dishonesty carries civil consequences, too. For example, the court can dismiss the debtor's case or deny the debtor a discharge. At the national level, the Office of the United States Trustee operates a civil enforcement program to insure that Chapter 7 is not abused.

21. 11 U.S.C.A. § 521(e)(2)(A).

examine (i.e., interrogate) the debtor, under oath, about the debtor's financial affairs. Therefore, at the 341(a) meeting, the debtor is asked questions confirming information about debts and assets reported in schedules and other forms the debtor filed along with her bankruptcy petition. She is also asked questions digging deeper and beyond the information already reported.

In the hunt for equity, the trustee may ask questions testing the debtor's valuation of property or the claim of exemptions. Another important line of questioning concerns any transfers of money or other property the debtor made before bankruptcy. It's possible for the trustee to avoid some of these transfers, including liens, and thereby increase equity for the estate.

If the trustee decides to sell property, she can do so herself or hire another professional. If she decides to file a proceeding in the case to avoid prepetition transfers, or decides to go to court to challenge exemptions or for any other reason, she can hire another lawyer to represent her (including another panel trustee acting in the role of private attorney). Alternatively, the case trustee can represent herself and get paid for her legal services.

Based on the schedules and other forms, the Kaddours' case appears to be a no-asset case and probably is. However, we won't know for sure until the 341(a) creditors' meeting. The trustee may uncover more information at the meeting or from some other source (such as an angry creditor) that leads to more property, changes the trustee's initial evaluation of the case, and triggers further action by her.

While this evaluation process is going on, other stuff is happening in (and because of) the bankruptcy case. Let's review some of it after you have seen the docket in the Kaddours' case. The docket lists everything filed with the bankruptcy court during the case and, more important, gives you a good idea of what happened in the case and when.

U.S. Bankruptcy Court Middle District of North Carolina (Winston–Salem) Bankruptcy Petition #: *[court assigned case number deleted]* In re: Ahmed Kaddour (Debtor) and Irshad Kaddour (Joint Debtor)		
Filing Date	**#**	**Docket Text**
01/21/2006	1	Chapter 7 Voluntary Petition. Fee amount $274 Filed by Ahmed Kaddour, Irshad Kaddour (Friedman, Larry)
P01/21/2006	2	Statement of Social Security Number(s) Filed by Debtor and Joint Debtor
01/21/2006		Receipt of filing fee for Voluntary Petition ($274.00)
01/21/2006	3	Certificate of Credit Counseling Filed by Debtor and Joint Debtor
01/21/2006	4	Document *Debtor's Claim for Property Exemptions Ahmed Kaddour*

Filing Date	#	Docket Text
01/21/2006	5	Document *Debtor's Claim for Property Exemptions Irshad Kaddour*
01/23/2006	6	Meeting of Creditors 341(a); meeting to be held on 2/17/2006 at 09:00 AM at Creditors Mtg Room, Winston Salem. CertOf-CompFinMgt Course Due: 4/3/2006. Last day to oppose discharge or dischargeability is 4/18/2006
01/25/2006	7	BNC Certificate of Mailing–Meeting of Creditors. (RE: related document(s) Meeting of Creditors Chapter 7 No Asset)
02/17/2006		Chapter 7 Meeting of Creditors Held
02/23/2006	8	Notice of Requirement for Financial Management Course
02/25/2006	9	BNC Certificate of Mailing. (RE: related document(s) Notice of Requirement for Financial Management Course)
02/27/2006	10	As required by 11 U.S.C. § 704(b)(1)(A), the Bankruptcy Administrator has reviewed the materials filed by the debtor(s). Having considered these materials in reference to the criteria set forth in 11 U.S.C. § 707(b)(2), and pursuant to 11 U.S.C. § 704(b)(2) and § 707(b)(2), the Bankruptcy Administrator has determined that the debtor's(s') case should be presumed not to be an abuse under § 707(b).
02/28/2006		Trustee's Report of No Distribution: Trustee of this estate reports and certifies that the trustee has performed the duties required of a trustee under 11 U.S.C. § 704 and has concluded that there are no assets to administer for the benefit of creditors of this estate. I have received no funds or property of the estate, and paid no monies on account of the estate. Wherefore, the trustee prays that this report be approved and the trustee be discharged from office.
03/01/2006	11	BNC Certificate of Mailing. (RE: related document(s) 10 BA's Statement of No Presumption of Abuse)
03/06/2006	12	Certificate of Financial Management Course Filed March 6, 2006 by Debtor and Joint Debtor
03/20/2006	13	Reaffirmation Agreement between Debtor and M & I Dealer Finance Filed by Debtor and Joint Debtor
03/21/2006	14	Hearing Set (RE: related document(s) Reaffirmation Agreement filed by Debtor, Joint Debtor.) Hearing scheduled 4/5/2006 at 02:00 PM at Courtroom, Winston–Salem.
03/22/2006	15	Reaffirmation Agreement between Debtor and Wells Fargo Financial Acceptance Filed by Debtor and Joint Debtor
03/22/2006	16	Reaffirmation Agreement between Debtor and Select Portfolio Servicing, Inc. Filed by Debtor and Joint Debtor
03/22/2006	17	Hearing Set (RE: related document(s)15 Filed Reaffirmation Agreement between Debtors and Wells Fargo Financial Acceptance, 16 Filed Reaffirmation Agreement between Debtors and Select Portfolio Servicing, Inc.) Hearing scheduled 4/5/2006 at 02:00 PM at Courtroom, Winston–Salem
03/23/2006	18	BNC Certificate of Mailing. (RE: related document(s)14 Hearing Set on Reaffirmation Agreement)
03/24/2006	19	BNC Certificate of Mailing. (RE: related document(s)17 Hearing Set on Reaffirmation Agreement)
04/05/2006		Hearing Continued (RE related document(s) 16 Reaffirmation Agreement Filed by Debtor, Joint Debtor. Hearing to be held on 4/19/2006 at 02:00 PM Courtroom, Winston–Salem
04/24/2006	20	Proposed Order *Approving Reaffirmation Agreement with Wells Fargo Financial Acceptance* Filed by Joint Debtor, Debtor (RE: related document(s) 15 Reaffirmation Agreement)

Filing Date	#	Docket Text
04/24/2006	21	Proposed Order *Approving Reaffirmation Agreement with M & I Bank (M & I Dealer Finance)* Filed by Joint Debtor, Debtor (RE: related document(s)13 Reaffirmation Agreement)
04/24/2006	22	Proposed Order *Approving Reaffirmation Agreement with Select Portfolio Servicing, Inc.* Filed by Joint Debtor, Debtor (RE: related document(s)16 Reaffirmation Agreement)
04/28/2006	23	Final Order GRANTING Reaffirmation Agreement (RE: related document(s)13 Reaffirmation Agreement filed by Debtor, Joint Debtor)
04/28/2006	24	Final Order GRANTING Reaffirmation Agreement (RE: related document(s)16 Reaffirmation Agreement filed by Debtor, Joint Debtor)
04/28/2006	25	Final Order GRANTING Reaffirmation Agreement (RE: related document(s)15 Reaffirmation Agreement filed by Debtor, Joint Debtor)
05/03/2006	26	BNC Certificate of Mailing—PDF Document. (RE: related document(s) 23 Reaffirmation Order (Final Order))
05/03/2006	27	BNC Certificate of Mailing—PDF Document. (RE: related document(s) 24 Reaffirmation Order (Final Order))
05/03/2006	28	BNC Certificate of Mailing—PDF Document. (RE: related document(s) 25 Reaffirmation Order (Final Order))
05/12/2006	29	Order Discharging Debtor
05/14/2006	30	BNC Certificate of Mailing—Order of Discharge. (RE: related document(s) 29 Order Discharging Debtor)
05/22/2006	31	Final Decree
05/22/2006		Bankruptcy Case Closed
05/24/2006	32	BNC Certificate of Mailing—Final Decree (RE: related document(s) 31 Final Decree)

§ 16.4 Stay Prevents Creditors From Visiting the Kaddours and Taking Property

Larry's filing the Kaddours' petition "operate[d] as a stay, applicable to all entities," enjoining and preventing all creditors from taking or continuing any action in or outside of court against the debtors to collect the creditors' claims. So, creditors cannot file lawsuits, enforce any judgments already won, or act in any other way "to collect, assess, or recover a claim that arose before the commencement of the case."

So, Circuit City, JC Penney, the credit card companies, and all of the Kaddours' other creditors are enjoined from calling, sending a letter, or emailing the Kaddours asking for payment. The creditors are not stopped from refusing to extend new credit to the Kaddours; but the creditors cannot condition giving new credit on the Kaddours paying their prepetition debts.

The stay is also an injunction against creditors' actions to obtain possession or otherwise exercise control over property of the estate. More particularly, the stay stops secured creditors from taking any actions with respect to liens they have on property of the estate or on property of the debtors.

So, the two creditors with mortgages on the Kaddours' double-wide mobile home, Select Portfolio and LSB Bank, cannot foreclose on the property even if the debtors are in default. The creditors, M & I and Wells Fargo, cannot repossess the 2003 Dodge truck and the 2004 Chrysler Pacifica to enforce their Article 9 security interests.

Please remember, however, that neither filing the petition nor triggering of the stay, by itself or in combination, cuts off the secured creditors' liens. Filing the petition which triggers the stay only prevents the secured creditors from taking any actions—exercising any rights given by state law or contract—with respect to their liens, except upon request to and agreement by the bankruptcy judge.

This kind of request is based on section 362(d) which lists grounds for the bankruptcy judge to give "relief" from the stay. Giving this relief is called "lifting" the stay, and the motion a creditor files to get this relief is called a "lift stay" motion.

The usual grounds for giving relief to a secured creditor in an individual Chapter 7 case is that "the debtor does not have an equity" in the collateral. It's the debtor's equity in property that is liquidated and distributed to unsecured creditors. If the debtor lacks any equity in collateral, the property lacks any value for the estate, and no reason exists for continuing to prevent the secured creditor from enforcing its state-law and contract rights.

The Kaddours own a little equity in their mobile home, but the bankruptcy estate won't get the equity. The property is valued at $81,500; and the two mortgages (in favor of Select Portfolio Servicing and LSB) total $78,764.23, which leaves about $2,736 in equity. The Kaddours, however, have claimed the equity as exempt property, which leaves nothing for the estate.

In any event, the mortgagees will not file lift stay motions. Look at the form "Debtor's Statement of Intention." It states that with respect to Select Portfolio Serving, which holds the first mortgage, the Kaddours will "retain the collateral and continue to make regular payments," which suits the mortgagee.

Even absent this declaration of intention by the debtors, Select Portfolio would not seek relief from the stay. Select Portfolio is fully secured; the Chapter 7 case will not last very long; the property will not depreciate during this time; Select Portfolio's mortgage will survive the bankruptcy case (unless very uncommon, very unlikely facts exists allowing the trustee to avoid the lien); and the debtors' discharge in bankruptcy will not affect the mortgage. Therefore, without substantial risk of loss, Select Portfolio can ride through the bankruptcy (which means do nothing) and foreclose, after the bankruptcy case ends, if the debtors are in default.[22]

For the same reasons, LSB Bank, which holds the second mortgage, will not seek relief from the stay. Additionally, filing and pursuing a lift stay motion would cost more than the amount of the mortgage debt owed LSB Bank, which is only $1,778.38.

The Kaddours have no equity in the Dodge truck and the Chrysler Pacifica which are subject to liens, respectively, in favor of Wells Fargo and M & I. In fact, the secured debts are way more than the value of the vehicles. Generally, absent avoidance by the trustee or debtor (which is uncommon), Article 9 security interests in personal property also survive a debtor's bankruptcy and are unaffected by the discharge. However, vehicles tend to depreciate quickly which increases the unsecured part of the creditor's claim, i.e., decreases the size and value of the lien. Therefore, compared to a real estate mortgage, it's more likely that an Article 9 secured party with a lien on a vehicle will file a lift stay motion in an individual Chapter 7 case.

In the Kaddours' case, however, even though the debtors lack equity in the vehicles, Wells Fargo and M & I are not certain to win immediate relief from the stay without a fight.[23] Look again at the form "Debtor's Statement of Intention." The debtors state an intention to avoid the creditors' liens. So, if Wells Fargo and M & I filed motions to lift stay, they would face challenges to their liens. How the debtors might argue for avoidance, and their chances of success, are discussed in a later section on exemptions and the debtors' very limited ability to avoid lien impairing exemptions.

§ 16.5 Property the Kaddours Lose and Property They Keep

Larry's fee for legal services and the filing and associated fees paid to the bankruptcy court are not, in theory, the debtor's biggest costs. The debtor's biggest cost (again, in theory) for getting the benefits of bankruptcy (such as the stay of creditors and the discharge of debts) is the loss of the debtor's property, which passes to the bankruptcy estate and is liquidated and distributed to unsecured creditors.

However, in some cases, not everything the debtor owns passes to the estate. Some property is excluded from the estate and the

22. To insure Portfolio against this risk and to insure the Kaddours against a lift-stay motion, the Kaddours agreed to reaffirm their debt to Select Portfolio. We discuss reaffirmation agreements later in this unit.

23. In the end, the Kaddours "bought" protection against M & I and Wells Fargo getting relief from the stay and taking the vehicles by making reaffirmation agreements, which we discuss later in this unit.

debtor gets to keep it, though these exclusions are rarely significant in the typical, individual Chapter 7 case.

Also, in the typical case, the debtor is allowed to take back some of the property that passed to the estate by exempting certain property from the estate. The debtor thereby loses this property when her bankruptcy case is filed, but she gets back the property by claiming the property as exempt.

Exemptions are always significant in the typical, individual Chapter 7 case. Also, in practice as opposed to theory, the debtor's exemptions largely or completely deplete the bankruptcy estate of property that would otherwise have been distributed to the unsecured creditors, as discussed below. So, in practice, the typical debtor doesn't really lose her property (or very much of it) as a cost of bankruptcy benefits.

(a) Property the Estate Gets—Debtor's Interests at Filing

In the Kaddours' case, and really in every other case, the basic law is very simple: all of the debtor's interests in property that she owns (or both debtors own in a joint case) when the petition is filed passes to the bankruptcy estate. As a general rule, the estate gets only property owned at the very instant the petition is filed. This transfer of such property to the estate happens immediately and automatically upon filing; and the transfer covers all of the debtor's interests in property wherever the property is located and even if the debtor failed to list the property in the schedules she filed with the bankruptcy petition.

Don't miss a very big point: the estate gets only the debtor's interests in property. If anybody else also owns an interest in the property, this other person's interest does not pass to the estate. The person's ability to exercise her rights with respect to her interest may be procedurally affected by the bankruptcy case; but her ownership of the interest is not taken from her.

This point applies most commonly to liens. Take, for example, Ahmed Kaddour's 2003 Dodge truck. Before bankruptcy, his property interest was title to the truck and all rights accompanying this interest. His title, however, was subject to a consensual lien, i.e., an Article 9 security interest, in favor of M & I which probably financed his purchase of the truck. M & I's interest limited and encumbered Ahmed's otherwise complete ownership.

When the Kaddours filed bankruptcy, Ahmed's property interest in the truck passed to the bankruptcy estate. M & I, however, kept its interest. The stay prevented M & I from exercising the rights associated with its interest, but the bankruptcy does not destroy M & I's interest. The interest can be attacked on the basis of the debtor's or trustee's avoiding powers (which we discuss later); but these powers are very limited and very rarely work against a lien such as M & I's security interest. In fact, the percentage of third-party interests avoided by the debtor or trustee in Chapter 7 cases is tiny.

The trustee is obligated to liquidate the property interests that have passed to the bankruptcy estate and distribute the money to unsecured creditors. However, with respect to Ahmed's interest in Dodge truck, the interest is worthless if the debtor's estimate of the truck's market value—$15,700—is correct. The reason is that Ahmed's interest secures a $22,839.48 debt owed M & I and secured by M & I's lien, which means the whole market value of the truck, is encumbered by (subject to) M & I's lien. Anybody buying the truck (i.e., Ahmed's interest in the truck) from the trustee would take the property subject to M & I's lien; and, because the truck has no market value beyond the amount of the lien, nobody will buy Ahmed's interest. It's worthless to the market and, concomitantly, worthless to the estate and the trustee.

The same analysis and conclusion apply to Irshad's Chrysler Pacifica and Wells Fargo's security interest in this vehicle. It, too, is worthless for bankruptcy purposes.

(1) Property Acquired After the Petition is Filed and Proceeds

The general rule in all Chapter 7 cases is that the bankruptcy estate does not include property the debtor acquires (which really means interests in property the debtor acquires) after the petition is filed. The estate includes only interests in property the debtor owns at the exact time of filing.

Of course, exceptions exist, but they are few. Also, in the typical Chapter 7 case, the circumstances do not exist that trigger any of the exceptions, aside from the exception dealing with proceeds.

Here's an example to illustrate. Suppose, when Larry filed the Kaddours' petition, Ahmed had a bank account containing wages paid him by his employer. This money becomes part of the bankruptcy estate.

Suppose, however, that the day after the filing, Ahmed's employer paid him for work performed before the filing. Technically, with respect to the payment itself, Ahmed acquired a property interest postpetition; and, under the general rule, the postpetition payment is not part of the estate.

Here's where the proceeds exception comes into play. The estate includes "[p]roceeds, product, offspring, rents, or profits of or from property of the estate. . . ." The postpetition payment for prepetition services is proceeds within this exception and thus is property of the estate. Ahmed had earned the right to payment before the bankruptcy filing. This right to payment was itself property that passed to the estate. The actual payment, though postpetition, was proceeds of the prepetition property and is included in the estate.

Here's a follow-up example. Suppose that two weeks after the bankruptcy filing, Ahmed's employer pays him for work done after the filing. This payment is not proceeds of prepetition property and is not property of the estate.

(2) Property Transferred Before the Petition is Filed and Avoidance

Once again, property of the estate is limited to the debtor's interest in property at the time the bankruptcy petition is filed. Interests the debtor owned but effectively transferred before the filing are not property of the estate. The reason: the debtor doesn't own the interests at the time of filing.

Here's where the trustee's avoiding (or avoidance) powers fit within the Chapter 7 bankruptcy process. These powers describe limited circumstances under which the bankruptcy court—upon request of the trustee through a proceeding in the bankruptcy court—can undo, i.e., avoid, the debtor's prepetition transfer of property even though the transfer was perfectly legal and perfectly done under state law.

The best examples are the trustee's powers to avoid certain prepetition preferences and prepetition transfers that are fraudulent. Also, on different grounds, the trustee can usually avoid a mortgage, Article 9 security interest, or other lien that the secured creditor failed properly to perfect under local law.

The effect of avoidance is to invalidate the transfer as a matter of federal law. As a result, because the transfer is unwound, the interest the debtor transferred no longer belongs to the transferee and passes to the bankruptcy estate. The transferee ends up with an unsecured claim against the estate to the extent of her loss resulting from the avoidance.

When a lien is avoided, the collateral is freed from the lien and equity is freed for the estate. The debt owed the creditor remains but only as an unsecured claim against the estate.

In reality, though, the typical, individual, Chapter 7 debtor has not made any prepetition, preferential or fraudulent transfers, of any significance, that are avoidable. More important, the debtor's secured creditors have perfectly perfected their mortgages and liens. So, the trustee's avoiding powers are not commonly used in the typical Chapter 7 case involving individuals, such as the Kaddours' bankruptcy case.

(b) Property the Kaddours Keep From the Estate Because of Exclusions

The general rule is that the bankruptcy "estate is comprised of . . . ***all*** legal or equitable interests of the debtor in property as of the commencement of the case." Actually, in theory, the debtor's interests in some kinds of property are excluded from the estate. However, in practice, an individual debtor in the typical Chapter 7 cases doesn't have interests in these kinds of property, with a couple of important, possible exceptions.

Section 541(c)(2) provides: "A restriction on the transfer of a beneficial interest of the debtor in a trust that is enforceable under applicable [state or federal] nonbankruptcy law is enforceable in a [bankruptcy] case . . . ." We know: this provision is meaningless gobbledygook to you. However, you can easily see and understand the importance of its main effect.

Suppose the debtor is a beneficiary of a spendthrift trust created by her grandparents. The debtor gets regular income from the trust but cannot touch the corpus or principal. State law usually restricts the alienability of the debtor's beneficial interest in the trust by providing, as do the terms of the trust itself, that the beneficiary's interest in the principal cannot be transferred either voluntarily or involuntarily. The result of this restriction is that, under state law, creditors of the debtor-beneficiary likewise cannot get to the principal. So, because state law so restricts the transfer of the debtor's beneficial interest and puts it beyond creditors' reach, section 541(c)(2) excludes the principal of the trust from the estate and creditors of the estate if the debtor files bankruptcy.

Of course, the typical, individual Chapter 7 debtor is not the beneficiary of such a spendthrift trust. Often, however, such a debtor owns a retirement account that is inalienable under state or federal law in the sense that creditors cannot reach the principal of the account. So, section 541(c)(2) excludes the retirement account from the bankruptcy estate.

Also, because of amendments to the Bankruptcy Code enacted in 2005, education individual retirement accounts (IRAs) are separately excluded from the estate. Likewise excluded is the debtor's interest in a qualified, state tuition credit account or program.

The 2005 amendments also created limited exemptions for almost all retirement accounts, including retirement IRAs and the like. These exemptions are not dependent on or related to the section 541(c)(2) exclusion of retirement accounts.

Exclusions and exemptions sometimes overlap and often have essentially the same effect; but their sources in the Code and how they work are different. The main source of exclusions is section 541; and the effect of exclusion is that the property never becomes part of the bankruptcy estate. The debtor keeps the property free from the bankruptcy process and usually without regard to the property's value.

Section 522 is the main source of exemptions. An exemption is a law under which the debtor is allowed to take back certain property that she owned when the bankruptcy case commenced and that therefore passed to the estate. Very often, exemptions are limited in terms of the amount or value of exempt property the debtor can reclaim from the estate.

Here's an explanation of exemptions the Kaddours claimed in their bankruptcy case.

(c) Property the Kaddours Take Back From the Estate Because of Exemptions

Section 522 allows the debtor to exempt property from the estate that is exempt from creditors under the applicable law of exemptions. The Code allows the debtor to choose between the exemptions allowed by state law or a set of exemptions provided by the Code itself, unless the state has "opted out" by enacting a law eliminating this choice and requiring the debtor to use state-law exemptions.

Most states have opted out and therefore, in most cases the debtor's exemptions are mainly based on state law. We say "mainly" because the Code adds some federal exemptions even when the exemptions law of an "opted-out" state applies and also because the Code adds some limits or qualifications on state-law exemptions.

In the Kaddours' case, each of them claimed his and her own set of property exemptions.[24] They filed in North Carolina which has "opted out;" they have lived in North Carolina for several years; and their exemptions are therefore mainly governed by North Carolina law.[25]

24. With some restrictions, each debtor in a joint case can usually, separately claim applicable exemptions with respect to property in which he or she has interests.

25. The state law that governs exemptions is that law of the state in "which the debtor's domicile has been located for the 730 days immediately preceding the date of the filing of the petition or if the debtor's domicile has not been located in a single State for such 730–day period, the place in which the debtor's domicile was located for 180

North Carolina law allows a debtor to exempt the debtor's "aggregate interest, not to exceed eighteen thousand five hundred dollars ($18,500) in value, in real property or personal property that the debtor or a dependent of the debtor uses as a residence," which is known as the homestead exemption. Generally speaking, however, a homestead exemption applies to the debtor's equity, which is the value of the property in excess of a purchase-money mortgage, other mortgages, and maybe other kinds of liens, too.

In the Kaddours' case, the equity in their home is only $2,735.77. Ahmed claimed one-half of this amount. Irshad claimed the other half.

North Carolina law also exempts "the debtor's interest, not to exceed three thousand five hundred dollars ($3,500) in value, in one motor vehicle." Ahmed claimed the 1967 Ford truck worth $400, which he owns free-and-clear of any liens.

Under the vehicle exemption, Irshad listed the 2004 Chrysler Pacifica. However, the value of the vehicle is $16,475, and Wells Fargo has a consensual lien for $25,313.36. So, there is no equity unless the lien is avoided in bankruptcy; and, in North Carolina and most other states, exemptions are inapplicable to a creditor's claim "[f]or contractual security interests in the specific property affected."

Together, the Kaddours owned clothing valued at $750, jewelry valued at $750; and assorted household goods valued at $1,500. Each of the debtors claimed one half of this property as exempt, which is well within the state law exemption of more than $5,000 for "household furnishings, household goods, wearing apparel, appliances, books, animals, crops, or musical instruments, that are held primarily for the personal, family, or household use of the debtor or a dependent of the debtor." Ahmed also exempted hunting equipment worth $750.

State law exempts qualified individual retirement accounts (IRAs) and also exempts college savings plans not exceeding $25,000. Ahmed claimed a 401k account worth $400. Irshad claimed her 401k worth $1,200 and a college savings account worth $40.

Any unused portion of the homestead exemption, not to exceed $5,000, can be used to exempt any property, which is called a "wildcard" exemption. On the basis of this exemption, Ahmed listed the following property:

- LSB savings account of $400 (one-third interest equaling $133)
- 2003 Dodge truck (but there is no equity)

days immediately preceding the 730–day period or for a longer portion of such 180–day period than in any other place." 11 U.S.C.A. § 522(a)(3)(A).

- Two utility trailers together worth $1,000
- Golf cart valued at $1,500 (one-half interest equaling $750)
- 1952 Ford tractor worth $1,500 (one-half interest equaling $750)

Irshad used her wildcard exemption for this property:

- LSB savings account of $400 (one-third interest equaling $133)
- Golf cart valued at $1,500 (one-half interest equaling $750)
- 1952 Ford tractor worth $1,500 (one-half interest equaling $750)
- 22 shares of Sara Lee stock worth $400

When state law exemptions control in a bankruptcy case, as in the Kaddours' case, the debtor is also allowed to exempt "any interest in property in which the debtor had, immediately before the commencement of the case, an interest as a tenant by the entirety or joint tenant to the extent that such interest ... is exempt from process under applicable nonbankruptcy [i.e., state] law." Several states, including North Carolina, recognize the ancient property estate known as "tenancy by the entirety," at least with respect to real property. This estate is created and only applies to property acquired by a couple as husband and wife.

In North Carolina, when a debtor owns real property as a tenant by the entirety, the property is immune from judicial liens without regard to size or value of the property. In terms of state law, this effect results from the nature and incidents of the estate, not because of state exemption law. It's only bankruptcy law that refers to tenancy by the entirety as an exemption.

It's not certain that the Kaddours owned their homestead as tenants by the entirety. Some technicalities apply in creating such an estate that may not have been satisfied. If the Kaddours were tenants by the entirety with respect to their homestead, they probably could have removed their interests from the estate on this basis rather than on the basis of the state, homestead exemption law.

However, owning the property as tenants by the entirety would not have affected the two mortgages on their homestead. Tenants by the entirety acting together can subject their collective and individual interests to consensual liens; and the secured creditors are not prevented by state law from exercising whatever rights their liens give them. So, at most, only the Kaddours' collective "entirety" equity could be exempted as property held as tenants by the entirety. Therefore, they had no reason to rely on this basis to protect this homestead interest because the size of the statutory, homestead exemption statute covered their equity. It's true that using the homestead exemption reduced the size of their wildcard exemption; but they didn't need a larger wildcard to cover everything they could exempt.

Even when the source of a debtor's bankruptcy exemptions is state law, section 522 allows the debtor to exempt additional property within the scope of certain exemptions created by federal law. First, the debtor can exempt property that fits within a set of federal, nonbankruptcy exemptions;[26] but these exemptions are very limited and almost never applicable in Chapter 7 cases and not in the Kaddours' case.

Second, and much more important, is the exemption created by bankruptcy law, section 522, for retirement accounts. It is very broad and exempts virtually all retirement accounts, including IRAs. However, this exemption (or some part of it) is limited to "$1,000,000 in a case filed by a debtor who is an individual, except that *such amount may be increased if the interests of justice so require*." We're not kidding. This language is an exact quote from the statute.

Chapter 7 debtors have retirement accounts even in many, typical individual cases, as do the Kaddours. These retirement accounts are typically excluded under section 541 or exempted under section 522 even if the applicable exemption law is state law. The $1,000,000 limitation, which section 522 imposes, is never a problem in the typical case; and so the judge never gets the chance to consider when the "interests of justice" require raising it.

The applicable state law may also exempt retirement accounts and other property that federal law exempts or excludes from the estate, as in the Kaddours' case. In this event, however, some election is made by the debtors or forced on them. They cannot stack the duplicative state and federal exemptions.

26. Most of the exemptions protect various forms of retirement income and social welfare benefits paid by the United States or somehow regulated by federal law. Examples are: veterans' benefits, 38 U.S.C.A. § 3101(a); social security old age and disability benefits, 42 U.S.C.A. § 407(a); disability and death benefits paid to government employees injured while in the performance of their duties, 5 U.S.C.A. § 8130; federal civil service retirement, 5 U.S.C.A. § 8346(a); compensation and benefits paid under the Longshoremen's and Harbor Workers' Compensation Act, 33 U.S.C.A. § 916; annuities paid pursuant to the Railroad Retirement Act, 45 U.S.C.A. § 231m, and Railroad unemployment insurance benefits, 45 U.S.C.A. § 352(e); annuities paid to members of the armed forces or their survivors, 10 U.S.C.A. §§ 1440 & 1450(i); a foreign nation's property within the United States (except as otherwise provided by statute or international agreement), 28 U.S.C.A. § 1609; annuities to survivors of certain United States judicial officials, 28 U.S.C.A. § 376(n); injury or death compensation payments from war risk hazards, 42 U.S.C.A. § 1717; and seamen's clothing, 46 U.S.C.A. § 11110.

Section 522 also imposes some limits on a debtor's homestead exemption even if the source of the exemption is state law. For example, the "debtor may not exempt any amount of interest [in her homestead exceeding $125,000] that was acquired by the debtor during the 1215–day period preceding the date" bankruptcy was filed.

Suppose, for example, that before this period, the debtor's homestead was worth $300,000. During this period, before she eventually filed bankruptcy, the debtor added a couple of rooms and an additional acre of land, and the value of the homestead increased to $500,000. For the sake of simplicity, also suppose that state law governs her exemptions, and the state-law homestead exemption is unlimited in size and value and, in this example, is therefore $500,000. Nevertheless, because of the 522 limitation, the debtor's homestead exemption would be limited to $425,000. The increase in value of the debtor's exemptible interest acquired during the 1215–day period, which is actually $200,000, is limited to $125,000.

In reality, this limitation and the other limitations that section 522 impose on the debtor's homestead exemption will almost never apply in the typical Chapter 7 case. First, state-law homestead exemptions are commonly very limited, as in North Carolina where the Kaddours' homestead exemption is limited to $18,500. Second, the typical Chapter 7 debtor typically lacks the means to grow her homestead exemption any where near $125,000 during the 1215–day period before she files bankruptcy.

In sum, please notice something very important: the total of the debtor's exemptions equals or exceeds the total equity of the bankruptcy estate (equity meaning the value of the debtor's interest in property exceeding the amount of all liens and other encumbrances the trustee cannot avoid). If the exemptions stand, and if the trustee cannot find or recover other property for the estate by use of her avoiding powers or otherwise, the value of the estate—that would have been distributed to unsecured creditors—is completely exhausted by the debtor's claim of exemptions. The case is a "no-asset" case. It's true of the Kaddours' case. It's true of the typical individual Chapter 7 case everywhere.

(1) Valuation and Stripping Liens From Exempt Property

Remember that many of the exemptions available to the Kaddours under North Carolina law are limited in value. The homestead exemption is limited to the debtor's "aggregate interest, not to exceed eighteen thousand five hundred dollars ($18,500) in value...." The exemption for a vehicle is "the debtor's interest, not to exceed three thousand five hundred dollars ($3,500) in value ...."

Remember, too, that these laws do not exempt the house or vehicle itself. They exempt the debtor's interest in the property; and the debtor's interest is, for all practical purposes, the debtor's equity in the property, which is the market value of the property less the amount of consensual liens and maybe some other kinds of liens on the property.

So, although North Carolina allows an $18,000 homestead exemption, the Kaddours' homestead exemption was limited to $2,735.77 which was the amount of their equity in the mobile home (market value of the mobile home less the two mortgages). The same math applies to the vehicle exemption; and, therefore, the Kaddours could not exempt anything with respect to either the Dodge truck or the Chrysler Pacifica because they had no equity whatsoever in either vehicle.

In theory, a debtor can attack in two, principal ways this problem of exemptions being diluted or worthless because of liens on the property. First, the debtor can state and argue for a market value of the property that exceeds the value of the liens (probably, but only coincidentally, a market value that equals or exceeds the total of the amount of the liens and the size of the allowable exemption). This strategy is shaky because the debtor's valuation of property, in her schedules or otherwise, is not final and conclusive. The trustee or secured creditor can challenge the debtor's valuation; and the market value will be determined by the court (1) conducting a hearing in which the judge hears everybody's evidence of value and decides, as a fact, the property's market value or (2) allowing a sale of the property that determines the true market value and then allowing the debtor to claim her exemption from any surplus proceeds that remain after satisfying the liens.

The debtor's other possible attack is based on section 522(f). It gives the debtor the power, with court agreement, to avoid certain liens on certain property when the liens "impair" an exemption. Impair basically means that the lien prevents the debtor from exempting an interest in property that she could have exempted *but for* the lien on the property, i.e., if the lien didn't exist at all or to some extent. The debtor's section 522(f) avoiding power is different from and in addition to the trustee's avoiding powers; and these powers belong to the debtor rather than the trustee.

Be forewarned: the avoiding powers under section 522(f) are very limited. They work only against a judicial lien or a nonpossessory, nonpurchase-money security interest in certain kinds of personal property. In practice, section 522(f) is rarely used successfully to any significant effect, but here's a short explanation of when it's supposed to work and why it's usually of no use to a Chapter 7 debtor.

Section 522(f) begins by providing: "the debtor may avoid the fixing of a lien on an interest of the debtor in property to the extent that such lien impairs an exemption to which the debtor would have been entitled .... if such lien is ... a judicial lien...." A judicial lien is a "lien obtained by judgment, levy, sequestration, or other legal or equitable process or proceeding."

For example, suppose that before bankruptcy, a creditor gets such a judicial lien on the debtor's boat. The market value of the boat is $15,000, which is also the amount of the debt the judicial lien secures.

Debtor files bankruptcy. State law governs exemptions, and this law allows the debtor to exempt her interest in a boat not to exceed $5,000. Apart from section 522(f), this exemption is worthless to the debtor because she lacks any equity in the boat. On the basis of section 522(f), however, the debtor can avoid the judicial lien to the extent of $5,000 (the amount of the allowable exemption) and use the exemption to take this value from the estate. The judicial lienor is left with a $10,000 secured claim and a $5,000 unsecured claim.

In most cases, however, section 522(f) doesn't work this way and adds nothing in terms of protecting the debtor's exemptions. The reason is that state law usually controls the debtor's exemptions in bankruptcy; and state law itself usually prevents a judicial lien from attaching to property to the extent that state law exempts the debtor's interest in the property. So, in this example, the creditor's judicial lien—before and after bankruptcy—would attach to the boat, by reason of state law, only to the extent of $10,000. Thus, the debtor's exemption would not have been impaired; and section 522(f), by its own terms, would not apply and would not be necessary.

Section 522(f) also empowers the debtor, within large limits, to avoid security interests, which the Code defines as "a lien created by an agreement." This power is potentially a bigger deal than avoiding judicial liens because most states do not exempt property from consensual liens.

The power to avoid security interests, however, is very small. To begin with, the power is limited to nonpossessory, nonpurchase-money security interests. In the typical, individual Chapter 7 case, the security interests that impair exemptions are purchase-money security interests. In the Kaddours' case, the creditors holding liens on the Dodge truck and the Chrysler Pacifica are probably the creditors who financed the purchase of the vehicle. So, their liens are purchase-money security interests. Section 522(f) won't work against them.

Also, even the power to avoid nonpurchase-money security interests is limited to such interests in a limited set of property:

- household furnishings, household goods, wearing apparel, appliances, books, animals, crops, musical instruments, or jewelry that are held primarily for the personal, family, or household use of the debtor or a dependent of the debtor;
- implements, professional books, or tools of the trade of the debtor or the trade of a dependent of the debtor; or
- professionally prescribed health aids for the debtor or a dependent of the debtor.

In the real world, creditors may very occasionally finance the purchase of some of these kinds of property and take purchase-money interests in the property; but they don't typically create nonpurchase-money interests to secure debts otherwise incurred. An exception is a pawn shop, but section 522(f) won't apply in such a case because the debtor's section 522(f) power to avoid security interests is limited to *nonpossessory*, nonpurchase-money interests. A pawn shop's security interest, if any, is nonpurchase-money but is also possessory and therefore beyond the scope of section 522(f).

Furthermore, some or all of the personal property section 522(f) protects against security interests is, to some extent, already exempted by some states' exemptions laws, which therefore separately renders the section 522(f) avoiding power unnecessary and not useful. An example is North Carolina where the stout, general rule, as everywhere else, is that exemptions are ineffective against consensual liens. North Carolina, however, recognizes a tiny exception by giving a tiny exemption against nonpossessory, non-purchase money security interests in the debtor's household goods. This exemption makes moot a significant chunk of section 522(f) because state law already immunizes the debtor's interest in these goods.

On the form "Chapter 7 Individual Debtor's Statement of Intention," which the Kaddours filed along with the bankruptcy petition, they claimed the Dodge truck and the Chrysler Pacifica as exempt property. With respect to each vehicle, they added this notation: "avoid lien." We're not sure about Larry's strategy because we don't know all the facts.

We do know, however, that avoidance under section 522(f) is unlikely. The liens are not judicial liens. They are security interests. However, they are also probably purchase-money security interests; also, vehicles don't fit within the categories of exempt property that section 522(f) protects even against non-purchase-money security interests. Section 522(f) won't work against the vehicles. For all these same reasons, the two mortgages on the homestead are safe from attack under section 522(f). For similar reasons, too, the small, state-law exemption against security interests does not apply.

Maybe Larry knows facts that would allow use of the trustee's very different, more powerful avoiding powers. However, the necessary facts are not commonly present, and even then the debtor cannot assert these powers. The trustee alone owns them.

We're sure, however, that Larry knows what he's doing. We don't know what's he doing because we lack Larry's full knowledge of the facts and circumstances and also lack his level of expertise in handling consumer cases in North Carolina.

In the end, the liens on the Kaddours' vehicles probably can't be avoided by the debtors under section 522(f) or by the trustee otherwise. This outcome would mirror what happens in the typical individual Chapter 7 case: nobody avoids any liens with respect to any property.

(2) Somebody Objecting to Exemptions

Sometimes, though not regularly, the trustee or a creditor will disagree in some respect with the debtor's claim of exemptions, and she can take her disagreement to the bankruptcy judge by "objecting." "[A] party in interest may file an objection to the list of property claimed as exempt within 30 days after the [section 341(a)] meeting of creditors ... or within 30 days after any amendment to the list or supplemental schedule is filed, whichever is later."[27] A hearing is held; the objecting party has the burden of proving that the exemptions are not properly claimed by the debtor; and the bankruptcy judge decides the matter.

Three kinds of objections are typical. The person objecting argues that a particular piece of property the debtor claims as exempt doesn't fit within the terms of any applicable exemption law. For example, a fur coat is not "necessary clothing." Another reason for objecting is that the size or value of the property the debtor claims as exempt exceeds the limitations of the exemption statute. For example, the exemption law allows exempting "the debtor's interest in a fur coat not to exceed $2,000," and the trustee or creditor argues that the debtor's fur coat is worth $5,000. (We have already explained alternative ways for resolving such disputes as to value.)

The third typical objection is that the debtor has offended or not satisfied some other qualification the exemption law imposes. Good examples are parts of section 522 that limit or deny a debtor's claim of homestead, even when state law governs exemptions,

27. Fed. R. Bankr. P. 4003(b)(1).

because of certain conduct by the debtor, including making fraudulent transfers or having being convicted of certain crimes.

In the typical, individual case, the Chapter 7 debtor will try to fit everything she owns, to the fullest extent possible, within the allowable exemptions, as did the Kaddours. Often, because the typical debtor doesn't own much property, the exemptions actually, fully cover everything she owns, that is, cover all of the debtor's interests in property. It seems true in the Kaddours' case.

So, it's not uncommon for lawyers, as a routine matter, to list all of a debtor's property as exempt. If it happens that some of the property isn't covered by any applicable exemption law, the trustee or creditors must object within the 30–day period. Otherwise, the property is exempted even though the debtor had no colorable basis for claiming the exemption.[28] In practice, it's called a "default" exemption.

(d) Unsecured Creditors Get What's Left

Stop for just a minute and remember what's happening to the Kaddours' creditors. Before bankruptcy, the creditors are owed money by the debtor who is personally liable to them for these obligations. The creditors have rights against the debtor under non-bankruptcy law to collect the money owed them.

When the debtor files bankruptcy, however, all of these creditors' rights are stayed; and, during the case, the debtor's personal liability to all of the creditors will be discharged. So, when the case ends, the creditors can't take any action to enforce this liability.

In theory, bankruptcy provides an alternative "remedy" for the creditor. She files a proof of claim against the bankruptcy estate. The proof of claim basically describes the kind and amount of the obligation the debtor owes her. The trustee can challenge the existence or size of the obligation the creditor alleges in the proof of claim, but such a challenge is very uncommon in the typical case and didn't happen in the Kaddours' case.

Creditors who have filed proofs of claims are then paid from the estate which the trustee has liquidated. Remember, though, that the estate—what the trustee liquidates—is only the debtor's prepetition interests in property (value beyond liens) reduced by the prepetition property the debtor gets to keep (i.e., exclusions and exemptions). So, the estate is heavily discounted.

Moreover, when the trustee finally begins distributing the estate, certain "priority" claims are paid from the net estate before

28. Taylor v. Freeland & Kronz, 503 U.S. 638 (1992); see also 11 U.S.C.A. § 522(*l*) ("Unless a party in interest objects, the property claimed as exempt on ... [the debtor's list of exempt property] is exempt.").

the typical, unsecured creditor gets anything. These priority claims include administrative expenses and domestic support obligations, which can be very large. The net-net, after accounting for liens and paying priority claims, is then paid pro rata to creditors with unsecured claims.

Secured creditors don't participate in this distribution. Remember: their liens generally aren't substantively affected by the debtor's bankruptcy. A secured creditor may convince the court, during the case, to lift the stay so that the creditor can enforce her lien. In any event, the lien survives the case and is enforceable after the case ends. The discharge stops creditors from trying to enforce personal liability. The discharge does not prevent creditors or anybody else from enforcing their property interests; and a lien is a property interest.

Of course, to the extent that the creditor's collateral is less than the amount of the debt, the creditor has an unsecured claim. This part of the creditor's claim can be paid from the estate; and any remaining balance is personal liability that is within the discharge and cannot be collected from the debtor after the case ends.

In reality, as in the Kaddours' case, the estate is empty. There is little or nothing of value for the trustee to liquidate and distribute. It's a no-asset case, and creditors with secured claims don't even bother to file proofs of claims.

§ 16.6 Statement of Intention and the Kaddours' Home and Vehicles

Among the many schedules and forms that Larry filed along with the Kaddours' bankruptcy petition was a "Chapter 7 Individual Debtor's Statement of Intention." This form is required by section 521 whenever "an individual debtor's schedule of assets and liabilities includes debts which are secured by property of the estate." In this event, the debtor must file a form, the "Statement of Intention," stating "his intention with respect to the retention or surrender of such property and, if applicable, specifying that such property is claimed as exempt, that the debtor intends to redeem such property, or that the debtor intends to reaffirm debts secured by such property."

The Kaddours' schedules include debts secured by property of the estate: the debts owed with respect to the mobile home (their homestead), the Dodge truck, and the Chrysler Pacifica. So, their filing included the section 521 "Statement of Intention."

With respect to the mobile home, the Kaddours declared (surely on Larry's advice) that they would "retain [the] collateral and continue to make regular payments." Elsewhere, we have already discussed matters that explain this strategy and also the tiny extent to which the mobile home is exempt as their homestead.

With respect to the two vehicles, their "Statement of Intention" claims both of them as exempt and adds the notation "avoid lien." Elsewhere, too, we have already discussed that the debtors have no exemptible interest in the vehicles unless the liens of M & I and Wells Fargo can be avoided to some extent, which doesn't seem likely.

Surrendering the vehicles was an option. Surrender means giving the vehicles to the secured creditors who would sell them and file unsecured claims against the estate for deficiencies. In this case, these claims would go unpaid because the estate is essentially empty, but the Kaddours' liability for the deficiencies would be discharged. So, why didn't Larry advise the Kaddours to surrender the Dodge and Chrysler? The likely answer is simple: the Kaddours needed or wanted them.

Redeeming the vehicles under section 722 is, in theory, another option. The Kaddours would pay each creditor's secured claim, which is less than the full amount owed each creditor, and own the vehicles free and clear of liens. In reality, though, redemption isn't possible. It requires the debtors to pay each creditor's secured claim in full at the time of redemption, which means the Kaddours would have to find and pay M & I and Wells Fargo a total of $32,175 (the total of these creditors' secured claims).

Probably, the Kaddours and Larry would prefer that the debtors make their contract payments on the vehicles and simply allow the vehicle liens quietly to "ride through" the case without objection by the secured creditors. The discharge would not extinguish the liens; but, after the bankruptcy case ends, the debtors would continue making payments so that the secured creditors would have no cause to enforce their liens.

This approach probably won't work. First, a "ride through" is not an option that section 521 allows. Second, this approach would not necessarily appease M & I and Wells Fargo. The discharge would discharge the undersecured portions of the debts the Kaddours owe them. So, if the Kaddours defaulted after bankruptcy, the creditors could enforce their liens but could not sue for the likely large deficiencies.

So, during the bankruptcy case, M & I and Wells Fargo could make motions to lift stay. The court would likely grant the motions. The Kaddours would lose the vehicles they need or want to keep.

To avoid this result, the Kaddours could—and eventually did—agree to reaffirm the debts to M & I and Wells Fargo. Reaffirmation is an agreement between the debtor and a creditor in which the debtor promises to pay some of or the debtor's entire contract obligation, including any unsecured portion which bankruptcy will discharge. Bankruptcy law permits but closely scrutinizes reaffirmation agreements. An elaborate procedure exists to help insure that the debtor fully understands what she's doing and is doing so "freely." The end of this procedure is a hearing at which the bankruptcy judge must approve the agreement. The essential effect of a court approving a reaffirmation agreement is to sanction and re-instate the original contract between the debtor and the creditor and continue the debtor's personal liability for the full amount of the debt after the case ends.

Assuming court approval under bankruptcy law, a reaffirmation agreement is essentially a contract that survives bankruptcy and is enforceable, after bankruptcy, under state law. The creditor gives no new consideration, but state law enforces the contract despite the lack of consideration because of the old, exceptional rule "for promises to perform what could be regarded as a 'moral obligation.' "[29]

In the Kaddours' case, they made reaffirmation agreements with three creditors: Wells Fargo with respect to the Chrysler Pacifica; M & I with respect to the Dodge truck; and Select Portfolio with respect to the first mortgage on their mobile home. In each case, they promised to pay the creditor the full amount of the debt, not just the amount of the secured debt. So, if the debtors' default on any of these debts after bankruptcy, the creditor can enforce the lien and sue the debtors to hold them personally liable for any deficiency. In effect, because of the reaffirmation agreements, the discharge does not apply in any respect to these debts.

§ 16.7 Deciding Whether or Not to Dismiss the Case for "Abuse"

Any individual can file a Chapter 7 case. The Bankruptcy Code imposes no prerequisites, except the credit counseling briefing within 180 days before filing the case. However, an individual or anybody else who files Chapter 7 gets no guarantee of staying in Chapter 7 and has no absolute right to a discharge or other benefits that Chapter 7 provides debtors.

A discharge is limited and qualified, which we discuss later.

More important, a Chapter 7 case can be dismissed which means: the debtor must seek relief under another chapter of the Bankruptcy Code for which she qualifies, or, if she chooses not to seek the other relief, the debtor is shut out of and off from any

29. E. Allan Farnsworth, Contracts § 2.8 at 55 (3d ed. 1999).

bankruptcy protection. In this event, the debtor's rights against creditors are limited to the rights provided by state and nonbankruptcy, federal law, which are very tiny compared to a debtor's rights under bankruptcy law.

An individual, consumer debtor's Chapter 7 case can be dismissed for failing to comply with process or if the bankruptcy court "finds that the granting of relief would be an abuse of [Chapter 7] . . . ." Abuse is defined by three, alternative standards: filing the case in bad faith; the totality of circumstances; and the debtor having the financial means to repay a certain, statutory-prescribed percentage of her debts from future income during a three-to five-year period under a Chapter 13 plan. This last test for abuse is called the "means test." If the debtor fails this test, that is, she has such means, the court will dismiss the case unless the debtor agrees to convert the case to Chapter 13.

Applying the means test is somewhat complicated and requires a lot of math. We don't do math. So, we'll keep the explanation of means testing pretty simple.

Preliminarily, note that the completed forms that a debtor files with her bankruptcy petition require information about income and living expenses necessary for means testing. The debtor herself, in completing these forms, will do the math for deciding if she passes or fails the means test. The court, however, doesn't necessarily take the debtor's word for it. In every Chapter 7 case of an individual, consumer debtor, the United States Trustee (or Bankruptcy Administrator) is required to review the debtor's math and calculations and independently report if the debtor passes or fails the means test. Also, creditors and the court itself, on its own motion, can challenge a debtor's calculation that she passes the test.

Basically, means testing involves maybe two steps. The first step is always required: deciding whether or not the debtor is even subject to the means test. The test applies only if the combined, annualized, current monthly income (CMI) of the debtor and the debtor's spouse is more than the state median annual income for a family the size of the debtor's family. The forms a debtor files includes information for making this determination. Take a look at the Kaddours' Schedule I and Parts II and III of their "Statement of Current Monthly Income and Means Test Calculation" form.

The income of the typical Chapter 7 debtor is below the applicable median. Therefore, in the typical Chapter 7 case, the means test does not apply.

In this respect, the Kaddours and their case are atypical. Their annualized CMI ($67,308.84) exceeded the applicable state median ($55,117.00). Therefore, the means test applied in their case, and they and we must go to the second step of means testing.

The second step, which is reached only if the means test applies, is calculating whether or not the debtors' projected disposable income during the next three to five years is sufficient to pay a certain percentage of the unsecured debts they owed when they filed their petition. This calculation is performed in Parts IV, V, and VI of the "Statement of Current Monthly Income and Means Test Calculation."

If the debtor fails this test, which means she has sufficient disposable income to pay the statutorily-prescribed percentage of her unsecured debt, then a "presumption" of abuse arises. The debtor has the opportunity to rebut this presumption, but the grounds for rebuttal are narrowly tiny. Except in the rarest case, the presumption is not rebutted. As a result, the case is dismissed unless the debtor agrees to convert the case to Chapter 13.

By their own calculation (see Line 52 on Form B22A), the Kaddours passed the means test. Indeed, their disposable income is a negative number! And, if you look at the docket in the Kaddours case, which is reprinted earlier, you'll see that the Bankruptcy Administrator agreed and so reported to the court. So, the Kaddours' case could not be dismissed for failing the means test. Dismissal was still possible on the other, alternative grounds of bad faith and totality of circumstances, but nobody challenged their Chapter 7 case on these grounds.

The result could have been different, and the Kaddours could have failed the means test, or otherwise had their Chapter 7 case dismissed, if their calculations for means testing had been challenged and found wrong. Also, the Kaddours could have failed the means test if their income was somewhat higher, or they had filed bankruptcy in another state where the standard of living is lower and the allowable deductions used in calculating disposable income are smaller. In this event, their choice would be: convert to Chapter 13 or forgo any and all bankruptcy protection.

§ 16.8 How and Why the Trustee Finally Decides to Handle the Case

Remember that very soon after Larry filed the Kaddours' petition and accompanying stuff, their case was assigned to a Chapter 7 panel/case trustee. His job was to liquidate the estate and distribute the proceeds to unsecured creditors. Remember, too, that the estate consists of the debtor's interests in property less the property the debtors exempt and does not include the debtors' interests in property excluded from the estate.

Well, on the face of the Kaddours' filings, the Kaddours' bankruptcy estate was empty. The debtors had no equity in property (market value of the property less encumbrances) except the property they exempted.

Apparently, the section 341(a) creditors' meeting turned up no additional property. The trustee did not independently investigate, and he believed the Kaddours had reported everything they owned. Also, the trustee didn't uncover any significant, prepetition transfers of property that he could avoid and retrieve for the estate.

In the trustee's judgment, the bottom line was: the Kaddours' case was a "no asset" case, which means no property exists (or none that is worth selling) and thus nothing is available to distribute to creditors. Look at the docket, and you'll see that the trustee reported this conclusion to the bankruptcy court. Essentially, therefore, the trustee's job is done and he's finished with the case. Officially, however, he's still on the job in the unlikely event that something comes up that requires a case trustee's attention.

The trustee's conclusion that the Kaddours' case was a no-asset case is not atypical. Indeed, trustees across the country routinely reach the same conclusion in the vast majority of Chapter 7 cases filed by individual, consumer debtors.

§ 16.9 Kaddours' Debts (Some of Them) Get Discharged (or Not)

The Kaddours' main goal in filing Chapter 7 was to get a bankruptcy "discharge."

Section 727 provides that "[t]he court shall grant the debtor a discharge unless . . ." any of the reasons or circumstances for denying a discharge, which section 727 lists, is present. These circumstances are called "objections" to discharge.

Any party in interest, including creditors, can initiate a proceeding (by complaint) to object to a discharge on the basis of the reasons listed in section 727. Such a complaint, however, must be filed no later than 60 days after the first date set for the section 341(a) meeting of creditors. If a complaint is timely filed, the court conducts a trial on the complaint; and the plaintiff—the person who is objecting to the discharge—has the burden of proving the objection.

If no complaint objecting to discharge is timely filed, "the court shall forthwith grant the discharge" except for a few, small reasons of process or if the debtor "has not filed with the court a statement regarding completion of a course in personal financial management . . . ." The debtor completing such a course is required for discharge.

As is typical, no complaint objecting to discharge was filed in the Kaddours' case. If you look at the docket, you'll see that the

Kaddours filed certificates of having completed a financial management course; and you'll also see that the judge thereafter, on May 12, 2006, entered an order discharging the debtors. The order is one sentence: the debtors are "granted a discharge under section 727 of title 11, United States Code (the Bankruptcy Code)."

Different from objections are "exceptions" to discharge, which are listed in section 523. An objection to discharge is a reason why none of the debtor's obligations will be discharged. An exception to discharge is a reason for shielding a particular debt from the effects of discharge.

The exception to discharge most important to law students is the exception for student loans. In every kind of bankruptcy case, educational loans and similar credit owed by an individual debtor is unaffected by the discharge whether the loans are government sponsored or private. There is a limitation on this exception: student loans can be discharged to the extent that not doing so "would impose an undue hardship on the debtor and the debtor's dependents." To take advantage of this limitation, the debtor must initiate a proceeding before the bankruptcy court and prove that requiring her to repay her student loans constitutes an undue hardship. Trust us: convincing a bankruptcy judge of "undue hardship" is very difficult and rarely accomplished. So, it's a good thing the Kaddours had no student loans.

Except for a few exceptions to discharge, they are not litigated during the bankruptcy case. Instead, an exception is claimed after bankruptcy if a creditor sues the debtor—in state or nonbankruptcy, federal court—and the debtor's defense is the bankruptcy discharge. Read on and, within a few paragraphs, you'll better understand how this works.

Among the exceptions that must be decided during the bankruptcy case is the so-called "credit card" exception, though the language of the exception says nothing about credit cards. It's section 523(a)(2)(C). Here's generally how it works.

The opening language is section 523(a)(2): an individual debtor is not discharged from "any debt ... for money property, services, or an extension or refinancing of credit to the extent obtained by ..." and then the section lists two circumstances in subsections (a)(2)(A) & (B). They are debts obtained by:

(A) false pretenses, a false representation, or actual fraud, other than a statement respecting the debtor's or an insider's financial condition; or

(B) use of a statement in writing (i) that is materially false; (ii) respecting the debtor's or an insider's financial condition; [and] (iii) on which the creditor to whom the debtor is liable for such money, property, services, or credit reasonably relied.

This language is the foundation for excepting credit card debt in most bankruptcy cases in which any such debt is excepted from the discharge, which is a small percentage of cases. The language, however, says nothing specifically about credit card debt, and proving the circumstances required by section 523(a)(2)(A) & (B) is very difficult and not commonly done.

The kicker is section 523(a)(2)(C) which presumes that a certain amount of consumer debts incurred shortly before bankruptcy are presumed nondischargeable for purposes of section 523(a)(2)(A). These debts are:

- consumer debts owed to a single creditor and aggregating more than $500 for luxury goods or services incurred . . . on or within 90 days before filing bankruptcy, and
- cash advances aggregating more than $750 that are extensions of consumer credit . . . on or within 70 days before filing bankruptcy.

Although section 523(a)(2) doesn't use the words "credit card," this section—because of the subsection (C) presumption—is typically the basis for excepting credit card debt. However, it doesn't commonly happen; and, even in a case in which credit card debt is excepted under section 523(a)(2)(A) & (C), relatively small amounts of debt ($500 and $700) are excepted. The amounts of credit card debt excepted are small in comparison to the typically large amounts discharged.

Also, to except any debts under section 523(a)(2), the creditor must initiate a proceeding requesting the court to grant the exception. The court then makes the determination after notice and a hearing. Moreover, if the creditor loses, the court "shall" award costs and attorney's fees if the court also finds that the creditor's argument for the exception was not substantially justified.

The Kaddours' credit card debts amounted to almost $44,000. None of the creditors who were owed this money asked the court for an exception to the Kaddours' discharge. So, all of the Kaddours' credit card debts were discharged, which is pretty typical.[30]

So, what's the effect of a bankruptcy discharge? According to section 727, "a discharge . . . discharges the debtor from all debts that arose before the date of the order for relief under this chapter

30. A commonly held suspicion is that the 2005 amendments to the Bankruptcy Code were the work of the "greedy" credit card companies. We don't know if these companies are truly greedy. We do know, however, that any benefits from the 2005 amendments are not based on creating a really generous, easy exception of credit card debts from the discharge.

[which means the time the petition was filed] ...." Section 524, which applies in all kinds of bankruptcy cases, is more specific in providing that a discharge:

- voids any judgment at any time obtained, to the extent that such judgment is a determination of the personal liability of the debtor with respect to any debt discharged under section 727 ..., whether or not discharge of such debt is waived; [and]
- operates as an injunction against the commencement or continuation of an action, the employment of process, or an act, to collect, recover or offset any such debt as a personal liability of the debtor, whether or not discharge of such debt is waived; * * *

Carefully notice four things. First, the discharge does not extinguish any debt. It creates an injunction against creditors acting to collect debts that are discharged. So, if a creditor sues the debtor after bankruptcy in state or nonbankruptcy, federal court, the debtor will assert the bankruptcy discharge as a defense. If the creditor responds that her claim was not discharged because it's not a debt that fits section 524 or 727, or is a debt that is excepted from the discharge under section 523, the court where the action is pending will interpret and apply these sections of bankruptcy law; and this court will decide whether or not the plaintiff's claim was discharged by the debtor's earlier bankruptcy. On these issues, the parties will not return to the bankruptcy court because the bankruptcy case is closed and, for the most part, the bankruptcy court no longer has jurisdiction.

Second, the discharge applies only to debts that arose before the debtor filed her bankruptcy case. Debts incurred thereafter are not affected by the discharge.

Third, the subject of the discharge, i.e., the debt that is discharged, is the debtor's personal liability for the debt. Liens that are not avoided during the bankruptcy are not affected by the discharge, which is especially important with respect to undersecured debts. For example, suppose the debtor owed a creditor $20,000 on a prepetition debt which was secured by collateral worth only $15,000. After bankruptcy, and despite the discharge, the creditor can enforce her lien on the property according to her rights under state law and any relevant contract between the parties. If and when circumstances occur allowing the creditor to enforce her lien, the bankruptcy discharge does not stop her. However, the discharge does prevent the creditor from acting to collect the $5,000 deficiency. Under other law, the debtor remains personally liable for the deficiency; but the bankruptcy discharge gives her a defense to this personal liability.

Fourth, which is an exception to the third, the discharge does not shield the debtor from personal liability on a prepetition debt, including any deficiency owed an undersecured creditor, if debtor effectively reaffirmed the full amount of the debt during the bankruptcy case. Remember: the Kaddours reaffirmed the full amounts of the debts owed Select Portfolio (first mortgage on the mobile home), M & I (lien on the Dodge truck), and Wells Fargo (lien on the Chrysler Pacifica). Remember, too, that reaffirmation agreements with secured creditors are typical in Chapter 7 cases.

In the end, therefore, see who's really affected by the bankruptcy discharge in the typical, individual Chapter 7 case. Look at the Kaddours' Schedule F, which lists creditors holding unsecured, nonpriority claims. Together, the creditors listed there are owed almost $44,000. None of them got a dime from the bankruptcy case. The discharge enjoins all of them from suing the debtor, after the bankruptcy case, for anything they are owed, except to the extent that any of the debts is excepted from the discharge under section 523. Probably, none of the debts is excepted.

The Kaddours end up keeping and walking away with their property and walking away from $44,000 of personal liability. The $1,800 or so they paid for Larry's services and bankruptcy fees was a pretty good investment. (Are you still wondering where they got the $1,800?)

On the other hand, the Kaddours' credit score is affected. For many years, their credit report will show their bankruptcy. Also, even though section 525 gives them some protection against discriminatory treatment, creditors are generally free to refuse loans and any other credit because of the Kaddours' bankruptcy.

In reality, however, lots of credit is always, almost immediately available—for a price—to debtors who have been discharged in Chapter 7. A related reality is that the Kaddours or any other debtor discharged in Chapter 7 is ineligible for another Chapter 7 discharge at any time during the next eight years.

§ 16.10 Kaddours' Case Ends and is Closed

The Kaddours' bankruptcy case was filed on January 21, preceded by a couple of weeks of activity and preparatory work by them and Larry. Lots of stuff was filed which triggered activity by the bankruptcy court and the trustee, who had lots of questions, issues, and work that he could potentially pursue with the right facts. Early in the Kaddours' case, however, it became clear to the trustee and the court that those facts weren't present in this case. It was a no-asset case. Consequently, very little activity occurred beyond the usual creditors' meeting, reaffirmation agreements, and pro forma entry of discharge.

Therefore and thereafter, the case ended by the court entering a final decree which simply provided:

> "The estate of the above named debtor(s) has been fully administered.
>
> "IT IS ORDERED THAT:
>
> > "[The trustee] is discharged as trustee of the estate of the above named debtor[s].
> >
> > "The Chapter 7 case of the above named debtor[s] is closed."

On May 22, the bankruptcy judged signed and dated the decree, which was almost exactly five months after the petition was filed.

Upon the closing of a case, the section 362 automatic stay ends; but, to some extent, the discharge injunction has taken its place. The bankruptcy court is done with the case and, essentially, loses jurisdiction. In theory, the court can reopen a closed Chapter 7 case, but it's rare and doesn't ever happen in the typical case. We're pretty sure it won't happen in the Kaddours' case.

Unit 17

A TYPICAL CHAPTER 13 CASE

Table of Sections

---

§ 17.1 Good News and Bad News for the Kaddours

(a) Ahmed Gets a Raise

We met Ahmed and Irshad Kaddour in Unit 16 and followed and examined their Chapter 7 bankruptcy case. They made it through the process; kept all of their property; and discharged more than $40,000 in unsecured debt.

We also told you, however, that under certain circumstances, the Kaddours' case would have been dismissed, and they would have been forced to choose between converting their case to Chapter 13 and foregoing any kind of bankruptcy protection. The most likely circumstance that could have forced this choice is their failing the section 707(b) "means test" of Chapter 7 because: (1) their income was somewhat higher; (2) they lived and filed bankruptcy in another state where the standard of living is lower and allowable deductions are correspondingly lower; or, (3) a combination of higher income and smaller deductions.

In this unit, let's put the Kaddours in Chapter 13 and see how the process, issues, and outcome of their case are different from those same matters in Chapter 7. We'll keep them in North Carolina so the allowable deductions for means testing and otherwise are the same. Also, all of the financial and other factual information we reported about the Kaddours in Unit 16 still applies, except information about income. For purposes of this Unit 17, we'll make a change in their income which, as you'll see, prevents them from maintaining a Chapter 7 case.

Remember that Ahmed is an electrical engineer. His actual, annual, gross salary is close to $30,000. Nationally, the average, annual salary of an electrical engineer is about $50,000. So, for purposes of this unit, let's give Ahmed a raise. We're sure he's above-average, having spent some time in Minnesota years ago. However, for purposes of realism, let's just give him a $20,000 raise so that he's earning the national average of $50,000 a year. And let's make the raise effective six months before the bankruptcy filing.

This raise would increase the Kaddours' actual, net, monthly cash flow (as reported on their Forms I and J) by more than $1,000. Possibly, with this additional income, they would not need bankruptcy protection of any kind. It's not certain, however, because we don't know the exact demands from creditors on cash flow or the demands made by the Kaddours themselves with respect to their discretionary spending.

We'll assume that even with Ahmed's raise, he and Irshad decide to file bankruptcy. Their lawyer, Larry Friedman, whom we also met in Unit 16, will tell the Kaddours that a Chapter 7 case would be dismissed. If they want bankruptcy protection, their only practical option is filing a Chapter 13 case.[1]

(b) The Court Would Dismiss a Chapter 7 Case

Upon motion by the United States Trustee, a Chapter 7 case trustee, a creditor, or the bankruptcy court itself, a Chapter 7 case can be dismissed for various reasons, including "abuse." Abuse includes the debtor having the ability to repay a certain percentage of her debts over a period of years through a Chapter 13 plan. To a large extent, the percentage is set and calculated according to a complicated, statutorily-prescribed formula.

The Kaddours lacked this ability to repay their debts in the original bankruptcy case (Unit 16) and could therefore liquidate under Chapter 7. With Ahmed's raise, however, they are able to repay enough of their debts so that allowing them to stay in Chapter 7 would be an abuse; and they would be forced to choose between converting to Chapter 13 and foregoing any bankruptcy protection.

1. In theory, anyone who files a case under Chapter 13 could have filed, alternatively, under Chapter 11. In reality, filing under Chapter 11 makes no sense if you can file under Chapter 13.

Here's why. Go back to Unit 16 and look again at the "Statement of Current Monthly Income and Means Test Calculation," which Larry filed with the Kaddours' petition. In particular, look at lines 51 and 52 of the Statement. Line 51 reports the Kaddours' projected, disposable income over the next five years. Line 52 explains that if this amount is less than $6,000, the "presumption [of abuse] does not arise," which means they lack the ability to fund a Chapter 13 plan. They can stay in Chapter 7.

In the Kaddours' original case, their projected, disposable income over the next five years was less than $6,000. It was a negative number! They stayed in Chapter 7.

Now, let's factor in Ahmed's raise. Making $50,000 a year, his "current monthly gross" salary is $4,166.67. So, for purposes of line 12 of the "Statement of Current Monthly Income and Means Test," the "current monthly income [both debtors]" would be $7,349.07. The 60–month disposable income (after subtracting allowable deductions) for line 51 would be more than $10,000, and Line 52 would therefore direct that "the presumption [of abuse] arises;" which means a case filed under Chapter 7 would be dismissed. The Kaddours would be required to convert their case to Chapter 13 if they wanted any bankruptcy protection.

(c) How Chapter 13 is Different

Here's how a Chapter 13 case is fundamentally different from a Chapter 7 case. In Chapter 7, the debtor (in theory) loses her property to the bankruptcy estate. The trustee liquidates the estate and distributes the money to unsecured creditors. The debtor gets a discharge of personal liability for existing debts and gets to keep her right to future income and other property she acquires postpetition. In sum, existing debts are paid to some extent from existing property.

In Chapter 13, the debtor's interests in property pass to a bankruptcy estate, but the debtor keeps possession. The property is not sold to satisfy existing debts. Instead, the debtor submits a plan for court approval (confirmation) whereby she proposes to pay existing creditors from future income during the next several years, but the plan need not provide for paying creditors in full. The debtor gets a discharge when the plan is completed. In sum, existing debts are paid to some extent from future income. In theory and often in practice, unsecured creditors usually do better under Chapter 13 than they do under Chapter 7.

(d) Larry's Services (and Fee) Change

For the most part, everything written in Unit 16 about the Kaddours meeting Larry and Larry advising them is the same, except that he's advising them to file Chapter 13 instead of Chapter 7. Larry specializes in consumer bankruptcy cases. So, he's an expert in 13 as well as 7; and his office "systems," including people, handle 13s just as efficiently as they handle 7s.

By filing a Chapter 13 case, the Kaddours don't avoid having to provide Larry with all the information about their assets, liabilities, and incomes. They also don't avoid having to get a credit counseling briefing before Larry can file their case. The Bankruptcy Code requires such a briefing, within 180 days before the date of filing, for any "individual" filing any kind of bankruptcy case.

The Kaddours also don't avoid having to pay fees. The filing and other fees paid to the court for a Chapter 13 case are about the same as fees paid in a Chapter 7 case. However, Larry's fee for legal services is significantly higher in a Chapter 13 case. The fee can range between $2000 and $5000, depending on the services provided, market forces, and (most important) court approval.

The stuff Larry must file doesn't change much in a Chapter 13 case. However, Larry otherwise works more in a Chapter 13 case. He must develop a debt repayment, Chapter 13 "plan" that he can get the court to confirm, which we discuss later; and getting a plan confirmed sometimes requires fighting with the Chapter 13 trustee and creditors. Also, issues requiring Larry's attention may arise after a plan is confirmed while the debtor is repaying her debts under the plan.

Fortunately for the Kaddours, the lawyer's fee is typically not paid up front, at least not all of it. Much of the fee will be paid in installments under the Chapter 13 plan.

(e) What Larry Files—Form B22C

To commence the Kaddours' Chapter 13 case, Larry files basically the same stuff he filed to begin the Chapter 7 case described in Unit 16, with a few differences. The petition is the same with this difference: in the space for indicating the chapter of the Bankruptcy Code under which the petition is filed, Larry checks the box for Chapter 13 rather than the box for Chapter 7.

A bigger difference is that in a Chapter 13 case, the filing does not include a "Statement of Current Income and Means Test Calculation." Instead, Larry will file Form B22C, which is a "Statement of Current Monthly Income and Calculation of Commitment Period and Disposable Income." The two forms are similar and contain and use much of the same information; but they serve different purposes.

The statement filed in a Chapter 7 case determines whether or not the debtor can stay in Chapter 7 or is required to convert to

Chapter 13. Form B22C is filed only in a Chapter 13 case in which the debtor—over time—will repay existing debts. In calculating how much time, i.e., the "commitment period," Form B22C determines how long the plan lasts, i.e., how long the debtors must pay their future income to satisfy existing debts. The "disposable income" calculation determines how much of their total, gross income they must pay each month throughout the commitment period. The debtor wants the shortest possible commitment period and the smallest possible disposable income. Creditors want the opposite.

§ 17.2 The Chapter 13 Plan

With the Chapter 13 petition, or within 15 days of filing the petition, the debtor must file her Chapter 13 plan. This plan details how much money from future income the debtor intends to pay monthly to which creditors for some period of time. The amount of future income the debtor must commit to the plan, the creditors who are paid and which of them are preferred, and the length of the plan are matters the Bankruptcy Code regulates. They are also matters often disputed among the debtor, creditors, and Chapter 13 trustee.

(a) What the Statute Requires and Allows

The debtor's objectives in designing a Chapter 13 plan are to pay as little as possible of her future income for the shortest possible period of time. At first glance, the provisions of Chapter 13 governing the plan seem to allow the debtor great flexibility in achieving these objectives.

Section 1322(a) begins with the obvious: the plan must provide for the debtor submitting such portion of future income as is necessary for the execution of the plan. And, section 1322(b) describes what the plan "may" do, which includes modifying (i.e., eliminating) the rights of both unsecured and secured creditors. So, if the debtor can simply wipe out rights and debts, executing the plan isn't very costly.

On closer look, however, the Bankruptcy Code imposes some stringent, baseline requirements that significantly frustrate the debtor's quest to get through Chapter 13 quickly and cheaply. To begin with, the plan lasts for several years.

i. How Long (Commitment Period)

The length of the Chapter 13 plan, i.e., how long the debtor must pay her future income to existing creditors, is either three or five years. It's five years if the annualized current monthly income (CMI) of the debtor and the debtor's spouse equals or exceeds the applicable state median income for a family the size of the debtor's family. Otherwise, the plan is three years long, unless the court for cause approves a longer period not to exceed five years.

Debtors whose joint, annualized CMI is less than the state median are likely to file Chapter 7 and are not subject to means testing, which means they can stay in Chapter 7. Commonly, therefore, debtors who file Chapter 13 are the debtors whose joint, annualized CMI equals or exceeds the state median. So, the length of the plan in Chapter 13 cases is usually five years.

ii. How Much (Disposable Income)

In terms of the bottom line, a debtor's concern about the length of the plan is related to the amount of future income she is required to pay each month under the plan. The less she is required to pay, the less she is concerned with how long she must pay.

Chapter 13 establishes some minimums for how much the debtor must pay. To begin with, section 1322(a)(2) requires the plan to provide for the full payment, in deferred cash payments, of all priority claims. Assuming the debtor has no or only a few priority claims that aren't too large, this requirement isn't so bad. Each month, for five years, the debtor's income is reduced by the amount of these claims spread over a five-year period.

It gets considerably worse, however. The court must confirm the debtor's plan. Section 1325(a) sets out the requirements for confirmation. Two requirements are the most important. First, each unsecured creditor must be paid, over the life of the plan, as much as the creditor would have received if the debtor had filed a Chapter 7 case and the bankruptcy estate had been liquidated and distributed to creditors.

- So, the debtor's lawyer hypothesizes a Chapter 7 case to determine the amount that each unsecured creditor would have received from the hypothetical distribution of the hypothetical estate.
- This total is paid in installments over the entire life of the plan or some part of it.
- The lawyer then adds interest because section 1325(a) requires paying each unsecured creditor "the value" of what she would have received in a Chapter 7 "as of the effective date of the [Chapter 13] plan."

Well, this requirement isn't such a big deal because most unsecured creditors would have received nothing or very little if the debtor had filed and liquidated under Chapter 7. The same is probably true in the Kaddours' case. Just because Ahmed got a raise doesn't mean the couple would have owned more property to fund a Chapter 7 estate. Their unsecured creditors would still have received nothing.

The second, most important requirement for confirmation concerns secured creditors. Unless the holder of a secured claim agrees otherwise, the plan must provide that the secured creditor retains her lien and is paid the amount of her secured claim plus interest if the plan provides for paying the secured claim in installments. Here, as with unsecured claims, the "present value" requirement applies.

Again, this requirement isn't such a big deal when you consider (1) that secured claims would have been paid in full, one way or another, in or following a Chapter 7 case and also consider (2) that the debtor in Chapter 13 gets to keep all of her property. It's true that the debtor's interests in all her property pass to a bankruptcy estate, as in Chapter 7; but, in Chapter 13, nothing is sold and the debtor keeps possession of all the property whether or not the property is exempt. So, even though the debtor files a claim of exemptions in Chapter 13, as in Chapter 7, it's mostly a moot exercise in Chapter 13. Creditors are paid from future income, not present property.

Here's where things get bad for the debtor in Chapter 13. Upon objection (by motion) of any unsecured creditor or the trustee, the court cannot confirm a plan unless all of the debtor's disposable income for the next five years is committed to the plan. An unsecured creditor can thereby prevent confirmation and trigger this additional requirement even if the plan provides for paying the creditor the present value of her hypothetical Chapter 7 dividend.

See what's happening. The debtor has figured that with respect to unsecured claims, her future income will be reduced with respect to paying unsecured creditors only by the little amounts (if any) these creditors would have received in a Chapter 7 case. Moreover, the debtor can spread these payments on unsecured claims over five years (with interest). So, the debtor's monthly income really won't be largely affected by these payments.

The unsecured creditors see the same thing, and they don't like what they see. They believe that to the extent the debtor will earn "excess" income beyond what's necessary for the debtor's basic needs, the excess income should be paid to them. The Bankruptcy Code agrees.

So, because unsecured creditors will always object to a plan that only gives them amounts equaling Chapter 7 dividends, the debtor's plan must commit all of the debtor's projected "disposable income," for five years, to paying unsecured claims. "Disposable income" basically means the debtor's current monthly income (CMI) reduced by statutorily allowed deductions for reasonably necessary expenses for the maintenance or support of the debtor and family. When the debtor's annualized CMI is more than the state median family income, which is common in Chapter 13 cases, disposable income is basically calculated by subtracting, from the debtor's CMI, mostly the same deductions used in Chapter 7 means testing.

In essence, the debtor's monthly income is turned over, or paid directly, to the Chapter 13 trustee. The debtor gets an allowance for expenses (which is not overly generous), and the trustee pays the balance to creditors according to the terms of the Chapter 13 plan. This process repeats itself every month for the life of the plan unless, as often happens, the Chapter 13 case is dismissed because the debtor cannot complete the plan. In real life, many more Chapter 13 cases are dismissed than are completed.

(b) Calculating Commitment Period and Disposable Income

In preparing a Chapter 13 plan for the Kaddours, the starting place for Larry is the Form B22C that he filed with the Kaddours' bankruptcy petition. Using the information the Kaddours supply, Larry decides how to complete the B22C; and, in completing the form, Larry is calculating the "commitment period" of whatever plan he proposes and also the amount of "disposable income" the Kaddours must pay under the plan each month of the commitment period. So, here's the Form B22C filed in the Kaddours' Chapter 13 case preceded by Forms I and J which, as you'll see, report that actual net income is different from the disposable income calculated using Form B22C. We'll discuss later the significance of the difference.

Schedule I. Current Income of Individual Debtor(s)

INCOME: (Estimate of average monthly income)		DEBTOR	SPOUSE
1.	Current monthly gross wages, salary, and commissions	4,166.66	3,182.40
2.	Estimate monthly overtime	0.00	0.00
3.	SUBTOTAL	4,166.66	3,182.40
4.	LESS PAYROLL DEDUCTIONS		
	a. Payroll taxes and social security	514.39	593.95
	b. Insurance	0.00	498.03
	c. Union Dues	0.00	0.00
	d. Other (specify): 403(k)/401(k)	87.97	0.00
	401k		258.18
5.	SUBTOTAL OF PAYROLL DEDUCTIONS	602.36	1,350.16
6.	TOTAL NET MONTHLY TAKE HOME PAY	3,564.30	1,832.24
7.	Regular income from operation of business or profession or farm	0.00	0.00
8.	Income from real property	0.00	0.00
9.	Interest and dividends	0.00	0.00
10.	Alimony, maintenance or support payments payable to the debtor for the debtor's use or that of dependents listed above	0.00	0.00
11.	Social security or other government assistance	0.00	0.00
12.	Pension or retirement income	0.00	0.00

13.	Other monthly income (specify)	0.00	0.00
14.	SUBTOTAL OF LINES 7 THROUGH 13	0.00	0.00
15.	TOTAL MONTHLY INCOME (Add amounts shown on lines 6 and 14)	3,554.30	1,832.24
TOTAL COMBINED MONTHLY INCOME			$5,396.54
Describe any increase or decrease in income reasonably anticipated to occur within the year following the filing of this document:			

Schedule J. Current Expenditures of Individual Debtor(s)

1.	Rent or home mortgage payment (include lot rented for mobile home) a. Are real estate taxes included? NO b. Is property insurance included? NO	499.95
2.	Utilities a. Electricity and heating fuel b. Water and sewer c. Telephone d. Other: Cell phone Cable	 100.00 25.00 45.00 56.72 81.00
3.	Home maintenance (repairs and upkeep)	25.00
4.	Food	516.00
5.	Clothing	83.33
6.	Laundry and dry cleaning	0.00
7.	Medical and dental expenses	166.67
8.	Transportation (not including car payments)	480.00
9.	Recreation, clubs and entertainment, newspapers, magazines, etc.	25.00
10.	Charitable contributions	20.00
11.	Insurance (not deducted from wages or included in home mortgage payments) a. Homeowner's or renter's b. Life c. Health d. Auto e. Other:	 136.57 0.00 0.00 117.00 0.00
12.	Taxes (not deducted from wages or included in home mortgage payments) Specify: property taxes	70.30
13.	Installment payments: (In Chapter 11, 12 and 13 cases, do not list payments to be included in the plan.) a. Auto b. Other: Truck c. Other: Second mortgage	 561.00 428.00 100.00
14.	Alimony, maintenance, and support paid to others	0.00
15.	Payments for support of additional dependents not living at your home	0.00
16.	Regular expenses from operation of business, profession, or farm (attach detailed statement)	25.00
17.	Other: Miscellaneous Child care	 100.00 404.00
18.	TOTAL MONTHLY EXPENSES	4,065.54
19.	Describe any increase or decrease in expenditures reasonably anticipated to occur within the year following the filing of this document:	
20.	STATEMENT OF MONTHLY NET INCOME a. Total monthly income from Line 16 of Schedule I b. Total monthly expenses from Line 18 above c. **Monthly net income**	 5,396.54 4,065.54 **1,277.54**

Form B22C (Chapter 13) (10/05)

According to the calculations required by this statement [or form]:

- ☐ **The applicable commitment period is 3 years.**
- ■ **The applicable commitment period is 5 years.**
- ■ **Disposable income is determined under § 1325(b)(3).**
- ☐ **Disposable income is not determined under § 1325(b)(3).**

(Check the box as directed in Lines 17 and 23 of this statement.)

STATEMENT OF CURRENT MONTHLY INCOME AND CALCULATION OF COMMITMENT PERIOD AND DISPOSABLE INCOME

	Part I. Report of Income		
1	Marital/filing status [This space contains a set of boxes to check, and the Kaddours check the box "Married," which then requires completing Columns A and B for Lines 2–10 below.]	**Col A Debtor's Income**	**Col B Spouse's Income**
2	Gross wages, salary, tips, bonuses, overtime, commissions	4,166.66	3,182.40
3	Income from the operation of a business, profession or farm	0.00	0.00
4	Rents and other real property income	0.00	0.00
5	Interest, dividends, and royalties	0.00	0.00
6	Pension and retirement income	0.00	0.00
7	Regular contributions [from anyone] to the household expenses of the debtor or the debtor's dependents	0.00	0.00
8	Unemployment compensation	0.00	0.00
9	Income from all other sources	0.00	0.00
10	Subtotal. Add Lines 2 through 9 in Column A, and, if Column B is completed, add Lines 2 through 9 in Column B. Enter the total.	4,166.66	3,182.40
11	Total [both debtors]		7,349.06
	Part II. Calculation of § 1325(b)(4) Commitment Period		
12	Enter the amount from Line 11.		7,349.06
13	Marital adjustment.		0.00
14	Subtract Line 13 from Line 12 and enter the result.		7.349.06
15	Annualized Current Monthly Income for § 1325(b)(4). Multiply the amount from Line 14 by the number 12 and enter the result.		88,188.72
16	Applicable median family income. Enter the median family income for the applicable state and household size.[2]		56,985.00
17	Application of §1325(b)(4). Check the applicable box and proceed as directed. ☐ The amount on Line 15 is less than the amount on Line 16. Check the box for "The applicable commitment period is 3 years" at the top of page 1 of this statement and complete Part VII of this statement. Do not complete Parts III, IV, V or VI. ■ The amount on Line 15 is not less than the amount on Line 16. Check the box for "The applicable commitment period is 5 years" at the top of page 1 of this statement and continue with Part III of this statement.		
	Part III. Application of § 1325(b)(3) for Determining Disposable Income		
18	Enter the amount from Line 11.		7,349.06
19	Marital adjustment.		0.00
20	Current monthly income for § 1325(b)(3). Subtract Line 19 from Line 18 and enter the result.		7,349.06
21	Annualized current monthly income for § 1325(b)(3). Multiply the amount from Line 20 by the number 12 and enter the result.		88,188.72
22	Applicable median family income. Enter the amount from Line 16.		56,985.00
23	Application of §1325(b)(3). Check the applicable box and proceed as directed. ■ The amount on Line 21 is more than the amount on Line 22. Check the box for "Disposable income is determined under § 1325(b)(3)" at the top page 1 of this statement and complete the remaining parts of this statement.		

2. In the Kaddours' case, the applicable state is North Carolina and the family size is four (4).

	☐ The amount on Line 21 is not more than the amount on Line 22. Check the box for "Disposable income is not determined under § 1325(b)(3)" at the top of page 1 of this statement and complete Part VII of this statement. Do not complete Parts IV, V, or VI.	
	PART IV. CALCULATION OF DEDUCTIONS ALLOWED UNDER § 707(b)(2)	
	SUBPART A: DEDUCTIONS UNDER STANDARDS OF THE INTERNAL REVENUE SERVICE (IRS)	
24	National Standards: food, clothing, household supplies, personal care, and miscellaneous	1,546.00[3]
25A	Local Standards: housing and utilities; non-mortgage expenses	421.00
25B	Local Standards: housing and utilities; mortgage/rent expense Enter in Line a below the amount of [the IRS allowance for] mortgage/rent expense for your county and family size; enter on Line b the total of the Average Monthly Payments for any debts secured by your home, as stated in Line 47; subtract Line b from Line a and enter the amount here. Do not enter an amount less than zero. a. [Amount of IRS allowance:] $1,011.00 b. [Less] average monthly payment for any debts secured by your home, if any, as stated in Line 47: $1,312.73[4] c. Net mortgage/rental expenses	0.00
26	Local Standards: housing and utilities; adjustment	0.00
27	Local Standards: transportation; vehicle operation/public transportation expense Check the number of vehicles for which you pay operating expenses ☐ 0 ☐ 1 ■ 2 or more Enter the amount [the IRS allows] for the applicable number of vehicles	343.00
28	Local Standards: transportation ownership/lease expense; Vehicle 1 Check the number of vehicles for which you claim an ownership/lease expense ☐ 1 ■ 2 or more Enter in Line a below the amount of the IRS Transportation Standards, Ownership Costs, First Car; enter in Line b the total of the Average Monthly Payments for any debts secured by Vehicle 1, as stated in Line 47; subtract Line b from Line a and enter the result in Line 28. Do not enter an amount less than zero. a. [Amount of IRS First Car allowance]: $475.00 b. [Less] average monthly payment for any debts secured by Vehicle 1 [Dodge truck] as stated in Line 47: $380.66 c. Net ownership/lease expense Vehicle 1	94.34
29	Local Standards: transportation ownership/lease expense; Vehicle 2 [Chrysler Pacifica] [which is essentially calculated as in Line 28] [$338 less $421.89 = (-$83.89)]	0.00
30	Other necessary expenses: taxes	898.00
31	Other necessary expenses: mandatory payroll deductions	346.15
32	Other necessary expenses: life insurance	0.00

3. This and other amounts allowed by the IRS are different than the amounts for some of the same expenses in the Kaddours' Chapter 7 case (which we discussed in Unit 16). The reason is that some of the expenses are based on income as well as family size; and, in this unit, the Kaddours' family income is higher because of Ahmed's $20,000 raise.

4. This total represents the sum of actual, monthly payments to LSB Bank and Select Portfolio on the home mortgages owed them.

33	Other necessary expenses: court-ordered payments	0.00
34	Other necessary expenses: education for employment or for a physically or mentally challenged child	0.00
35	Other necessary expenses: childcare	404.00
36	Other necessary expenses: health care	166.67
37	Other necessary expenses: telecommunication services	56.72
38	Total Expenses Allowed under IRS Standards (Lines 24–37)	**4275.88**
	SUBPART B. ADDITIONAL EXPENSE DEDUCTIONS UNDER § 707(b) **Note: Do not include any expenses that you have listed in Lines 24–37**	
39	Health Insurance, Disability Insurance and Health Savings Account Expenses	498.03
40	Continued contributions to the care of household or family members	0.00
41	Protection against family violence	0.00
42	Home energy costs in excess of the allowance specified by the IRS Local Standards	0.00
43	Education expenses for dependent child less than 18	0.00
44	Additional food and clothing expense	47.00
45	Continued charitable contributions	20.00
46	Total Additional Expense Deductions under § 707(b)	565.03
	SUBPART C: DEDUCTIONS FOR DEBT PAYMENT	
47	Future payments on secured claims. For each of your debts that is secured by an interest in property that you own, list the name of the creditor, identify the property securing the debt, and state the Average Monthly Payment. The Average Monthly Payment is the total of all amounts contractually due to each Secured Creditor in the 60 months following the filing of the bankruptcy case divided by 60. LSB Bank — Second mortgage; doublewide mobile home and 2 acres land — 29.64 Select Portfolio — First deed of trust; double-wide mobile home and 2 acres land — 1283.09 M & I — Lien on motor vehicle; 2003 Dodge truck — 380.66 Wells Fargo — Lien on motor vehicle; 2004 Chrysler Pacifica — 421.89	2115.28
48	Past due payments on secured claims	0.00
49	Payments on priority claims	0.00
50	Chapter 13 administrative expenses. If you are eligible to file a case under Chapter 13, complete [a chart following in this space to calculate the average monthly administrative expense of a Chapter 13 case based on your circumstances].	50.00
51	Total Deductions for Debt Payment (Lines 47–50)	2115.28
	SUBPART D: TOTAL DEDUCTIONS ALLOWED UNDER § 707(b)(2)	
52	Total of all deductions allowed under § 707(b)(2). Enter the total of Lines 38, 46, and 51	6956.19
	PART V. DETERMINATION OF DISPOSABLE INCOME UNDER § 1325(b)(2)	
53	Enter the amount from Line 20	7,349.06
54	Support income.	0.00
55	Qualified retirement deductions	0.00
56	Total of all deductions allowed under § 707(b)(2). Enter the amount from Line 52.	6956.19
57	Total adjustments to determine disposable income. Add the amounts on Lines 54, 55, and 56 and enter the result.	6956.19
58	Monthly Disposable Income under § 1325(b)(2). Subtract line 57 from Line 53 and enter the result.	342.87
	PART VI. ADDITIONAL EXPENSE CLAIMS	
56	Other Expenses. List and describe any monthly expenses, not otherwise stated in this form, that are required for the	

	health and welfare of you and your family and that you contend should be an additional deduction from your current monthly income under § 707(b)(2)(A)(ii)(I). All figures should reflect your average monthly expense for each item. Total the expenses.	0.00
Part VII. Verification		
57	I declare under penalty of perjury that the information provided in this statement [form] is true and correct. (If this is a joint case, both debtors must sign.) [The Kaddours both added dated signatures.]	

The commitment period for a Chapter 13 plan is five years if the debtor's annualized current monthly income (CMI) is equal to or greater than the state median family income. In the Kaddours' Chapter 13 case, Ahmed's CMI is $4,166.66 (with his raise); Irshad's CMI is $3,182.40. Together, their combined CMI is $7,349.06. This amount annualized is $88,188.72, which is way above the North Carolina median family income of $56,985.00. So, as Lines 1–17 of Form B22C calculate, the Kaddours' Chapter 13 plan will last five years.

With Ahmed's raise, the Kaddours' monthly disposable income—calculated according to Form B22C—is $342.87. See Lines 53–58. So, over the life of a five-year plan, their 60–month disposable income is $20,572.20. We'll discuss the importance of this amount later. For now, it's enough to say that unsecured creditors will get a "fair" amount under the plan in terms of the percentage of their debts—or dividend—unsecured creditors typically receive in a Chapter 13 case.

(c) What Larry Plans for the Kaddours (Their Proposed Chapter 13 Plan)

As we've already explained, Larry is stuck with preparing a five-year Chapter 13 plan.

In deciding how much to pay creditors during this period, Larry begins with M & I and Wells Fargo. They have purchase-money liens on the Dodge truck and Chrysler Pacifica, respectively. The plan will spread their secured claims over the five years paid in equal monthly installments with interest.

Remember, however, that both M & I and Wells Fargo are undersecured. The Kaddours owe M & I $22,839.48 on the truck which, they claim, is worth only $15,700.00. By this calculation, M & I has a secured claim of $15,700 and an unsecured claim of $7,138.48. They owe Wells Fargo $25,313.36 on the Pacifica, which the Kaddours claim is worth only $16,475. So, Wells Fargo has a secured claim of $16,475, and an unsecured claim of $8,838.36.

So what? Here's what. Section 1325(a) requires a Chapter 13 plan to pay, over the term of the plan, the full amount of each allowed, secured claim plus interest. (A secured claim is the lesser of the amount of the secured debt or the value of the collateral.)

And, section 1322(b) allows a Chapter 13 debtor to modify the rights of holders of secured claims with only a few exceptions.

For this reason, the Kaddours can "strip down" M & I's lien on the Dodge truck to $15,700, which is the value of the creditor's secured claim. Therefore, their plan can provide for paying only this lesser amount in full, not the full amount of the debt owed M & I. The balance of the debt, i.e., M & I's unsecured claim, is paid what every other unsecured claim is paid. At the end of the plan, the Kaddours are discharged from any unpaid portion of M & I's unsecured claim. And, during the period of the plan, the stay stops M & I from enforcing its reduced, secured claim as long as the Kaddours are making payments according to the terms of their Chapter 13 plan.

Stripping down purchase-money car liens is not possible with respect to purchase-money car debts incurred within 910 days before the bankruptcy petition is filed. The purchase-money lien of Wells Fargo with respect to the Chrysler Pacifica was incurred within the 910–period. It's a 2004 model, but new car models are usually released in the fall of the preceding year. The Kaddours bought and financed their Pacifica in early October, 2003, which was about 830 to 840 days before they filed their Chapter 13 case on January 21, 2006.

As a result, the Kaddours cannot strip down Wells Fargo's lien on the Pacifica. Their plan must provide for paying the full amount of the debt they owe Wells Fargo even though the value of Wells Fargo's collateral is less than this debt.

Also, a Chapter 13 debtor cannot strip down a mortgage or other consensual lien on real estate that is the debtor's principal residence. Even absent this exception, the Kaddours couldn't strip down the mortgages on their home—the doublewide mobile home—because its value exceeds the amounts of both mortgages on the property. These secured creditors are over secured, not undersecured.

The secured claim of the first mortgagee, Select Portfolio, is $76,985.85. Probably, the remaining term of this mortgage is more than five years. The Kaddours are not required to shorten the term and pay off the mortgage in five years. Section 1322(b) allows a Chapter 13 plan "to provide for . . . maintenance of payments while the case is pending on any unsecured or secured claim on which the last payment is due after the date on which the final payment under the plan is due."

Therefore, with respect to Select Portfolio's secured claim, Larry will propose that the Kaddours pay Select Portfolio according to the exact terms of the mortgage. In other words, the Kaddours will make their usual, monthly payments of principal and interest.

However, Larry is not required to include these payments within the plan itself. Instead, he will propose paying the mortgage "outside" the plan, which (as we'll explain later) will reduce administrative costs.

The second mortgagee, LSB bank, has only a small, secured claim amounting to $1,777.38. Larry will also propose paying this claim outside the plan and in accordance with the terms of LSB's mortgage.

The Kaddours' unsecured, nonpriority debts, as reported in their Schedule F, are $43,770.88. This amount climbs to $50,910.36 after adding M & I's unsecured claim which the Kaddours claim is $7,139.48 (e.g., the difference between the debt owed M & I and the value of M & I's collateral as calculated by Larry and the Kaddours).

The Kaddours' plan must pay each of the unsecured creditors the amount the creditor would have received had the Kaddours liquidated. However, if any creditor or the trustee objects, the plan must commit all of the debtors' "projected disposable income" to paying unsecured creditors after satisfying priority and secured claims. Somebody will object.

So, the plan must provide for paying the Kaddours' projected disposable income to unsecured creditors over a five-year period. As calculated by Form B22C, the Kaddours' disposable monthly income is $342.87; and, using this amount, the total disposable income for their five-year plan is $20,572.20.

This total, however, is not enough to fully satisfy the total of unsecured claims. So, the Kaddours' plan proposes that unsecured creditors share the projected disposable income on a pro-rata basis and that each creditor receives a dividend of 40% ($20,572.20/$50,910.36), which means 40% of the total amount owed each unsecured creditor.[5]

Finally, but no less important, Larry will include in the plan a provision for the Kaddours to pay his legal fee, which is $2,500, over a five-month period at the beginning of the plan.

In standard form, here's the Kaddours' proposed Chapter 13 plan which Larry filed:

NOTICE TO CREDITORS AND PROPOSED PLAN

The Debtor(s) filed for relief under Chapter 13 of the United States Bankruptcy Code on January 21, 2006.

5. Actually, the percentage (called the "dividend") paid unsecured creditors will be somewhat less if other claims are later allowed and if actual, administrative expenses are higher than originally projected. Also, the dividend "tax" for administrative expenses will include Lawyer Larry's attorney's fees, which reduces the payments to unsecured creditors.

The filing automatically stays collection and other actions against the Debtor, Debtor's property and certain co-debtors. If you attempt to collect a debt or take other action in violation of the bankruptcy stay you may be penalized.

Official notice will be sent to creditors, which will provide the name and address of the Trustee, the date and time of the meeting of creditors, and the deadline for objecting to the plan. The official notice will include a proof of claim form.

A creditor must timely file a proof of claim with the Trustee in order to receive distributions under the plan. The Trustee will mail payments to the address provided on the proof of claim unless the creditor provides another address in writing for payments. If the claim is subsequently assigned or transferred, the Trustee will continue to remit payment to the original creditor until a formal notice of assignment or transfer is filed with the Court.

CHAPTER 13 PLAN SUMMARY

The Debtor proposes an initial plan, which is subject to modification, as follows:

I. Plan Payments

The plan proposes a payment of $1026.43 per month for 60 months. The debtor shall commence payments to the Trustee within thirty (30) days from the date the petition was filed.

II. Administrative Costs

1. **Attorney fees.** The Attorney for the Debtor will be paid the base fee of $2,500.00. The Attorney has received $0.00 from the Debtor prepetition and the remainder of the base fee will be paid by the Trustee as funds are available after scheduled monthly payments to holders of domestic support obligations and allowed secured claims.

2. **Trustee costs.** The Trustee will receive from all disbursements such amount as approved by the Court for payment of fees and expenses.

III. Priority Claims

All pre-petition claims entitled to priority under 11 U.S.C. § 507 will be paid in full in deferred cash payments unless otherwise indicated.

1. **Domestic Support Obligations ("DSO")**

   NONE

2. **Other priority claims to be paid by Trustee**

   NONE

IV. Secured Claims

1. Real Property Secured Claims

a. Check here ____ if none

b. All payments on any claim secured by real property will be paid by the Trustee unless the account is current, in which case the Debtor may elect to continue making mortgage payments directly. Arrearage claims will be paid by the Trustee as separate secured claims over the term of the plan without interest.

Creditor	Residence or Non–Residence R/NR	Current Y/N	Monthly Payment	Arrearage Amount	If Current Indicate Payment by Debtor (D) or Trustee (T)
Select Portfolio*	R	Y	$499.95	$0.00	Debtor
LSB Bank*	R	Y	Demand	$0.00	Debtor

* Debtors elect to continue making these mortgage payments directly to the creditors and outside of the plan.

2. Personal Property Secured Claims

a. Check here if ____ None

b. Claims secured by personal property will be paid by the Trustee as follows:

Creditor	Collateral	Secured Amount	Purchase-money Y/N	Undersecured Amount	Pre-confirmation payment per § 1326(a)(1)	Post-confirmation Equal Monthly Amount (EMA)	Proposed Interest Rate
M & I	2003 Dodge Truck	15,700.00[6]	Y	7,139.48	261.67	261.67	10%
Wells Fargo	2004 Chrysler Pacifica	25,313.36[7]	Y	NONE	421.89	421.89	10%

The Trustee will disburse pre-confirmation adequate protection payments to secured creditors holding allowed purchase-money secured claims. Claims having a collateral value of less than $2,000.00 will not receive adequate protection payments.

To the extent that the valuation provisions of 11 U.S.C. § 506 do not apply to any of the claims listed above, the

6. The plan must provide for fully paying secured claims. A secured claim is the greater of the value of the collateral or the size of the debt. At this point, the Kaddours claim that the value of the collateral, and thus the value of M & I's secured claim, is $15,700, which they propose to pay in full. In effect, therefore, the Kaddours' plan strips down M & I's lien to this amount and treats the balance owed M & I, $7,139.47, as an unsecured claim which they aren't required to pay in full. Later in the case, M & I objects to this valuation; the parties settle on a higher value; and the court's order confirming the plan adopts the higher value and increases M & I's secured claim, which thus increases the monthly plan payment to M & I.

7. Wells Fargo is undersecured, too. The debt is more than the value of the collateral. However, for reasons we discuss elsewhere, the Kaddours cannot strip down Wells Fargo's lien. The debt is treated as fully secured, and the Kaddours' plan must provide for paying all of it.

creditor's failure to object to confirmation of the proposed plan shall constitute the creditor's acceptance of the treatment of its claim as proposed, pursuant to 11 U.S.C. § 1325(a)(5)(A).

3. Collateral to be Released

The Debtor proposes to release the following collateral: NONE

4. Liens to be Avoided

The debtor pursuant to 11 U.S.C. § 522 proposes to avoid the following liens on property to the extent that such liens impair the Debtor's exemption: NONE

V. Co–Debtor Claims

The Debtor proposes to separately classify for payment in full the following claims for consumer debts on which an individual is liable with the Debtor: NONE

VI. Unsecured Claims

General unsecured claims with be paid on a pro-rata basis with payments to commence after priority unsecured claims are paid in full. The estimated dividend to general unsecured claims is 40%.

VII. Executory Contracts

NONE

VIII. Special Provisions

a. Check here ____ if NONE

b. Other classes of unsecured claims and treatment: NONE

c. Other Special Terms: NONE

Date: January 21, 2006

/s/ Larry Friedman
Larry Friedman
Attorney for Debtors

Larry files this proposed plan along with the Chapter 13 petition and basically all of the other stuff he filed in the Kaddours' Chapter 7 case (which we described in Unit 16). The Kaddours haven't changed where they live since Unit 16, and so Larry files in the same federal judicial district, the same city, and the same bankruptcy court.

The proposed plan is not effective, however, unless and until the bankruptcy court confirms it. Typically, several months will elapse between filing and confirmation.

During this period, creditors will get notice of the bankruptcy filing and the plan. They and the trustee will scrutinize the proposed plan to ensure that it complies with the requirements for confirmation. If any of the creditors or the trustee sees a problem, she will complain to Larry or the court.

Objections to confirmation are not uncommon. Any objection that sticks—either because the objection is settled out of court or because the court hears the objection and agrees with it—will cause Larry to file an amended plan.

As we discuss later, M & I objected to the proposed plan based on the valuation of its collateral. The dispute was settled, and the plan was changed to adjust the value of the property and, concomitantly, the size of M & I's secured claim.

Also, within 30 days after filing the plan which is well before confirmation, the debtor must commence making payment to the trustee as provided in the plan. The trustee retains these payments until the plan is confirmed and then pays them to the creditors in whatever amounts the plan provides for them.

Additionally, during the interim after filing and before confirmation, the debtor must make "adequate protection" payments directly to the holder of a purchase-money secured claim. The purpose and amount of this payment is to compensate the creditor for any depreciation in the amount of the collateral that would have the effect of reducing the size of the creditor's secured claim. This payment directly to a secured creditor reduces the amount of the debtor's interim, plan payments to the trustee. These "adequate protection" payments to secured creditors end when the plan is confirmed; and, in theory, the secured creditors are protected by the payments of principal and interest they receive under the plan.

§ 17.3 What Happens to the Kaddours After Filing

The immediate legal effects of filing the case under Chapter 13 are the same as the effects of filing under Chapter 7: the stay is triggered and the bankruptcy estate is created, but the stay and estate operate a little differently in Chapter 13. Also, as under Chapter 7, the case is assigned to a trustee. In a Chapter 13 case, however, the trustee is different and works differently and with very different purposes, which includes closely analyzing the proposed Chapter 13 plan Larry filed on the Kaddours' behalf.

(a) The Stay and Property of the Estate

In every kind of bankruptcy case, including the Kaddours' Chapter 13 case, the filing of the petition "operates as a stay, applicable to all entities." This section 362 stay enjoins and prevents all creditors from taking or continuing any action in or outside of court (except the bankruptcy court) against the debtors, their property, or property of the estate to collect the creditors' claims.

A difference in Chapter 13 is whom the stay protects. In every other kind of bankruptcy case, the stay protects only the debtor against creditors' collection efforts. Creditors cannot start or continue lawsuits against the debtor; can't call the debtor asking for payment; and can't do anything else against the debtor or property to collect the debts owed the creditors.

Sometimes, however, individual debtors in Chapter 7 or 13 cases owe debts on which somebody else is also liable as a surety. If the debtor files Chapter 7, the stay does not prevent the creditor from suing the surety or taking other actions to collect the debt.

In Chapter 13, however, the section 362 stay is supplemented by section 1301 which imposes a stay against certain sureties called "codebtors." Under section 1301, upon and after the filing of a Chapter 13 petition, "a creditor may not act, or commence any civil action, to collect all or any part of a consumer debt of the debtor from any individual that is liable on such debt with the debtor . . . ." This stay protects only a surety who is an "individual," which means a natural person; and it applies only if the debt on which the surety is liable is a "consumer debt," which means a debt "incurred by an individual primarily for a personal, family, or household purpose."

For example, suppose the debtor borrowed money from a bank to buy a car for her personal use. The debtor's parents "co-sign" the note. They are sureties. They are individual codebtors on a consumer debt. If the debtor filed Chapter 7, the bank could go after the parents because, as sureties, they are liable on the debt. If the debtor files Chapter 13, however, section 1301 prevents the bank from taking any collection action against the parents.

Generally speaking, the effects of sections 362 and 1301 last until the case is dismissed or closed, which basically means the case is completed and done with as far as the bankruptcy court is concerned. In a Chapter 7 case, the case is closed several months after the case begins. In a Chapter 13 case, the case remains open and is not closed until the debtor's payments under the plan are completed or the case is earlier dismissed. The length of the plan is either three or five years and is usually the latter; and the effects of 362 and 1301 continue the entire time.

As in Chapter 7, a creditor can make a motion for relief from the stay so the creditor can do something the stay prevents. Almost always, the creditor making such a "lift stay" motion is a secured creditor who wants to enforce her lien.

In a Chapter 7 case, the court will grant the relief if the debtor lacks any equity in the property. Remember: the purpose of Chapter 7 is to squeeze the debtor's equity out of property and distribute the proceeds to unsecured creditors. So, if a secured creditor seeks to lift the stay with respect to collateral in which the debtor lacks equity, the court will typically grant the lift-stay motion.

In a Chapter 13 case, however, the debtor's lack of equity in property is not a sufficient basis for lifting the stay. If the same creditor files the same kind of motion under Chapter 13, the court will lift stay only if the debtor lacks equity AND the property is not necessary to an effective reorganization.

In the typical Chapter 13 case, the collateral is the debtor's vehicle or her home. The debtor needs to keep the property to succeed under Chapter 13. Also, the debtor really wants to keep the property and will often do whatever is necessary in the Chapter 13 process to make the secured creditor happy enough that the creditor won't file a lift-stay motion.

As in every kind of bankruptcy case, the property the stay protects in a Chapter 13 case includes property of the debtor and, even more widely, property of the estate. And, under Chapter 13, the estate is wider than under Chapter 7.

For the most part, the estate in a Chapter 7 case is only the debtor's interests in property that the debtor owns at the time the petition is filed. The estate generally does not include property the debtor acquires postpetition. This property belongs to the debtor. Nevertheless, as long as the case is open, the stay protects it; and, thereafter, the property is variously or indirectly protected by the discharge.

In a Chapter 13 case, the bankruptcy estate includes all of the debtor's interests in property she owns when she files her petition. Also, and very differently, the Chapter 13 estate includes property the debtor acquires after the case is commenced and anytime during performance of the plan, especially including "earnings from services performed by the debtor after the commencement of the case."

The Chapter 13 estate, however, is not sold and distributed to creditors. Also, the debtor keeps possession of the property even though it belongs to the estate. The purpose of funneling all of this property into a bankruptcy estate is to ensure effective administration of the case and, especially with respect to future income, to help ensure that this property is funneled to creditors according to the terms of the Chapter 13 plan.

Nevertheless, a Chapter 13 debtor is entitled to exempt property from the estate under the applicable law that governs exemptions. Typically, therefore, the debtor files a claim to exempt property along with her Chapter 13 petition. The purpose, though, is not so much to take the property out of the estate because: the estate property is not sold, and the debtor gets to keep possession of all the property, except future income that is committed to the Chapter 13 plan.

The debtor claims exemptions mainly for two other purposes. First, deciding how much to pay creditors under the plan depends, in part, on deciding how much creditors would have received in a Chapter 7 case. How much they would have received in a Chapter 7 case depends on the size of the estate in the Chapter 7, which partly depends on how much property the debtor would have exempted from the estate.

The other reason for the debtor claiming exemptions in a Chapter 7 case is more important to the debtor. Remember from Unit 16 that, to some extent, section 522(f) allows the debtor to avoid liens that impair exemptions. Avoiding such a lien in a Chapter 13 case eliminates or reduces the creditor's secured claim and converts the claim, correspondingly, into an unsecured claim. A Chapter 13 plan must provide for fully paying secured claims but can pay unsecured claims much, much less than their full amounts and maybe even nothing. The result is to reduce the amount of the debtor's future income that she must commit to the Chapter 13 plan.

In the Kaddours' Chapter 7 case, Larry implied in the "Debtor's Statement of Intention," which is a form he filed with the petition, that the debtors intended to avoid the liens on the Dodge Truck and Chrysler Pacifica. Larry is not required to file the same form in a Chapter 13 case, but in a Chapter 13 case he can try to avoid liens that impair the Kaddours' exemptions. However, as we said in Unit 16, the section 522(f) avoiding power is very small and rarely used successfully in any significant way. Also, we concluded in Unit 16 that Larry probably couldn't avoid the car liens to any extent under section 522(f) in the Kaddours' Chapter 7 case; and we reach the same conclusion in their Chapter 13 case.

In a Chapter 7 case, the trustee is given powers to avoid liens and prepetition transfers, such as preferences and fraudulent transfers. In a Chapter 13 case, the debtor splits some administrative rights with the Chapter 13 trustee; but the general, broad avoidance powers (that the trustee gets in a Chapter 7 case) belong exclusively to the Chapter 13 trustee. The debtor's power to avoid prepetition transfers is limited to the narrow power given her by section 522(f).

The Chapter 13 trustee, however, is really not motivated to exercise these avoidance powers. Recovering prepetition transfers of property does not increase future income. And, avoiding prepetition liens, which otherwise could be paid fully through the debtor's plan, converts them to unsecured claims, which will be paid much less through the plan. The result is to reduce how much the trustee is paid for her role in the case, which we now explain.

(b) Meet the Chapter 13 Trustee

After filing, the Kaddours' case is assigned to a Chapter 13 trustee. The trustee's role is to oversee Chapter 13 cases; study the proposed plans to ensure they comply with the Bankruptcy Code and Rules; and administer confirmed plans. Payments due under a Chapter 13 plan are paid to the trustee, and the trustee distributes the money to the creditors in accordance with the terms of the plan.

Like Chapter 7 trustees, Chapter 13 trustees are appointed by the Office of the United States Trustee which oversees Chapters 7 and 13 trustees. A Chapter 13 trustee is usually a lawyer but, unlike a Chapter 7 trustee, she generally does not practice on the side. Being a Chapter 13 trustee is usually a full-time job. Indeed, it's a business with assistant trustees and staff that is funded by confirmed, Chapter 13 cases.

The Chapter 13 trustee receives a fee or commission that is a percentage of the money disbursed to creditors under and through a Chapter 13 plan; and with this money she pays her employees and other costs of operating her business. The trustee's commission percentage varies around the country. In the Middle District of North Carolina, where the Kaddours filed their case, the commission is five percent.

Therefore, a Chapter 13 trustee is motivated to help the debtor get her plan confirmed but, at the same time, is motivated to inflate as much as possible the size of the plan, i.e., the total amount of money the debtor pays creditors under the plan. So, the trustee will advise the debtor, through the debtor's lawyer, about the rules and process for getting a plan confirmed; and, if the plan is confirmed, the trustee will assist the debtor in performing the plan, including ensuring that the debtor makes timely payments.

On the other hand, the Chapter 13 trustee has standing to challenge the debtor's plan. She, as well as any party in interest (i.e., any creditor), can object to the court's confirmation of the plan. So, the Chapter 13 trustee can contest any and every aspect of a debtor's proposed plan, specifically including the value of a creditor's collateral. In sum, the Chapter 13 trustee is a major player in shaping the size and terms of a plan and in keeping the debtor true to the performance of a plan the court confirms.

Because funding a Chapter 13 plan depends on future income, not present property, the Chapter 13 trustee has a special interest in verifying the debtor's Schedule I which reports the debtor's current income. This amount is also the starting point for calculating the commitment period and disposable income under Form B22C.

For verification, the trustee relies on pay stubs and other evidence of wages and income paid by the employer prepetition, which the debtor must file with her petition. The trustee also relies on the debtor's income tax return. Section 521 requires the debtor to "provide [to the trustee], not later than 7 days before the date first set for the first [341(a)] meeting of creditors, . . . a copy of the Federal income tax return . . . for the most recent tax year ending immediately before the commencement of the case. . ." or a transcript of the return. Any creditor can request a copy of the return or transcript.

If the debtor fails timely to provide the tax return, "the court shall dismiss the case" unless the debtor proves that failing to provide the information is due to circumstances beyond her control. The debtor having failed to file a tax return is not a good excuse. Indeed, section 1308(a) requires the debtor, before the first scheduled 341(a) creditors' meeting, to "file with appropriate tax authorities all tax returns for all taxable periods ending during the 4–year period ending on the date of the filing of the petition." Also, the debtor can be required to provide tax returns filed for any subsequent tax year date ending while the case is pending. So, if a Chapter 13 plan is confirmed, the debtor will typically provide the court with her tax returns filed during the three-or five-year period of the plan.

As the foregoing suggests, the Chapter 13 process involves, as in Chapter 7, a section 341(a) meeting of creditors held within a reasonable time after the petition is filed. A Chapter 13 meeting is run by the Chapter 13 trustee; creditors can attend; and the meeting serves the purposes of interrogating the debtor about her property and financial affairs and, in a Chapter 13, especially getting more details about the debtor's prepetition, present, and future income.

§ 17.4 Trustee's Possible Concerns with Larry's Proposed Plan for the Kaddours

Acting for herself and unsecured creditors, the Chapter 13 trustee may object to confirmation of the Kaddours' proposed Chapter 13 plan on several different grounds.

(a) Ignores Any Actual, Future Income

Section 1325(b) requires that upon complaint by an unsecured creditor or the trustee, the debtor's plan must commit all of her "projected disposable income" to paying creditors. The Bankruptcy Code defines "disposable income" as "current monthly income" (CMI) less the statutorily-defined deductions. CMI is also defined: "the average monthly income from all sources that the debtor receives (or in a joint case the debtor and the debtor's spouse receive) . . . during the 6–month period ending on . . . the last day of the calendar month immediately preceding the date of the commencement of the case. . . ."

CMI is backward looking from the time of the petition. So, in the Kaddours' case, the forms Larry filed calculated the CMI by adding together Ahmed's and Irshad's income for the six-month period and dividing this total by six.

The trustee may argue that because the statute requires "*projected* disposable income," the CMI should be inflated by increases in income that have occurred postpetition. By increasing the CMI in this way or any other, the effect is to increase the number from which the deductions (however determined) are subtracted and thereby increase the possibility and size of disposable income available for unsecured creditors.

As we write this book, the debate is ongoing about whether or not this argument of the trustee is sound. So far, it looks as though the courts are buying this argument. An earlier, influential decision is In re Hardacre.[8] Bankruptcy Judge Russell Nelms decided that in a Chapter 13 debtor's "projected disposable income," such as debtor is required to devote to payments under plan, is based on the debtor's actual, financial circumstances on the effective date of the plan, not just the debtor's prepetition CMI.

Judge Nelms reasoned that "a debtor who anticipates a significant enhancement of future income is provided strong incentive to file Chapter 13 as soon as possible. The amount of money that she would be required to commit to the plan would be based upon her lower average income prior to filing. On the other hand, a debtor who finds herself in the unfortunate circumstance of having a lower income after filing her petition might find that she is unable to confirm a plan because she cannot devote to the plan a 'projected disposable income' predicated upon her prepetition income."[9]

He anchored this reasoning squarely on the word "projected." The statute requires using CMI to calculate a debtor's "disposable income." The statute, however, requires that the debtor commit

8. 338 B.R. 718 (Bankr. N.D. Tex. 2006).

9. Id. at 722.

not "disposable income" but "*projected* disposable income." "Projected," he concluded, "necessarily refers to income that the debtor reasonably [actually] expects to receive during the plan,"[10] not income the debtor actually received before the plan.

The *Hardacre* case is not universally accepted. In In re Alexander,[11] the judge rejected the *Hardacre* notion that "projected disposable income" is based on the debtor's anticipated income during the plan. *Alexander* held that the Code plainly defines "disposable income" based on an average of the debtor's prepetition income; the modifier "projected" does not trump this definition; and the prepetition average is the projected income for purposes of the Chapter 13 plan.

Nevertheless, other courts are buying *Hardacre*. And they are buying it fully in the sense that "projected disposable income" can be inflated by postpetition increases in future income and also deflated by postpetition decreases in future income. In the Kaddours' case, however, there is no evidence that their income either increased or decreased postpetition. So, absent such evidence, the plan is calculated and based on CMI without additions or subtractions.

Distinguish a different situation: the debtor's income increases or decreases after the debtor's Chapter 13 plan is confirmed and she had begun performing under the plan. In this event, as we discuss later, the plan may be modified; or, in case income decreases, the case may be converted to Chapter 7.

(b) Ignores Actual, Present, Monthly Net Income

A trustee could possibly make another argument that looks the same as the argument above but is different. The argument above, e.g., *Hardacre*, essentially concerns how to calculate gross income going forward from which expenses are deducted to determine projected disposable income. Is the calculation of future, monthly income based solely on the CMI which is an average of prepetition income, or does the projected monthly income consider actual changes in the debtor's income that would raise (or lower) actual future income compared to CMI?

A different argument looks not at gross income but the deductions from income the court considers in deciding projected disposable income. Should the gross income (however determined) be reduced by the debtor's actual expenses (shown on Forms I and J) or expenses calculated by Form B22C?

10. Id. at 723.

11. 344 B.R. 742 (Bankr. E.D. N.C. 2006).

For example, in the Kaddours' Chapter 13 case, the Form B22C calculation of monthly disposable income is $342.87. Using this number, the Kaddours' proposed plan would pay unsecured creditors 40% of their claims. So, the Kaddours' proposed plan is a 40% plan.

However, the trustee will point to Schedules I and J the Kaddours filed with their bankruptcy petition. The bottom line of these schedules is that in terms of actual income and actual living expenses (including paying secured claims), the Kaddours' monthly, net income is $1,277.54. The trustee could argue that projected disposable income, which the Kaddours must pay unsecured creditors, should be based on the higher, actual number calculated on Forms I and J rather than the lower, formularized number calculated under Form B22C. In this event, the Kaddours could fully pay their unsecured creditors—pay 100% of unsecured claims—during the five-year term of their plan.

Lawyer Larry's response clings to the literal language of the statute. Section 1325(b) imposes the requirement that the debtors commit all of their projected disposable income to paying unsecured creditors under the debtor's Chapter 13 plan. The very same section explains how "disposable income" is determined, which is the foundation for Form B22C. "Disposable income" is the current monthly income of the debtors less the deductions detailed there and incorporated into Form B22C, which for above-median debtors are the IRS-based deductions of section 707(b)(2). By this calculation, the Kaddours' monthly, disposable income is only $342.87; and, therefore, they are required to pay unsecured creditors only about 40% of their claims over the next five years.

The Chapter 13 trustee's reply relies on section 1325(a). This provision conditions confirmation of a plan on the court finding several things, including the 1325(a)(3) condition that "the plan has been proposed in good faith and not by any means forbidden by law." The trustee argues that a plan is not proposed in good faith when the debtors' Schedules I and J show actual, net monthly income that the debtor does not propose committing to the Chapter 13 plan.

As we write this book, this debate is just beginning. A case that's likely to influence the outcome is In re Barr.[12] In this case, the debtor's Form B22C showed negative disposable income. Her Schedules I and J, however, showed actual, net disposable income of $2,038.00. The debtor's Chapter 13 plan proposed a 0% plan, which means zeroing out unsecured creditors and paying them nothing.

12. 341 B.R. 181 (Bankr. M.D. N.C. 2006).

The trustee and debtor's lawyer made the conflicting arguments described above. Bankruptcy Judge William Stocks sided with the debtor. He reasoned that "once section 1325(b) was adopted, a debtor's ability to pay became a matter to be addressed under section 1325(b) rather than section 1325(a)(3)." And, "[c]alculating 'disposable income' for above-median-income debtors under new section 1325(b) is now separated from a review of Schedules I and J ...."

The trustee argued that "such a result is unfair and contrary to the way that Chapter 13 should work and has worked in the past." Judge Stocks responded that "the language of section 1325(b)(3) is unambiguous in requiring that the expenses and deductions of above-median-income debtors be determined under section 707(b)(2)(A) and (B)," and "this court is not free to ignore revised section 1325(b) or replace it with a standard pulled from section 1325(a)(3)" because "[t]o do so ... would impermissibly undermine policy choices made by Congress."

Even if Judge Stocks is right, that "disposable income" determined by section 1325(b) is generally not trumped by section 1325(a), there is a newer, different argument supporting the trustee's position. *Barr* was decided at just about the same time as Judge Nelms in *Hardacre* and other courts began deciding, as we explained earlier, that in determining gross "projected future income," prepetition calculated CMI is not controlling. Rather, it's the gross income the debtor reasonably expects to receive during the term of the plan.

Well, if "projected" means actual income (not the formularized CMI) in terms of calculating gross income, maybe "projected" also means actual expenses rather than expenses calculated according to the section 1325(b) formula. In this event, calculating "projected disposable income" means determining actual, anticipated gross income and deducting the lesser of the total actual expenses the debtor reports on her Forms I and J and the total expenses resulting from the calculation under 1325(b). Applying this math to the Kaddours' case would mean that because no changes in income are anticipated, their projected disposable income is $1,277.54 monthly or $76,652.40 over five years, which exceeds the present, total value of their unsecured debts.

Their plan would not be a 40% plan. It would be a 100% plan. Instead of unsecured creditors getting only 40% of their claims, their claims would be fully, 100% paid.

The Kaddours would prefer a 40% plan. Nevertheless, they have good reasons for filing Chapter 13 even if they were required to fully pay unsecured claims. A 100% plan still allows the Kaddours to stretch out their payments for five years and, for the entire time, keep the creditors at bay because of the automatic stay.

We don't know how this debate will end. We don't know if the courts will ultimately decide that net, projected, disposable income is determined by the formularized, bottom line of Form B22C or the actual, bottom line of Forms I and J. For now, we'll assume that the calculations under section 1325(b) and Form B22C control at least in cases, such as the Kaddours' case, where the gap between actual disposable income (based on Forms I and J) and projected disposable income (based on Form B22C) is not unreasonable and the latter calculation yields a decent dividend for unsecured creditors.

(c) Makes Payments to Creditors Outside the Plan

Remember that the Kaddours' proposed plan would pay the mortgages on their mobile home according to the terms of the mortgages but outside the plan. The Kaddours would pay the mortgagees directly. The trustee would not disburse the payments to the mortgagees and, as a result, the Chapter 13 trustee's fee from this case is reduced. The trustee only gets a percentage of funds paid by her under and through the plan.

Several provisions of Chapter 13 seem to imply that all payments in Chapter 13 should be made through the plan.[13] On the other hand, section 1326(c) provides that the plan or the order confirming a plan can "otherwise provide" for payments to creditors under the plan.

So, the Bankruptcy Code doesn't prohibit payments outside the plan. The judge in her discretion can allow it. And, in practice, courts have generally allowed debtors to pay secured claims outside the plan and directly to the secured creditors if the claims have not been modified in any way.

In the Kaddours' case, therefore, paying the mortgages outside the plan is probably okay. They could not have paid the car loans outside the plan because those claims will be modified, i.e., the liens stripped down, if the court confirms the plan.

You might think the Kaddours wouldn't care about this issue and would just as soon pay the mortgages through the plan. The Kaddours do care. The commission the trustee is paid for adminis-

13. "Except as otherwise provided in the plan or in the order confirming the plan, the trustee shall make payments to creditors under the plan." 11 U.S.C. § 1326(c). Section 1322(a)(1) provides: "The plan shall (1) provide for the submission of all or such portion of future income of the debtor to the supervision and control of the trustee as is necessary for the execution of the plan." 11 U.S.C. § 1322(a)(1). Section 1326(a)(2) provides that upon confirmation of a Chapter 13 plan, "the trustee shall distribute any such payment in accordance with the plan as soon as is practicable." 11 U.S.C. § 1326(a)(2).

tering a Chapter 13 plan is paid by the debtor. So, by paying the mortgages outside the plan, the Kaddours pay lower administrative expenses.

§ 17.5 Secured Creditor's (M & I's) Possible Concern With Larry's Plan for the Kaddours'—Amount of Secured Claim

The trustee may have another concern with the Kaddours' proposed plan that is shared by M & I. Remember that this creditor has a lien on the Kaddours' Dodge truck. Remember, too, that the Kaddours' plan puts a value on the truck that leaves M & I undersecured (i.e., the debt is larger than the value of the collateral); and the plan proposes to strip down the lien to this value. Doing so leaves the balance of M & I's claim unsecured; none of the claim will be paid anything under the plan; and the debtor's liability for the unsecured claim will be discharged when the plan is completed.

The lower the value assigned to collateral, the more likely the creditor is undersecured. And, as the value gets lower, the size of the unsecured claim gets bigger; the secured claim gets smaller; and the amount the debtor is required to pay the secured creditor (which is the full amount of the secured claim) decreases.

The debtor wants the lowest possible valuation of collateral. The creditor with the secured claim wants the highest possible valuation. The trustee maybe wants the highest possible value, too, to increase the amount disbursed through the plan and thus increase the trustee's commission.

The Bankruptcy Code provides a standard for valuation when the debtor is an individual in a Chapter 7 or 13 case and the collateral is personal property. Under these circumstances, the value of the collateral "shall be determined based on the replacement value of such property as of the date of the filing of the petition without deduction for costs of sale or marketing." Also, if the collateral was acquired for personal, family, or household purposes, "replacement value shall mean the price a retail merchant would charge for property of that kind considering the age and condition of the property at the time value is determined."

M & I could challenge the Kaddours' valuation of its collateral, the Dodge truck. As a creditor, M & I can do so because any party in interest, which includes any creditor, has standing to object to court confirmation of the plan. Objecting to valuation of collateral is, in effect, a way of objecting to confirmation. The trustee, too, is authorized to appear and be heard on the value of a creditor's collateral.

Local "blue book" values are frequently good evidence of the retail, replacement value of a particular vehicle. At the time we're writing this book, local, retail, blue book values for a 2003 Dodge truck vary substantially. The range is huge depending on the model, the size of the bed, quad cab or not, mileage, accessories, etc. Some of the local, retail replacement values are far above the value assigned by the Kaddours, which is $15,700.

You get the idea. Even a statutory standard for determining value leaves plenty of room for disagreement.

M & I decided to challenge the debtor's valuation. It filed a motion initiating a proceeding that leads to a noticed hearing before the bankruptcy judge. The motion looked like this:

IN THE UNITED STATES BANKRUPTCY COURT
MIDDLE DISTRICT OF NORTH CAROLINA
WINSTON–SALEM DIVISION

IN RE:

AHMED KADDOUR
Chapter 13
IRSHAD KADDOUR

Case No.: 06–72C818
Debtors.

M & I FINANCIAL CORPORATION'S OBJECTION TO VALUATION/OBJECTION TO CONFIRMATION AND REQUEST FOR HEARING

M & I CORPORATION ("M & I") by and through counsel, moves this Court for valuation of its security interest pursuant to Bankruptcy Code Section 506 and Bankruptcy Rule 3012. In support of M & I's objection, M & I shows the Court as follows:

1. On or about December 22, 2002, Regal Dodge, Inc. ("Regal Dodge") extended credit to the male debtor in the principal sum of $38,785.14, and, as evidence of the obligation to pay such amount to Regal Dodge, Debtor executed and delivered a Security Agreement Retail Installment Contract ("Contract") to Regal Dodge. Under the Contract, Debtor was to make monthly payments to pay off the loan and to maintain physical damage insurance. A true and correct copy of the Contract is attached hereto as "Exhibit A" and incorporated herein and by reference.

2. The Contract was assigned by Regal Dodge to M & I as evidenced by the assignment in the Contract.

3. As security for the indebtedness owed to M & I, or its predecessor in interest, Debtor granted M & I a purchase-money security interest in a 2003 Dodge truck, VIN 1NKDL50X5WJJ795406 (hereinafter "Truck"), which Regal Dodge enabled Debtor to acquire by financing Debtor's purchase of the Truck.

4. M & I perfected its security interest by placing a lien against the title of the Truck as evidenced by a notation of first lien on the North Carolina Certificate of Title. A true and correct copy of the North Carolina Certificate of Title is attached hereto as "Exhibit B" and incorporated herein by reference.

5. The Debtors filed a voluntary petition for relief under Chapter 13 of the Bankruptcy Code on January 21, 2006, case no. 06–72C818. The debtor's proposed, 60–month Chapter 13 plan valued the Collateral at $15,700.00. M & I filed a proof of claim in the amount of $22,839.48. The Debtors' proposed monthly Chapter 13 plan payments to M & I, based on the Debtors' valuation of the collateral and M & I's secured claim, are $261.67.

6. The current 2006 N.A.D.A. Official Commercial Truck Guide values the Collateral as high as $23,515.00. A true copy of the relevant page is attached hereto as "Exhibit C" and incorporated herein by reference.

7. Counsel for M & I contacted Debtors' counsel to discuss the value Debtors placed on the Collateral and the fact that M & I asserted a higher value based on the N.A.D.A. valuation. M & I's counsel attempted to renegotiate the Plan value but a consensual agreement has not been met.

8. M & I also contends, based on the terms of the Contract, that the Chapter 13 plan must provide for repaying the debt at 13.5% interest rather than the lesser percentage the Debtors' Chapter 13 plan proposes.

9. Debtors assert that M & I's claim should be partially secured and partially unsecured, and thus Debtors are attempting to cram down M & I's claim while retaining the benefit of using the Collateral during the Bankruptcy.

10. The total amount owing to M & I as of the filing date was $22,839.48. The contractual annual percentage interest rate is 13.5%.

11. M & I objects to the Debtors' valuation of the Collateral and, on this basis, to the confirmation of the Plan.

WHEREFORE M & I prays unto this Court as follows:

1. That the value placed on the Collateral be increased to $23,515.00 and M & I be allowed a secured claim for the total amount owed to M & I with appropriate interest;

2. That, in the alternative, Debtors' case be dismissed;

3. That M & I be granted its attorneys' fees and costs in filing this objection; and

4. That M & I be granted such other and further relief as this Court deems just and proper.

This the 10th day of March, 2006.

POYNER & SPRUILL LLP

____

Deborah M. Tyson
301 South College Street, Suite 2300
Charlotte, North Carolina 28202
ATTORNEYS FOR M & I
FINANCIAL CORPORATION

[CERTIFICATE OF SERVICE to: Debtors; Larry Friedman, Attorney for Debtor; and Chapter 13 Trustee]
[ATTACHMENTS A, B, and C]

At the hearing on this motion, M & I will put on evidence of a high value for the Dodge truck. Lawyer Larry, for the debtors, will put on evidence of low value. In the end, the issue is a question of fact the judge decides. If the judge decides the collateral is worth more than the value assigned by the debtor, the Kaddours' proposed plan must be changed accordingly, which means the value of the secured claim is increased and so is the amount the plan must provide paying the creditor.

It turns out that just before the hearing, M & I and the Kaddours settled the issue. The parties agreed that the Dodge truck was worth $18,000.00. M & I filed a pleading to withdraw its objection to the valuation of its collateral; and Larry, the Kaddours' lawyer, filed an amended plan that provides for paying M & I $18,000 over the term of the plan.

With respect to the Chrysler Pacifica subject to Wells Fargo's lien, the Kaddours owe Wells Fargo $25,313.36; and the local, retail, blue book values range from as high as $28,000 or more and as low as $15,000 or less. In forms the Kaddours filed with their petition, they valued the Pacifica at $16,475 in the schedules they filed with the bankruptcy petition. Wells Fargo, however, will not file a motion challenging the Kaddours' valuation.

In the case of the Pacifica, the "true" value of the collateral doesn't matter because a debtor cannot strip down a purchase-money lien on a motor vehicle the debtor acquired within 910 days before filing the bankruptcy case. The value of the secured claim is the total amount of the debt owed the secured party even if the actual value of the collateral is less than the debt. So, for purposes of their plan, the Kaddours must treat Wells Fargo as though the value of its secured claim is the total debt owed Wells Fargo: $25,313.36. The "true" or actual value of the collateral doesn't matter in deciding the amount of a 910–secured claim.

So, the Kaddours' plan proposes monthly payments of principal to Wells Fargo based on a secured claim of $25,313.36. As a result, Wells Fargo will naturally not file a motion challenging the valuation of its claim.

In sum, and to review and repeat, the Kaddours acquired the Dodge truck outside the 910–day period but acquired the Chrysler Pacifica within the period. So, M & I's secured claim is stripped down to the value of the truck, which the Kaddours and M & I agreed is $18,000.00. Their amended plan must provide for fully paying this amount. The gap between this value ($18,000) and the full debt owed M & I ($22,839.48) is an unsecured claim which is paid a 40% dividend, as are all other unsecured claims, under the Kaddours' amended plan.

Wells Fargo's claim for the Pacifica is $25,313.36, which is the total debt the Kaddours owe Wells Fargo. Because this lien can't be stripped down, the Kaddours' plan must provide for paying fully this $25,313.36 debt during the period of the plan, even if the value of this vehicle is much lower.

§ 17.6 Interest Rate on Secured Claims of M & I and Wells Fargo

Separate from the issue of the size of a secured claim, which must be paid fully under the plan, is the closely related issue of the interest that must be paid on the secured claim. The size of the secured claim determines the principal amount of the debt to be paid. The plan will provide, however, for paying this debt over the period of the plan, which is 60 months in the Kaddours' Chapter 13 case. Whatever the size or amount of the secured claim, the plan must provide for paying interest on the amount.

In effect, section 1325(b)(5) requires that the plan compensates the secured creditor (through interest) due to the delay in getting paid because the creditor receives payments over the life of the plan. So, what's the rate of interest the plan must pay? There are several possibilities: the contract rate of interest; the market rate of interest; the prime rate of interest; the cost-of-funds rate of interest; the coerced-loan rate of interest; some other rate of interest; and some combination of these rates. The secured creditor wants the rate that yields the highest amount of interest; the debtor wants the opposite.

The Supreme Court "decided" this issue in 2004 in Till v. SCS Credit Corp.[14] The Supreme Court adopted the "formula" or "risk plus" analysis in determining the appropriate rate of interest, which means that the prime rate serves as a base rate and is adjusted for the risk of default associated with payments over the term of a Chapter 13 plan. The size or amount of "adjustment" is decided by the bankruptcy court on a case-by-case basis.

Under *Till*, "prime rate" means the "national prime rate, reported daily in the press, which reflects the financial market's estimate of the amount a commercial bank should charge a credit-worthy commercial borrower to compensate for the opportunity costs of the loan, the risk of inflation, and the relatively slight risk of default."[15] The "adjustment" is added "[b]ecause bankrupt debtors typically pose a greater risk of nonpayment than solvent commercial borrowers ...."[16]

Okay. How much is the adjustment? "The appropriate size of that risk adjustment depends, of course, on such factors as the circumstances of the estate, the nature of the security, and the duration and feasibility of the reorganization plan."[17]

Okay. How is the adjustment decided? "The [bankruptcy] court must ... hold a hearing at which the debtor and any creditors may present evidence about the appropriate risk adjustment. Some of this evidence will be included in the debtor's bankruptcy filings, however, so the debtor and creditors may not incur significant additional expense."[18]

Okay. Who has the burden of proof? Well, "starting from a concededly *low* estimate [e.g., the prime rate] and adjusting *upward* places the evidentiary burden squarely on the creditors, who are likely to have readier access to any information absent from the debtor's filing ..."[19]

Some lawyers have argued that *Till* doesn't apply after the 2005 amendments to the Bankruptcy Code, at least not with respect to secured claims on vehicles that cannot be stripped down because of the 910–day rule. This argument has been especially

14. 541 U.S. 465, 124 S.Ct. 1951 (2004).

15. Id. at 479, 124 S. Ct. at 1961.

16. Id.

17. Id.

18. Id.

19. Id.

popular with lawyers for secured creditors when the contract rate of interest is more than the "prime rate plus" rate of interest under *Till*.

The debate continues as we're writing this book. So far, most courts have rejected the argument that *Till* no longer applies. They reason that the 2005 amendments did not change the key language of section 1325 that requires paying interest on secured claims. So, *Till* continues to apply; and the applicable interest rate on secured claims in Chapter 13 plans is "prime rate plus" without regard to the contract rate (whether higher or lower) or any other rate of interest.

In a typical case involving this issue, In re Soards,[20] Bankruptcy Judge Joan Cooper summed it up: "Simply stated, where the plan proposes to pay the secured claim in installments over time, the *Till* rate of interest must be added to the payment [of the secured claim] to arrive at the present value of the claim and the contract rate of interest is irrelevant to the analysis."[21]

Judge Cooper also concluded in *Soards* that "[i]n the absence of evidence of the risks associated with a default, . . . [adding] an additional two percentage points to the prime rate is the appropriate rate to be applied on . . . [secured] claims in these cases."[22] Other courts applying the prime rate plus approach "have generally approved adjustments of 1% to 3%."[23]

Therefore, the Kaddours' Chapter 13 plan commits to pay M & I and Wells Fargo the principal amounts of $15,700 and $25,313.36, respectively, in 60 monthly installments. The interest rate is 10% annually, which is about the prime rate at the time they filed their plan plus about two percent or so.

§ 17.7 Confirmation of the Plan

Section 1324 requires the court to hold a hearing on the plan at which any party in interest can object. The confirmation hearing is supposed to occur "not later than 45 days after the date of the [341(a)] meeting of creditors." In a Chapter 13 case, the 341(a) meeting is held sometime between 20 and 50 days after the petition is filed, which can be extended if a motion to dismiss the case is pending or for other reasons. Commonly, the confirmation hearing on a Chapter 13 plan is three months or so after the case is filed.

20. 344 B.R. 829 (Bankr. W.D. Ky. 2006).

21. Id. at 832.

22. Id.

23. Till v. SCS Credit Corp., 541 U.S. 465, 480, 124 S.Ct. 1951, 1962 (2004).

Section 1325 requires the court to confirm the debtor's plan if the requirements listed there are satisfied. These requirements, such as the debtor having paid required fees and how much creditors must be paid, are the bases for objections that creditors and the trustee will likely already have made if the debtor's proposed plan fails to satisfy any of them.

Typically, any such objections will have been settled or otherwise decided before the actual confirmation hearing, as in special hearings on valuation or other aspects of the debtor's proposed plan that troubled the trustee or a creditor. So, by the time for the confirmation hearing, the debtor will have amended her plan to make changes she agreed to or the court ordered.

Also, prior notice of the hearing and a copy of the final version of the debtor's plan (however amended) are sent to interested parties. The notice explains that anybody wishing to object to the confirmation must do so within 25 days and that no confirmation hearing will be held unless a timely objection is filed. Typically, no objection is filed as a result of this notice. Creditors have been noticed earlier and maybe repeatedly about the bankruptcy and the debtor's plan, and any of them objecting to the plan will already have done so.

As a result, confirmation itself becomes largely pro forma with the judge issuing an order of confirmation that incorporates the debtor's amended plan to which, by this time, nobody objects. Don't get us wrong. The judge is not required to confirm a plan just because nobody objects. She, too, must be personally satisfied that the requirements for confirmation are met. However, throughout the process with creditors and the trustee complaining to her about issues, the judge will have learned the case; and any questions she personally harbors will already probably have been answered, too, by the time of the confirmation hearing.

Also, in real life, a bankruptcy judge's caseload is very heavy; and she heavily relies on the Chapter 13 trustee to monitor cases and get things right. So, if the trustee is happy with the plan by the time for confirmation and thus doesn't object to the plan, the judge will typically confirm it. This reality partly explains why amended plans are often filed by the Chapter 13 trustee rather than the debtor. It clearly signals the trustee's approval.

Here is the judge's confirmation order in the Kaddours' Chapter 13 case, which adopts and approves the Kaddours' amended plan increasing the size of M & I's secured claim:

UNITED STATES BANKRUPTCY COURT
MIDDLE DISTRICT OF NORTH CAROLINA

Winston-Salem Division

In Re:	)	**ORDER CONFIRMING**
	)	**PLAN**
Ahmed Kaddour xxx-xx–0019	)	**CHAPTER 13**
Debtor.	)	
	)	
Irshad Kaddour xxx-xx–9132	)	
Joint Debtor.	)	
	)	**No. 06–72C818**
	)	

This case came before the Court, after notice and opportunity for hearing, for confirmation of the Chapter 13 plan proposed in this case; and

IT APPEARING to the Court as follows:

A. The Trustee in this case is [Chapter 13 trustee's name and address].

B. The attorney for the Debtor is Larry Friedman;

C. Under the final plan proposed by the Debtor:

1. The Debtor is to make monthly payments to the Trustee which are to be disbursed by the Trustee in accordance with the plan and this confirmation order;

2. The monthly plan payment to the Trustee is $1,064.76[24] beginning February 20, 2006,[25] for a total period of 60 months;

3. Any timely filed priority claims will be paid in full in deferred payments;

4. The treatment for secured creditors and additional provisions of the plan are as follows:

* M & I FINANCIAL CORP. (2003 Dodge truck)	$300.00 + 10% APR	$18,000.00

24. This amount is the sum of the monthly payment of principal and interest to M & I and Wells Fargo, plus monthly disposable income of $342.87.

Interestingly, the Kaddours' car and truck payments were over $900 a month (see Forms I and J) before bankruptcy and drops to about $722 a month under their Chapter 13 plan, which thereby inflates their actual, monthly disposable income to more than $1,400.00.

25. Section 1326 requires the debtor to begin making payments not later than 30 days after the date of filing which, of course, is weeks and months before the court finally confirms the plan. The beginning date of this plan, February 20, 2006, is 30 days after the Kaddours' petition was filed, and the Kaddours had begun and continued making payments from that date.

** WELLS FARGO (2004 Chrysler Pacifica)	$421.89 + 10% APR	$25,313.36

* The M & I claim is partially secured and partially unsecured. The 2003 Dodge truck was valued, by agreement between the debtors and M & I, at $18,000.00; and, there being no further objection, the vehicle is so valued. The balance of the claim is unsecured.

** The Wells Fargo claim is fully secured. Because the 2004 Chrysler was acquired within 910 days of the filing of the bankruptcy case, the secured claim is equal to the entire debt owed the secured creditor, $25,313.36.

5. The Debtor will pay THE GREATER OF the amount necessary to pay all allowed costs of administration, priority and secured claims in full, with the exception of continuing long-term debts,[26] and 40% to allowed unsecured general claims OR 60 monthly plan payments subject to the plan being reviewed periodically for adjustments to plan payment;
6. Payments to priority, secured and specially classified creditors will be prorated according to the balance of their claims except where a specific monthly payment is indicated herein;
7. There will be no separate payment on arrearage claims unless indicated herein;
8. The Debtor will be responsible for payment of continuing long-term nondischargeable debts after completion of plan payments;
9. The estimated return to unsecured creditors is 0%; and

IT FURTHER APPEARING to the Court that

(a) the plan complies with the provisions of Chapter 13, and with other applicable provisions of Title 11 of the United States Code;

(b) any fee, charge, or amount required under Chapter 123 of Title 28 of the United States Code, or by the plan, to be paid before confirmation has been paid;

(c) the plan has been proposed in good faith and not by any means forbidden by law;

26. Remember that the Kaddours are paying the mortgages on their home outside of the plan, directly to the mortgagees, and in accordance with the terms of the mortgages without any change or impairment.

(d) the value, as of the effective date of the plan, of property to be distributed under the plan on account of each allowed unsecured claim is not less than the amount that would be paid on such claim if the estate of the Debtor were liquidated under Chapter 7 on such date;

(e) with respect to each allowed claim provided for by the plan:

(i) the holder of such claim has accepted the plan; or

(ii) the plan provides that the holder of such claim retain the lien securing such claim and the value, as of the effective date of the plan, of property to be distributed under the plan on account of such claim is not less than the allowed amount of such claim; or

(iii) the Debtor surrenders the property securing such claim to such holder;

(f) to the extent that the plan calls for payments for a period longer than three years, good cause has been shown for the longer plan period; and

(g) the Debtor will be able to make all payments under the plan and to comply with the plan, and that the plan should be confirmed in accordance with the terms and conditions of this order; therefore, it is

ORDERED as follows:

1. The plan is confirmed.

2. The Trustee shall collect and disburse the plan payments in accordance with the plan and this confirmation order as soon as practicable.

3. The plan payments shall continue as provided in the plan and this order until voluntarily increased by the Debtor or until further orders are entered affecting the plan or the payments.

4. The attorney for the Debtor is allowed a fee in the amount of $2,500.00 to be paid by the Trustee as funds are available unless otherwise ordered by the Court.

5. The Trustee shall receive from plan payments such expenses and compensation as provided under the Bankruptcy Code and orders of this Court.

6. The Debtor shall not incur any indebtedness without the approval of the Trustee or this Court. All credit cards shall be canceled and surrendered immediately.

7. The Debtor shall not transfer any interest in property without the prior approval of this Court.

8. The Debtor shall maintain collision insurance on any vehicle on which there is a lien. If insurance is not maintained, the Debtor is ordered to store the vehicle as directed by the Trustee.
9. The employer of the Debtor shall deduct and remit funds from the wages, salary or commissions of the Debtor as directed by the Trustee.
10. Providing for a claim under this plan does not bar objections to the claim.
11. Notwithstanding any provision of the plan to the contrary, all property of the estate, as specified by 11 U.S.C. §§ 541 and 1306, shall continue to be property of the estate following confirmation.
12. The property serving as collateral for secured claims is valued at the amounts allowed herein with the exception of fully secured claims for which the value is deemed to be equal to or greater than the allowed secured claim. The property serving as collateral for secured claims is required by the Debtor for successful completion of the plan.
13. Notwithstanding the allowance of a claim as secured, all rights under Title 11 to avoid liens are reserved and confirmation of the plan is without res judicata effect as to any action to avoid a lien.
14. Any continuing long-term debt claimant being paid through disbursements by the Trustee is required to report any change in the monthly payment amount to the Trustee within 30 days from the effective date of the change. Any continuing long-term debt claimant being paid directly by the Debtor is required to report any change in the monthly payment amount to the Debtor within 30 days from the effective date of the change.
15. All insurance and warranty coverage on unsecured general claims is canceled and the claim must reflect cancellation and rebate to the account unless provided otherwise herein.
16. The Internal Revenue Service and the North Carolina Department of Revenue are authorized to offset any refund due the Debtor against any allowed secured or priority claim and to issue refunds directly to the Debtor unless otherwise ordered by this Court or instructed by the Trustee.
17. All creditors during the pendency of this case are restrained from commencing or continuing any civil action or attempting in any manner whatsoever to collect all or any part of a consumer debt proposed to be paid under this plan from any individual that is liable on such debt with the Debtor as

endorser, guarantor or co-maker unless further ordered by the Court.

18. The Trustee is authorized to record on the public records such documents as the Trustee may deem advisable for the purpose of giving all persons notice of this case.

May 17, 2006

/s/____________________
UNITED STATES BANKRUPTCY JUDGE

So, to summarize and review what's happened in the Kaddours' Chapter 13 case so far, here is the record of the case—the court docket—through the time of confirmation:

U.S. Bankruptcy Court
Middle District of North Carolina (Winston–Salem)
Bankruptcy Petition #: 06–72C818

Assigned to: [Bankruptcy Judge's Name]
Chapter 13 *Date Filed:* 01/21/2006
Voluntary

Ahmed Kaddour
[Address]
Winston–Salem, NC
SSN: xxx-xx–0019
Debtor

represented by **Larry Friedman**
[Address]
[Phone number]
[Fax number]
[Email address]

Irshad Kaddour
[Address]
Winston–Salem, NC
SSN: xxx-xx–9132
Joint Debtor

represented by **Larry Friedman**
(See above for address)

Filing Date	#	Docket Text
01/21/2006	1	Chapter 13 Voluntary Petition (attachments: schedules/forms). Fee Amount $189. Filed by Ahmed Kaddour, Irshad Kaddour
01/21/2006	2	Notice to Creditors and Proposed Plan Filed by Debtor Ahmed Kaddour, Joint Debtor Irshad Kaddour
01/21/2006	3	Application for Attorney Base Fee in Chapter 13 Case Filed by Debtor Ahmed Kaddour, Joint Debtor Irshad Kaddour
01/21/2006	4	Statement of Social Security Number(s) Filed by Debtor Ahmed Kaddour, Joint Debtor Irshad Kaddour
01/21/2006	5	Document Debtor's Claim for Property Exemptions. Filed by Ahmed Kaddour
01/21/2006	6	Document Debtor's Claim for Property Exemptions. Filed by Joint Debtor Irshad Kaddour
01/21/2006	7	Certificate of Credit Counseling Filed by Debtor Ahmed Kaddour

01/21/2006	8	Certificate of Credit Counseling Filed by Joint Debtor Irshad Kaddour
01/21/2006		Receipt of filing fee for Voluntary Petition (Chapter 13)(06–72C818) [misc,volp13] (189.00). Receipt number 876303, amount $189.00. (U.S. Treasury)
01/23/2006	9	Meeting of Creditors 341(a); meeting to be held on 3/3/2006 at 01:00 PM at Creditors Mtg. Room, Winston–Salem
01/23/2006	10	Chapter 13 Restraining Notice
01/25/2006	11	BNC Certificate of Mailing—Chapter 13 Restraining Notice (RE: related document(s) (10) Chapter 13 Restraining Notice); Service Date 01/25/2006. (Admin.)
01/25/2006	12	BNC Certificate of Mailing—Meeting of Creditors. (RE: related document(s) (9) Meeting of Creditors Chapter 13) Service Date 01/25/2006. (Admin.)
02/02/2006	13	Trustee's Motion to Collect Noticing Fees Filed by Trustee[27]
02/03/2006	14	Order Granting Motion to Collect Noticing Fees (Related Doc #13); Order is effective immediately upon expiration of time for filing objections
02/11/2006	15	Notice of Appearance and Request for Notice by Deborah Tyson Filed for Creditor M & I Financial Corp.
03/03/2006		Chapter 13 Meeting of Creditors Held
03/10/2006	16	Document (re: related document(s) (2) Objection to Valuation of 2003 Dodge Truck/Objection to Confirmation). Filed by Creditor M & I Financial Corp.
03/14/2006	17	Hearing Set (re: related document(s) (16) Motion Objecting to Valuation regarding a 2003 Dodge truck, filed by M & I Financial Corp.). Hearing scheduled 04/14/2006.
03/26/2006	18	Withdrawal of Document Filed by Creditor M & I Financial Corp. (re: related document(s) (16), Objection to Valuation of 2003 Dodge Truck/Objection to Confirmation)
04/02/2006	19	Amended Document Filed by Debtor Ahmed Kaddour, Joint Debtor Irshad Kaddour (re: related document(s) (2) Notice to Creditors and Proposed Plan Filed by Debtor Ahmed Kaddour, Joint Debtor Irshad Kaddour)
04/15/2006	20	Notice and Proposed Order of Confirmation (Chapter 13 Trustee)
04/17/2006	21	BNC Certificate of Mailing—PDF Document. (RE: related document(s) (20) Notice and Proposed Order of Confirmation) Service Date 04/17/2006. (Admin.)
04/18/2006	22	Certificate of Financial Management Course Filed by Debtor Ahmed Kaddour
04/18/2006	23	Certificate of Financial Management Course Filed by Joint Debtor Irshad Kaddour
05/17/2006	24	Order Confirming Chapter 13 Plan
05/19/2006	25	BNC Certificate of Mailing—PDF Document. (RE: related document(s) (24) Order Confirming Chapter 13 Plan) Service Date 05/19/2006. (Admin.)

27. The trustee mails notices to creditors. In this case, she estimates the number of these notices and estimates that the cost of mailing each notice is 50 cents; and she requests the court for an order allowing reimbursement from plan payments of the total cost of mailing the notices.

Please note, however, that the docket will not end here (with the reports of confirmation and the mailing of notice of confirmation) because confirmation is not the end of the case. Note, too, that confirmation effects no discharge of debts. Confirmation is when performance of the plan officially begins; and the bankruptcy discharge awaits and depends on completion of the plan.

So, the Chapter 13 case is not closed until performance of the plan is completed or the case is dismissed for lack of performance or some other reason. Until then, the Chapter 13 case remains open; the automatic stay remains in effect; the court's jurisdiction continues; and noticeable happenings in the case are reported in the docket.

§ 17.8 What Happens After Confirmation

The main effect of confirmation is to "bind the debtor and each creditor, whether or not the claim of such creditor is provided by the plan, and whether or not such creditor has objected to, has accepted, or has rejected the plan."[28] Most obviously, the debtor makes whatever payments the plan describes.

(a) Performing and Completing the Plan (Discharge)

Except for payments made outside the plan, the debtor's payments are made to the trustee and not directly to the creditors. The debtor monthly pays the trustee whatever amount is required by the plan, and the trustee disburses this payment to creditors according to the terms of the plan.

Actually, the debtor will have begun making payments to the trustee prior to confirmation and "not later than 30 days after the date of the filing of the plan." After confirmation, the trustee will notify the debtor's employer to withhold from the debtor's income and pay to the trustee some or all of the monthly amount the plan requires the debtor to pay the trustee. The debtor is expected to live on the balance.

As in the typical case, the Kaddours' plan lasts five years. So, for 60 months, their income is taxed for the monthly payment their plan requires them to make to the trustee. By doing so and thus completing their Chapter 13 plan, the Kaddours earn a right to discharge under section 1328(a), which provides: "as soon as practicable after completion by the debtor of all payments under the plan, ... the court shall grant the debtor a discharge of all debts

28. Confirmation also vests all property of the estate in the debtor unless the order confirming the plan provides otherwise. Typically, however, a Chapter 13 order of confirmation does provide otherwise, which is true in the Kaddours' case. The order in their case explicitly provides that "all property of the estate ... shall continue to be property of the estate following confirmation."

provided for by the plan" and also a discharge of all debts for claims the court has disallowed.

Please note that the 1328(a) discharge is triggered by the Kaddours completing all payments *required by the plan.* So, the discharge is not conditioned on paying creditors everything the creditors are owed under state or other nonbankruptcy law. The discharge is earned by paying creditors whatever the confirmed, Chapter 13 plan requires paying them. Therefore, if the Kaddours complete their plan, they will win a discharge even though their unsecured creditors were paid only 40% of the debts owed them.

Like a discharge under Chapter 7, the section 1328(a) discharge is subject to section 523(a) exceptions, i.e., debts that are unaffected by the discharge. The section 1328(a) discharge, however, is wider: it is subject to fewer 523(a) exceptions. For example, because of section 523(a)(6), a Chapter 7 discharge excepts, i.e., does not affect, a debt "for willful and malicious injury by the debtor to another entity or to the property of another entity." Chapter 13 discharges this kind of debt.

For the most part, however, the exceptions that apply in Chapter 7 but not in Chapter 13 are typically insignificant. As a result, the wider discharge in Chapter 13 is not usually sufficient to lure into Chapter 13 a debtor who could liquidate under Chapter 7.

In theory, the Kaddours or any other Chapter 13 debtor can earn a discharge even without completing all the payments required by the plan. It's called a "hardship discharge" under section 1328(b) but is available only if three, tough requirements are satisfied:

- Modifying the plan so that the debtor can complete all the required payments is not practicable; AND
- Each unsecured creditor has been paid the present value of what she would have been paid if the debtor had liquidated under Chapter 7; AND
- The debtor's failure to complete all of the payments required by the plan is due to circumstances for which the debtor should not justly be held accountable.

In practice, a hardship discharge is rare. And, when such a discharge is granted under section 1328(b), it is subject to all of the section 523(a) exceptions to discharge that apply in a Chapter 7 case. A hardship discharge for a Chapter 13 debtor under 1328(b) is therefore more narrow than the 1328(a) discharge that occurs when the debtor completes all payments required by the plan.

Also, although objections to discharge that apply in Chapter 7 don't generally apply in Chapter 13, some reasons exist for denying a discharge of any debts under either 1328(a) or (b). These reasons are, in effect, conditions to discharge. Two of them are most important.

First, the debtor cannot be discharged under Chapter 13 unless and until she has completed "an instructional course concerning personal financial management." This "course" is different from, and in addition to, the credit counseling "briefing" that is a condition on an individual filing a bankruptcy case.

Second, the debtor cannot be discharged in Chapter 13 if she has previously received a discharge (1) in another Chapter 13 case filed within two years before the present case was filed or (2) in any other kind of bankruptcy case filed within the preceding four years. These time limitations don't prevent the debtor from filing a later Chapter 13 case; they only prevent a discharge in the later-filed case.

In addition to discharge, either by completing the payments required by the plan or getting a hardship discharge, the Kaddours also get something else when, in either way, payments under a Chapter 13 plan are finished. The case will be closed, and the property of the estate will re-vest in them. The debtors will have lost title to their property to the estate; have nevertheless kept possession of the property during performance of the plan; paid their debts from their income to the extent possible; and, at the end, have title to the property of the estate, i.e., the property interests, returned to them.

(b) The Kaddours Get Another Raise

The Kaddours' income could increase during the performance of the plan. In this unlikely event, the trustee or unsecured creditor will request the court to modify the plan for the purpose of increasing the payments made to unsecured creditors. Section 1329 clearly creates a right for the trustee or an unsecured creditor to make such a request for this reason.

The statute does not clearly, expressly say that in such a case, the court must modify the plan to increase the dividend to unsecured creditors. It's true that section 1322 requires the plan to provide for the submission of all future income necessary to carry out the plan; and section 1325 requires the plan to commit all of the debtor's projected disposable income. However, whether and how these requirements apply to modifications under 1329 has long been uncertain; and, there is new uncertainty about the extent to which projected disposable income encompasses actual, future income.

We believe, however, that in the unlikely event that the debtors' income increases during the performance of a Chapter 13 plan, a court is very likely to modify the plan to increase payments to unsecured creditors. It seems pretty clear to us that in practice, creditors—not the debtors—get the benefit of increases in actual, future income that were not anticipated at the time of confirmation but occur during the performance of a plan.

(c) Kaddours Want More Credit

Between the times of getting their plan confirmed and completing it, the Kaddours must live on the balance of their income that remains after making the required, monthly payments to the trustee. Living on this balance is often difficult and challenging. Help in the form of increases in actual income is very unlikely and even rare and, in any event, is discounted because the court would most likely modify the plan to increase the dividend paid to unsecured creditors.

Help in the form of new credit is also not likely. The reason is not that new credit is unavailable. The main reason is the order of confirmation which commands: "[a]ll credit cards shall be canceled and surrendered immediately" and "[t]he Debtor shall not incur any indebtedness without the approval of the Trustee or this Court."

In the event a debtor disobeys and incurs new debt without the necessary approval, the creditor faces major problems in collecting the debtor. First, the creditor can't expect to receive anything from the trustee because the plan does not provide for paying this creditor. Second, the creditor is stopped from collecting directly from the debtor because the stay remains in effect.

Section 1305 provides some relief for creditors in the event of postpetition consumer debts "for property or services necessary for the debtor's performance under the plan." Such a creditor can file a proof of claim for the postpetition debt. If the claim is allowed, provision can be made for paying the debt within and under the plan; and, the debt is excepted from the Chapter 13 discharge.

The claim will be disallowed, however, "if the holder of such a claim knew or should have known that prior approval by the trustee of the debtor's incurring the obligation was practicable and was not obtained." In this event, the creditor gets nothing under the plan; the stay stops collection efforts; and the debt is excepted from the discharge. So, creditors who know that the trustee's approval is required for new credit are strongly encouraged to get this approval. Otherwise, they risk getting nothing of the new credit repaid.

On the other hand, if the creditor lacked this knowledge and the claim for new credit is allowed, the debt is excepted from the discharge if the debtor failed to obtain trustee's approval when doing so was practicable. The intended effect, of course, is to encourage debtors to get the trustee's approval. Otherwise, the debtor's Chapter 13 discharge will have a large hole that leaves the debt for new credit unaffected.

(d) Ahmed or Irshad Loses a Job or They Otherwise Can't Make Plan Payments (Dismissal or Conversion)

The most likely contingency to occur during the performance of a plan is not an increase in the debtor's income or the debtor's credit. What's most likely is that the debtor's income decreases because she loses her job; or, even if her income stays steady, the debtor is simply unable to sustain a subjectively acceptable lifestyle while making plan payments.

In this event, the debtor has three, basic options. The debtor's first choice is to ask the court for a hardship discharge. This option is least likely to work because of the tough conditions on such a discharge and, practically speaking, won't ever work in the absence of a fortuitous loss of income that the debtor can't reasonably replace.

The debtor's second-best choice is to request the court to modify the plan to reduce the amount of payments to unsecured creditors. Basically, though, the debtor must show either that the original plan was not realistically, accurately predictive or that some change of circumstances has occurred which, though not justifying a hardship discharge, nevertheless justifies a reduction in payments. Either showing is difficult to make. And debtors like the Kaddours, whose plan is five years, cannot avoid the difficulty simply by extending the length of the plan. The court can extend a three-year plan but not a five-year plan.

The debtor's final option is procedural: either dismiss the Chapter 13 case or convert it to Chapter 7. A Chapter 13 debtor enjoys a largely unfettered right to dismiss the case, but the consequences are not good. She loses the benefit of bankruptcy protections, including the stay and discharge; and her creditors enjoy an almost unfettered right to collect their debts.

According to Chapter 13, the debtor's right to convert the case to Chapter 7 is largely unfettered, too; and, upon conversion, she gets the benefits of Chapter 7 bankruptcy, as we described in Unit 16. However, she must pay the costs of Chapter 7, which we also described in Unit 16.

The principal cost, as we said there, is loss of title and possession to her property that becomes property of the estate, which upon conversion includes property of the estate on and after the filing of the petition that remains in the possession of or is under the control of the debtor on the date of the conversion. Also, upon conversion, any valuation of collateral and lien stripping done in

Chapter 13 is undone for purposes of the Chapter 7 case, which reinvigorates the strength of any affected secured creditor.

Beyond such costs is a possible problem for a Chapter 13 debtor wanting to convert her case to Chapter 7. The problem is section 707(b) "means testing," which limits the availability of Chapter 7 relief. When a case is converted from 13 to 7, "means testing" may still apply according to the circumstances existing at the time the case was filed or the time of conversion.[29] If so, and to this extent, "means testing" effectively limits converting a case from Chapter 13 to Chapter 7.

Therefore, under the right circumstances, a debtor who cannot complete the payments required by a Chapter 13 plan may also fail the Chapter 7 "means test," which means she cannot sustain a case under Chapter 7. Practically speaking, therefore, the debtor's only options are to dismiss the case and get out of bankruptcy altogether or "gut it out" under Chapter 13. This Hopson's choice may prove to be an important, unintended consequence of Chapter 7 "means testing:" the test can force a debtor into Chapter 13, and it can also keep her there.

29. Which time is correct—the time of filing or the time of conversion—may make a very big difference; but, as we write this book, the courts have not yet decided the issue. It's an issue because with respect to other matters in a converted case, the critical time is the time the Chapter 13 case was filed, not the later time when the case is converted to Chapter 7.

*

Last Comments to Students

It has been a pleasure for us to write this book. We hope that it has been a pleasure for you to read the book and that it will be a pleasure to read the grade on your bankruptcy exam.

One last comment about the exam. Before you start writing, be sure that you have read your law school exam at least as carefully as you have read this book. In reading your exam questions, look for the following 4 pieces of information: (1) Who is the "debtor," i.e., who is the person who is in bankruptcy? (2) What did she do, e.g., did she incur a credit card debt or did she pay a creditor, or . . . (3) When did she do this, i.e., before bankruptcy, after bankruptcy but before discharge, or . . . and (4) Who are the other people involved—creditors, buyers, trustee . . . .

With that information and the information gained from this book, you will make an "A" in bankruptcy. And, after you make that "A," please celebrate by going to eat at Eppie's in Charlottesville, Virginia (owned and operated by Charles and Daniel Epstein).

DGE
SHN

*

Table of Cases

R

S

T

U

Index

References are to Pages

V

W

†